AGING AND TIME

Multidisciplinary Perspectives

Edited by

Jan Baars
University for Humanistics, Utrecht
Tilburg University

Henk Visser
Maastricht University, The Netherlands

Society and Aging Series
Jon Hendricks: Series Editor

Routledge
Taylor & Francis Group
LONDON AND NEW YORK

First published 2007 by Baywood Publishing Company, Inc.

Published 2020 by Routledge
2 Park Square, Milton Park, Abingdon, Oxon OX14 4RN
52 Vanderbilt Avenue, New York, NY 10017

Routledge is an imprint of the Taylor & Francis Group, an informa business

Library of Congress Catalog Number: 2006048446

Library of Congress Cataloging-in-Publication Data

Aging and time : multidisciplinary perspectives / edited by Jan Baars and Henk Visser.
p. cm. - - (Society and aging series)
Includes bibliographical references and index.
ISBN-13: 978-0-89503-367-3 (cloth)
ISBN-10: 0-89503-367-4 (cloth)
1. Gerontology. 2. Aging--Philosophy. I. Baars, Jan. II. Visser, Henk, 1939-

HQ1061.A42483 2006
305.26--dc22

2006048446

ISBN-13: 978-0-89503-367-3 (hbk)

Table of Contents

Acknowledgments

The editors want to express their gratitude to some people who have been particularly important in producing this volume. To begin with, we want to thank the contributors who have remained committed and patient during the years that this project was under way. We feel privileged to have been able to work with these talented people. The enthusiasm of Jon Hendricks, the editor of the *Society and Aging Series* and an early pioneer in theorizing aging and time, has been a great support throughout the process. We are especially grateful to Peter van Huizen for his advice and textual corrections. Last but certainly not least, we are thankful to Julie Krempa and Bobbi Olszewski from Baywood Publishing Company for their professional expertise in handling the final stages of the publishing process.

Jan Baars
Henk Visser

CHAPTER 1

Introduction

Chronological Time and Chronological Age: Problems of Temporal Diversity

Jan Baars

It is the aim of this volume to revitalize the debate about the concepts of time implicit in the study of aging. A potentially interested but already overburdened reader may wonder whether one needs or whether there is a need for such a book. Time seems such an ordinary unproblematic topic that a work devoted to it might appear to be a digression from many pressing problems of aging. Indeed, aging can lead to many problems that must be taken care of. This has put an enormous pressure on the gerontological community to provide or seek practical applications and solutions. It is not important to read this book so as to counterbalance such practically oriented work. Its importance is the exploration of real issues concerning temporal concepts and approaches to aging: whatever concepts of time are used determine to a large extent the way aging is approached.

There is a seemingly self-evident time that we read on clocks and calendars and use to determine the ages of cars, buildings and (why not?) human beings. This *chronological* time serves many purposes well but is actually quite problematic when it comes to aging, especially when it gets more credit than it deserves. That aging is poorly indicated by higher chronological ages may often be admitted, but this does not appear to lead to much change in research practices. The vast majority of studies of aging still use a chronological approach to define populations for research purposes (determine who the "aged" are that should be studied) and try to establish how (social, economic, health, etc.) characteristics of people change as a function of their chronological age. This may lead to an accumulation of data, but in itself not to *explanatory* knowledge.

The issue at stake is not whether chronological time should be abandoned; that would be to neglect the role it has to play in every empirical study, also of aging processes. There is, however, an unreflected overemphasis on chronological time that leads to problems, as if the precision of chronological time would in itself give a solid foundation to the study of aging. This idea is even more tempting as this concept of time has been institutionalized to measure and coordinate processes and actions all over the world, leading to a calendar that makes it possible to localize anybody's birth in time and precisely determine his or her "age." The grand ambition of gerontology still seems to be to establish how this chronological or calendar age of persons determines the characteristics of aging persons or even of all humans. This would eventually reduce gerontology to a straightforward set of simple formulas in which scientific precision and practical use would be united. Almost 50 years ago this option was already stated with much self-assurance: "Chronological age is one of the most useful single items of information about an individual if not the *most* useful. From this knowledge alone an amazingly large number of general statements or predictions can be made about his anatomy, physiology, psychology and social behavior" (Birren, 1959, p. 8). Although the author of these lines has later expressed serious reservations about them, a large part of the gerontological community is still under their spell.

One of the practical issues at stake is whether gerontology does not, in its search for clear links between age and characteristics, reinforce conventional generalizations about aging and the aged. Furthermore, even unfounded generalizations about categories of people with certain ages can be implemented in policies regarding, for instance, specific forms of care or housing for "the aged" and thus contribute to a reality which forces aging people to fit in, because there are no other options offered. Consequently, later research can affirm the earlier generalizations, not because they grasped the realities of aging, but because gerontological expertise has again played its unreflected role in co-constituting the realities of aging. In such cases, the analytical apparatus of gerontology runs the danger of becoming an uncritical instrument catering to all kinds of organizational contexts, in which aging people are mainly relevant as the subjects of planning procedures and average estimates. Such bureaucratic operations may be necessary, but should not dominate the way aging is approached or understood. Although aging processes can be measured chronologically, they are not regulated by chronological time. The step from chronological time to chronological age should be taken very cautiously if we want to take aging processes seriously, especially because chronological age is widely used in contemporary societies to regulate all kinds of processes with many consequences for the people concerned (see Baars, this volume). To counteract these tendencies, it is good to emphasize that the search for aging characteristics based on chronological age has established much counterevidence, testifying to the many differences in aging processes. This counterevidence comes hardly as a surprise when we try to imagine persons with the same chronological age but living in very different circumstances. Think, for instance, of 60-year-olds: one would expect enormous differences in terms of empirical data and personal experiences between, let us say, a contemporary poor African woman, a Japanese man, or a homeless American of that age; not to mention 60-year-olds in prehistoric times, in the Roman Empire, in classical China or among nineteenth-century factory workers. The fact that in Western Europe the average life expectancy for males has practically doubled in the last 150 years (Imhoff, 1981) implies that chronological age cannot by itself give any precise reference to (a phase of) aging processes.

Chronological definitions of life expectancy must presuppose more or less regular cycles of human life in specific historical contexts. But also within the *same* historical period, different socioeconomic and cultural contexts, gender, genetic codes, medical histories, and individual choices or fates have been shown to be statistically associated with different aging processes. Even a "cohort identity," established by contrast with other cohorts within the same historical context, remains to a high degree an abstract construction which has to tolerate a considerable amount of internal differentiation. Major longitudinal studies like the Berlin Aging Study (Baltes & Mayer, 1999) or the Seattle Longitudinal Study (Schaie, 1996) offer many examples of these differences (cf. also Daatland & Biggs, 2004).

Because human beings with the same chronological age can show, even from a mere biological point of view, very different aging characteristics, we can no longer assume that aging processes develop in synchrony with chronological time. As organisms age at different rates and even different tissues, organs, and organ systems within an organism may age at different rates, chronological age turns out to be even a poor predictor of remaining life expectancy, leading here and there to other directions for research, such as the quest for "biomarkers" of aging (Sprott, 2002). The many faces of aging between the extremes of a teenager suffering from progeria and a vibrantly alive centenarian are mirrors in which the hidden and profoundly puzzling varieties of aging as living in time stare us in the face. Maybe the many different processes of aging all have their own dynamical properties, but these may include, to make it even more complicated, an openness to the environment. These processes must be discovered in their *specificity,* and in the course of this discovery chronological time can only function as an instrument and should not be extended to represent a chronological age with an implicit gerontological surplus. Chronological age is only the amount of chronological time that has passed since somebody was born.

To avoid any misunderstanding, these arguments are no denial of the finitude of human life, nor do they deny that aging can be observed in any human being, if we compare characteristics of the same person over a relatively long period of time. The question is how to approach these themes to get a better understanding. To achieve this, it is essential to understand the specific significance and relativity of chronological time and its unfounded seductions in relation to aging.

A MISTAKEN IDEA BEHIND CHRONOLOGICAL AGE: TIME WORKING AS A REGULAR CAUSE

Generalizations about people with a certain calendar age actually presuppose a *causal* concept of time: because time has worked for a certain duration in aged people, certain inevitable effects should be reckoned with. Moreover, the effects are assumed to develop steadily and universally according to the rhythm of the clock. However, such a causal concept of time in aging can never generate knowledge that might explain something of the differences that exist between human beings of the same age, nor allow us to understand that aging is a generalizing concept that is actually composed of many specific processes. While it is true that all causal relations are *also* temporal relations, or relations working "in time," it would be wrong to identify causality with time or to reduce the process of aging to the causal effects of time. The same Jim Birren whose high expectations of the predictive power of chronological age I quoted earlier, has later dealt with time extensively and articulated a similar view: "By itself, the collection of large amounts of data showing relationships with chronological age does not help, because chronological age is not the cause of anything. Chronological age is only an index, and unrelated sets of data show correlations with chronological age that have no intrinsic or causal relationship with each other" (Birren, 1999, p. 460).

The elusive concept of time is usually made visible and calculable using *spatial* and *numerical* projections to explain what time is or how time works. A well-known example of such a spatial projection is drawing a straight line, which visualizes the time which is passing even during this action of drawing. This can easily be transformed into the "arrow of time" or into one of the axes in a diagram explaining changes as a function of time. But this visualization creates precisely the illusion that aging processes can be clearly and unequivocally related to chronological time. An important limitation of such projections is that they can clarify only those aspects that time has in common with space. But is it at all possible to concentrate on pure time as such and measure it precisely?

THE ABSTRACT RHYTHMS OF CHRONOLOGICAL TIME

Time is usually indicated by clocks, which make it possible to measure the duration of a process or locate an event (the birth of a baby, a future appointment) in time. We know that some clocks do not function well, that they are not precise. But how can we determine whether a clock really measures time as such? Usually, we establish the accuracy of a clock by comparing it with the clock of an institution with "more authority," such as the telephone company or television. But again, how can we determine the accuracy of such an authoritative clock? To what most "authoritative clock" or most "fundamental time" are these clocks attuned? To the movement of the earth around the sun? Is that time in an ultimate sense? Or something else? Unfortunately, following this line of questioning does not lead to ultimate time or an ultimate clock. In all chronological time concepts that we know of, a specific, more or less regular process has been selected as a standard to establish what time is. In most traditions, the movements of the celestial bodies have been taken to represent time: defining years, seasons, months, day and night, hours and minutes.

But in principle, there are many processes that might be used as the basis of a chronological time concept. In fact, all rhythms could be taken into consideration. But a *general* time concept must be based on processes that cannot be influenced by the different processes it should measure. Therefore the movements of the earth and the moon were excellent candidates to form the basis of a general time concept, as their regular movements are clearly independent of anything happening on earth. But eventually this way of defining time resulted in many problems of measurement since these basic cosmological movements turned out to be too irregular. The elliptic form of the movement of the earth around the sun and the precession of the equinoxes caused, in the long run, a lack of precision in the Holy Calendar, which already upset the Pope toward the end of the fifteenth century and urged the Church to have the Christian calendar improved; changing it in 1582 from the Julian to the Gregorian calendar. After this, the calendar has more or less been left to itself as human beings could live very well with small, long-term irregularities; but these were increasingly regarded as intolerable to the degree that ever more precise measurements became of vital importance to further the range of effective control over nature. Therefore the search has been intensified for still more delicate regular movements that could be used as a basis for a general standard to measure all other movements.

The technical criteria that must be met have become extremely demanding. To be able to establish a natural process as a standard for measuring time, we need a periodic process with extremely short phases, which can easily be reproduced and has outcomes that are highly stable with respect to possible external disturbances. In searching for this time standard, the frequency of the periodical processes has risen to the level of the cesium atomic clock, which is based on a cycle of over nine billion vibrations during one (old) astronomical second. This has become the basis of the International Atomic Time, which is continuously broadcast from stations in Colorado (U.S.), Rugby (U.K.), and Braunsweig (BRD) and is received by the authoritative clocks referred to above. On this atomic foundation it is, in principle, possible to make chronological measurements extending from the millions of years that astrophysicists work with to the nanoseconds that are needed in other areas of physical research.

This time is indicated precisely by the clock, but this is in no way "time as such." Its foundation is only a specific stable movement that has been selected to function as a standard for chronological measurement. It is only a very sophisticated convention that enables time to be measured by offering a precise instrument everyone can use for the abstract temporal coordination of their actions.

An important implication is that the constructed chronological concept of time, to be able to measure all possible processes (except its own), must be totally devoid of any content and be completely abstract. This abstract nature implies that of any process, only those aspects are relevant that can be measured according to this chrono-logic. All other possible aspects are neglected: the measurement of time has nothing to do with its meaning. The anthropological paradox is, however, that the chronological subject is *theoretically* completely detached, but *practically* necessarily *involved* in time.

That gerontology is seduced to let chronological age play such an undeserved prominent role has something to do with this paradox, which leads to specific problems of studying aging as living in time.

First, it is impossible to study processes of aging as we would study other processes because we cannot observe aging in an experimental group and compare the results with a control group that does not age. We are, like everything that exists around us, embedded in time and although (unlike stones or trees) we can be aware of this, we cannot step out of time or aging to observe it purely. Getting a clear understanding of time is hard because it is always difficult to distance ourselves from what we take for granted. Time slips away *because we are living in time* and cannot distance ourselves from it. This fundamental human condition, discussed in this volume by Jan Baars, leads to problems in even the most sophisticated research strategies. The notorious Age-Period-Cohort problem, which is addressed here by Warner Schaie, is just another example of the *enveloping* and *elusive nature* of time: we cannot step out of time to pinpoint it clearly. We can never find aging in a pure form: aging can only be experienced or studied in specific situations that influence and co-constitute the processes that are involved.

Second, we have no organ to perceive time like we can see objects in space. And although what we can see for ourselves may often seem self-evident but actually be self-deceiving, grasping time is even more difficult. Therefore spatial or metric figures are mostly used to represent time, but they already presuppose specific ways of dealing with it.

Every step in studying or even discussing aging already involves metaphors, images, or vague ideas about time, and they make an uneasy contribution to the results of these studies or discussions. Moreover, as aging involves many different processes at different levels, all these processes must be precisely understood in their own temporal qualities, which requires adequate theories and concepts. Because time and aging cannot be perceived directly, the dynamics of aging cannot be grasped without concepts. More clarity about concepts of time should be a major priority for gerontology because only if we can specify more precisely the nature of different aging processes will it be possible to arrive at better explanations of the variations in aging among humans of the same chronological age, which are often hidden in average scores.

A further exploration of the implicit concepts of time and aging appears not only to be important for most individual disciplines which study aging, but is certainly relevant for the interdisciplinary pretensions of the endeavor called gerontology. During the last years, there have been some important publications that have advanced the interdisciplinary theoretical debate in gerontology (e.g., Bengtson & Schaie, 1999), but it may be also fruitful to focus on a common theme such as time, which poses fundamental questions for all disciplines involved.

Apart from the scholarly virtue of furthering such a thematic interdisciplinary dialogue within gerontology, it appears that the only way to explain processes of aging lies in the study of the interrelations between the different temporal dynamics that are responsible for the heterogeneity of aging processes (see Visser, this volume).

Hendricks and Peters (1986), building on earlier work by Maltz and Riegel, distinguished chronological, individual, social, and ideational time; and parallel with these, inner/biological, individual/psychological, cultural/sociological, and outer/physical dimensions of time. These dimensions can be recognized in the contributions to this volume, which focus as a whole on methodological and epistemological aspects of time and aging.[1] The psychological, methodological, physical, and biological contributions are positioned between two chapters in which concepts of time and aging are approached from a broader metatheoretical perspective. The opening chapter by Jan Baars articulates the fundamental issues from the perspective of social theory, emphasizing the need to acknowledge three different approaches to aging and time. The final chapter, by Henk Visser, counterbalances this by analyzing the problem of interdisciplinary integration from the perspective of the philosophy of science.

INTRODUCING THE CHAPTERS

Chapter 2, by Jan Baars, includes sociological and philosophical perspectives as he combines a theoretical reflection about concepts of time with a reflection about their possible practical consequences for aging persons. The overemphasis on chronological time and age is set against the background of cultural developments in which chronological time tends to become the only *shared* temporal perspective, as inspiring narratives about aging as living in time are largely absent or fragmented. As chronological time is only partially adequate in an empirical sense and completely inadequate to grasp the meaning of aging, Baars seeks both in a personal and a broader cultural sense to revitalize other temporal perspectives. He reflects on a major debate in Western philosophy, arguing the importance of subjectively experienced time in opposition to objective, chronological time. The

[1] However, aging as living in time poses many problems of a more existential nature, which are often referred to but not elaborated in this volume. They are addressed in a more recently started project (cf. Baars, 2002, 2006).

ambition of both perspectives, represented in the briefly cited main positions of Aristotle, Augustine, the phenomenologist Husserl, and the existential philosopher Heidegger, has been to constitute time *as such* from their perspective. From the confrontation between these theoretical positions, which are still basic for contemporary thinking about concepts of time, it follows that the ambitions of both traditions to constitute the one and only essential time must be seen as a failure: *both* objective and subjective time are necessary. They cannot constitute each other's perspectives. Moreover, it becomes clear that a third temporal perspective is presupposed and must be acknowledged in its own right to allow a more adequate understanding of aging as living in time: narrative articulations of shared meaning.

Baars argues that in order to do justice to the complexity and meaningfulness of human aging, gerontology should be guided by a meaningful configuration of three fundamental temporal perspectives: chronological measurements, personal experience, and narrative articulations of aging as living in time. They should each play their own explicit role in a Triple Temporality of Aging.

In Chapter 3, Elke van der Meer presents an overview of the most recent results from cognitive research and brain-based research on psychological time. From this overview we can learn that temporal experiences are not only conceptually mediated, but also presuppose memory structures and processes in the "hardware" of the human brain. The chapter presents another fascinating encounter of the objective and subjective time Baars writes about, as experimental research proceeding with objective, chronological time is used to clarify the subjective experience of time. Van der Meer discusses temporal order (succession) and temporal duration and also the temporal perspective (past, present, and future) which is presupposed in viewing human lives diachronically. We can see how Augustine's ideas about the subjective mind that embraces past, present, and future have already captured some of the temporal functions of the brain.

Whereas Augustine, however, assumed the human mind to be without age, it has been amply demonstrated that time concepts are gradually acquired through childhood and that there are important differences between young and older adults in the ways they look at past, present, and future. As humans are living through time, their bodies are aging and their brains are also changing. On the one hand, the brain is an organ like other organs, but on the other hand its high level of differentiation and complexity once again precludes a simple formula: the aging of the brain does not proceed according to chronological age. Not only do different regions in the brain like the hippocampus, cerebellum, and prefrontal cortex play their own intricate roles, but cognitive functioning represents a complicated temporality of its own. Van der Meer emphasizes that there are many possible factors influencing cognitive functioning and that its decline is neither linear nor irreversible as regional dysfunctions can be overcome by compensating mechanisms, so that cognitive aging becomes a mixed process of change, gains, losses, and maintenance (cf. Baltes & Singer, 2001; Park & Schwarz, 2000). In this context, van der Meer discusses the possible reasons for the widely held impression that time seems to pass more quickly as we get older. Often this is explained by referring to an internal clock or "neuronal pacemaker" that might be running more slowly, resulting in the impression that "external" time moves faster. But maybe the experiences in childhood are more diverse and the years spent as aged persons are dominated more by routines, so that cognitive (and not hardware) components are constitutive of the experience that time moves faster, which also points to the relevance of age-structured social contexts.

Such cognitive components are explored in Chapter 4 by Freya Dittmann-Kohli, who delves deeply into the temporal perspective of the self, as she draws upon innovative research methods that integrate quantitative and qualitative approaches, allowing her to study large datasets. She shows that there is also a subjective experience of the temporality of the self who is living in time. During midlife, a different sort of subjective temporal perspective emerges, which focuses on the self as having limited duration and facing decline and eventual death. Also, in younger persons with a serious illness, it may happen that knowledge of mortality becomes more personalized and integrated into the cognitive structures of identity. This amounts to a cognitive integration of the basic facts of human life: being a person with a past, present, and future that may be unexpectedly short or very long but still limited. This awareness of the human condition leads, in many aging persons, to another view of time than they had before. A person who has been an ambitious achiever may develop a more hedonistic orientation toward the present, which is not a sign of shortsightedness or irresponsibility, but of wisdom and understanding of the value of the time that remains. This leads to such goals as continuity, preservation, and maintenance, which are different from the ones that are typical of the "achievement syndrome." It turns out that the usual constructs of the Future Time Perspective are typical of healthy young or middle-aged adults and not representative of people who are seriously ill or very old or of people in cultures that are less oriented toward achievement and ambition. In contrast to traditional studies on Future Time Perspective, Dittmann-Kohli therefore emphasizes the importance of an *existential time perspective,* which develops as a cognitive framework or cognitive structure of identity in later life, as persons become more directly aware that they are living in a finite time perspective in which they are advancing, gathering more past, and facing less possible future. This experience of aging spreads gradually to all domains of life; there is an increased salience of existential time in late life—an awareness that an important part of life has passed.

In Chapter 5, Warner Schaie addresses the problems connected with the concepts of time and aging by exploring a methodological approach that can avoid some of the pitfalls connected with the so-called APC problem. The complexity of this problem can be illustrated as follows: when we have gathered data concerning a certain group of people we call aging or elderly, we cannot be sure whether these data tell us something about the aging process in general, about the specific period of study, or about the specific cohort these elderly people belong to. A precise assessment of these three aspects evades us; they are all relevant but we don't know how. Almost 40 years ago, Schaie had already articulated this problematic constellation in terms of a "General Developmental Model," and his most recent methodological strategy is highly interesting and subtle. As the unconfounded estimation of all components of the APC, or General Developmental Model, still eludes us, it is important to find ways to break the dependencies in the model. One way is to redefine one of the components in such a way that it is no longer directly dependent upon calendar time. For this purpose, Schaie chooses time-of-measurement or period, the component that is concerned explicitly with the timing of events of interest to the researcher. By concentrating on events, chronological time becomes a dependent variable and "raw calendar time," as Schaie calls it, is transformed into something more meaningful: event time. Instead of beginning by gathering a population with a certain age, one can start by defining a transition (or maturational variable) and investigate specified characteristics (with their ages as just one option) of people who go through this transition. A methodological device called the "Cattell Cube" is called upon to construct an appropriate design for this analysis, which is differentiated further into substantive *type* of event, *impact* of event, *direction* of event, event *density*, and *perceptions* of the event. As Schaie notes, event density can refer to historical periods, maturational periods, or to an event density provided by the environment. Accordingly, event time can be constituted at several levels, including the chronological regimes that Baars is referring to, which define people as aged at a certain age and use ascribed characteristics of these persons to legitimize these regimes.

Next, there is a fascinating confrontation between Jos Uffink and Eugene Yates in the short Chapters 6 to 9, partly devoted to a debate that originated between them during the preparation of this volume. They introduce the ideas of authors, such as Albert Einstein, Niels Bohr, Max Planck, Ilya Prigogine, and Stephen Hawking, who have deeply influenced the way we look at the universe, into the discussion about time and aging. Uffink begins with reviewing basic conceptual issues concerning physical concepts of time, from which he proceeds to a clarification of some important issues such as time *scale*. Often but confusingly, a particular time scale is called a particular *time*, as if a different type of measurement would be the same as adopting a different time, although the underlying concept is still given by "the same qualitative temporal ordering," as Uffink writes. He distinguishes the *measurement* of time from its *meaning* and insists that even in theoretical physics the meaning of time still has to be grasped on the basis of everyday language or narratives. He denies that it would be possible to specify the meaning of time in terms of theoretical physics or to define time in terms of more fundamental, nontemporal notions. According to Uffink, we can learn a lot from physics concerning the measurement of time, but nothing regarding its meaning or subjective experience and very little about human aging. Thus he underscores the remarks made about the empty and abstract nature of chronological time that were made above.

From this rather skeptical perspective, Uffink analyzes the work of some gerontologists who argue that theoretical physics provides an important clue to the understanding of aging, most notably Eugene Yates. Because the Second Law of Thermodynamics is often referred to in such endeavors, Uffink focuses on the problems of such applications of thermodynamics. The first problem that he notes is that aging cannot be understood as an accumulation of entropy or disorder, because a loosening of constraints as human aging proceeds is only one aspect, the other being that constraints may also change or new constraints may rise. To define aging as an accumulation of entropy turns this precise terminology into a speculative metaphor that serves no clear purpose. The second problem that Uffink notes concerns the use of accumulation of entropy as a theoretical foundation for a so-called intrinsic time/age, as opposed to a time/age that is measured externally, without being grounded in the specific dynamics of the system. If this would work at all (which Uffink doubts) there might be as many intrinsic times as there are aging systems (humans, organs) and we would lose the possibility of comparing or measuring them. Moreover, the openness of the human living system undermines the idea of an intrinsic age, which may be deeply influenced by changes in the ecological or social environment.

Uffink also discusses the spectacular Twin Paradox and its famous time dilation effect which would, however, only arise if humans would travel through the galaxies at speeds close to that of light. The Twin Paradox may be a fascinating possibility for elementary particles, but does not contain a feasible perspective for humans as long as they remain earthbound and are not subjected to traveling at speeds that are hardly imaginable nor endurable.

However, this fundamental difference between the elementary particles of conventional physics and the dynamics of living organisms is precisely what has encouraged Eugene Yates to develop his "Homeodynamics." Although he maintains that *biological* entities are ultimately *physical*, he is convinced that they cannot be adequately understood by standard physics. Whereas conventional physics focuses on inanimate physical systems and tends to abolish time, Yates is looking for a new heuristic perspective that can generate new approaches to the temporal qualities that are inherent in living organisms, building on fluid mechanics and the thermodynamics of irreversible processes. He argues that all multicellular organisms that reach a fixed size after a period of growth inevitably grow old and die; they live in irreversible or anisotropic time, which they generate and scale to an important degree through their own activities. We know from other research (e.g., Albrecht, 2002) that human bodies are temporally organized and maintained by periodic processes such as biological clocks. Many of these appear to be dominated by circadian rhythms, having originated in an evolutionary environment in which the solar system imposes 24-hour-long rhythms on life. Most physiological processes show such relatively independent circadian rhythms, which are also maintained or disturbed by external "Zeitgeber" (time givers). Yates presents an elegant model in which gerontological discussions of age-related disturbances of such circadian rhythms can be connected to a dynamical process of aging from birth to death. He designs a helix in which the lifetime energy budget of humans is portrayed in the form of a truncated ellipsoid, thus making visible the gradually diminishing functioning of circadian processes over a lifetime: the lifetime energy budget is gradually used up. The homeodynamic cause of senescence is an accumulation of internal entropy, which displaces a system from its normal optimal operating condition of "orderly disorder."

The goal of these explorations is to find an approach to aging processes that does not depend on external generalizations, but is based on aging processes operating within the living organism, so that we may better understand why people age differently when they share the same chronological age. Yates emphasizes that measuring the dynamics of these processes in terms of chronological time does not offer much more than an externally applied categorization of the intrinsic dynamics of life. He is searching, therefore, for a biological time in terms of the coordination of the internal actions of a living system, resulting in its internal temporal organization. The intrinsic dynamics generate the irreversible time that is characteristic of living organisms, so he concludes that "homeodynamic processes do not occur in time—they *make* their time." The need to keep aloof from chronological age as an explanatory factor is again affirmed when Yates quotes from Barbour's early work: "Physics must be recast on a new foundation in which change is the measure of time, not time the measure of change." *Mutatis mutandis* could also be a motto for Schaie's contribution.

Finally, Henk Visser looks back from the perspective of philosophy of science and asks what the preconditions might be for interdisciplinary research on aging, discussing some of the obstacles as well as possibilities. One of the obstacles he notes is that scientific concepts of aging are often derived in an unclear way from commonsense concepts or notions. He suggests therefore, investing more research in a data-oriented approach, instead of the operationalization approach, which is typically oriented toward taking over commonsense concepts, trying to transform them into scientific concepts.

Visser emphasizes especially the systematic significance of concepts in their function to make multilevel or interlevel explanations of aging possible. Although he remains rather skeptical about the present potential of gerontology to arrive at such explanations, he points pragmatically to the perspective of studying aging processes as changing possibilities over time, working gradually upward in a data-oriented approach from lower-order theories to more comprehensive theories.

REFERENCES

Albrecht, U. (2002). Invited review: Regulation of mammalian circadian clock genes. *Journal of Applied Physiology, 92,* 1348-1355.

Baars, J. (2002). *Ouder Worden en de Fragiliteit van de Intermenselijke Conditie* [Aging and the fragility of the interhuman condition]. Utrecht: University for Humanistics Press.

Baars, J. (2006). *Het Nieuwe Ouder Worden. Problemen en Perspectieren van leven in de týd* [Aging in a new light. Problems and perspectives of living in time]. Utrecht: University for Humanistics Press.

Baltes, P., & Mayer, K.U. (1999). *The Berlin Aging Study: Aging from 70 to 100.* New York: Cambridge University Press.

Baltes, P. B., & Singer, T. (2001). Plasticity and the aging mind: An exemplar of the bio-cultural orchestration of brain and behavior. *European Review, 9,* 59-72.

Bengtson, V. L., & Schaie, K. W. (1999). *Handbook of theories of aging.* New York: Springer.

Birren, J. (1959). Principles of research on aging. In J. Birren (Ed.), *Handbook of aging and the individual: Psychological and biological aspects* (pp. 2-42). Chicago: University of Chicago Press.

Birren, J. (1999). Theories of aging: A personal perspective. In V.L. Bengtson & K. W. Schaie (Eds.), *Handbook of theories of aging*. New York: Springer.

Daatland, S. O., & Biggs, S. (2004). *Ageing and diversity. Multiple pathways and cultural migrations.* Bristol: Policy Press.

Hendricks, J., & Peters, C. B. (1986). *The times of our lives.* In J. Hendricks & M. M. Seltzer (Eds.), *Aging and time. American Behavioral Scientist, 29*(6), 662-678.

Imhoff, A. E. (1981). *Die gewonnenen Jahre*. München: Beck.

Maddox, G. L., & Lawton, M. P. (Eds.). (1988). Varieties of aging. *Annual Review of Gerontology and Geriatrics, 8.*

Park, D., & Schwarz, N. (2000). *Cognitive aging. A primer*. Philadelphia: Taylor & Francis.

Schaie, K. W. (1996). *Intellectual development in adulthood: The Seattle Longitudinal Study.* New York: Cambridge University Press.

Sprott, R. L. (2002). Biomarkers of aging. In D. J. Ekerdt (Ed.), *Encyclopedia of aging.* New York: Macmillan Reference.

CHAPTER 2

A Triple Temporality of Aging: Chronological Measurement, Personal Experience, and Narrative Articulation

Jan Baars

Time is organized and interpreted at different levels in societies and cultures (Hendricks & Seltzer, 1986). We can think of the most general level of the Christian or Muslim calendar in which religious holidays structure the year, often in connection with a national calendar in which the year is structured by the remembrance of major events such as wars, disasters, declarations, or constitutions. Next we can think of yearly cycles in which the rhythms of the natural environment are coordinated with specific seasonal activities such as fishing, sowing, harvesting, or socializing in warm homes during cold and dark winters; usually combined with seasonal festivities, markets, contests, and holidays. Such cyclical representations of time are also implicit in social settings in which human beings are born, grow up, begin their own adult lives, get older, and eventually die.

Cultural representations of living in time are often highly colored by specific characteristics of regions and traditions, which are typically transferred by socialization (Zerubavel, 1981). As situations change and communication reaches beyond cultural boundaries, these representations tend to become targets of criticism because people want to choose their own ways of living without following ethnocentric, often gender-biased dictates (Arber, Davidson, & Ginn, 2003; Baars & Thomése, 1994; Settersten, 2002). Such criticism is inevitable and necessary as culture and society change. Aging, especially, poses many new questions as life expectancy has in a relatively short period of time broken through all previous frames of reference. Being "aged" has on the one hand become formally regulated (e.g., age of entrance, entitlements) but has, on the other hand, developed into a long and rather empty perspective. An empty space ahead may offer individuals maximal possibilities to go their own way, supported or distracted by the numerous suggestions for aging or anti-aging that are commercially explored and exploited. Living together, however, also implies a minimal basis of shared ideas, expectations, and values according to which people respect and take care of each other. As the representatives of communitarian and neoliberal positions fight each other's caricatures (suffocating sociality versus ruthless individualism) (cf. Avineri & De Shalit, 1992; Rosenblum, 1989), an inspiring contemporary culture of aging as living in time becomes difficult to envisage. All the more because aging individuals become, in spite of age-related generalizations, increasingly different from each other. This poses the difficult question of how to develop an inspiring *shared* culture of aging in which the realities of aging are acknowledged and *personal* experiences and perspectives of aging humans are respectfully articulated. This requires a meaningful configuration of three fundamental temporal perspectives: chronological measurements, personal experience, and narrative articulations of aging as living in time.

We are confronted, however, with an overemphasis on one of these three temporal perspectives. As traditional representations of aging are seen as outdated and unfit to give meaning to aging in an increasingly complex and differentiated world, chronological time tends to remain as the *only* time perspective that is shared with other people. Of course, there are still the calendars and yearly cycles of festivities and transitions, but they tend increasingly to be seen from a chronological perspective: as exact dates that must be incorporated and efficiently dealt with by chronological planning; hence the numerous self-help books on time management. But there is no chronological reason to celebrate anything; in the perspective of the clock, any moment is the same as any other (Hendricks, 2001). This leads to paradoxical situations as people are rushing in and out of situations that were originally meant to tone down the importance of chronological time. The dominant position that is given to chronological time has problematic effects as it has nothing to offer regarding the *meaning* of aging as living in time. Although chronological age is empirically not a very informative category (see the Introduction, this volume), it has become of constitutive importance as measurements of chronological time tend to dominate the understanding of aging, with many theoretical and practical consequences.

CHRONOLOGICAL REGIMES: MEASUREMENT WITHOUT MEANING?

The abstract nature of chronological time is present throughout the aging processes, hence voiding them of meaning because chronological *age* and chronological *duration* are used as primary instruments in the organization of the life course (Leisering & Leibfried, 1999). The identification of aged research populations, for instance, builds on chronological age and presupposes an organization of the life course in which chronological time has become an important instrumental perspective (Kohli, 1986; Mayer & Müller, 1986). Concepts such as age groups, age norms, or age grading presuppose chronological age as the typical instrument to regulate many transitions or entitlements. Concepts used in the discussions of aging societies, such as age-structure, birth cohorts, dependency ratio, age/cost profile, and all kinds of tables in which ages are associated with particular characteristics, pretending to give a quick informative overview, have become so general that their gerontological meaning is rarely questioned.

Chronological age is, however, nothing more than the result of a measurement of the chronological time that has elapsed since someone was born. We are getting older with every tick of the clock, but this "older" has a precise meaning only in a chronological, not gerontological sense. The aged have no more in common than a certain minimal calendar age. Age-related generalizations may be practical or even necessary for certain purposes, but for gerontological purposes this can hardly be satisfactory.

One of the problems that have arisen during the development of gerontology is that its analytical apparatus has become involved, in unclear and ambiguous ways, in organizational contexts, where aging people are mainly relevant as the subjects of planning procedures and average estimates. Such bureaucratic tasks may be necessary, but should not dominate the way aging is approached or understood. The scientific precision that is associated with chronological *time* has led to an uncritical acceptance of certain constructions of chronological *age*. We have reasons to doubt whether chronological age is really the "independent" or even "explanatory" variable much research assumes it to be, which also leads to the question whether the definitions and demarcations of the relevant populations that constitute the subject matter of gerontological studies, which are mostly built on chronological age, make sense.

Chronological time appears to be indispensable, also for research on aging processes, but this covers only a part of the complex realities of aging. As far as gerontology limiting its approach to chronological age because of its readiness to be used in generalizations and planning procedures involving large numbers of people, it becomes involved in processes that neglect meaning. That personal dimensions of aging processes cannot always be acknowledged may be unavoidable, because social entities such as institutions, communities, and societies want to assure their continuity while individuals fade away, sooner or later. Therefore these entities tend to use perspectives that are detached from limited personal horizons, and the chronological perspective may be useful for such long-term planning as it can interrelate the average chronological *duration of activities* with the chronological *ages* or average life expectancies of the actors involved. But the one-sided emphasis on chronological time tends to neglect not only personal meaning but *all* meaningful dimensions of aging.

Calculations with time and aging that run the risk of using shortsighted generalizations as aging processes, as has been repeatedly emphasized, are complex and differentiated. Moreover, the all too abstract categorical status of "being aged" is often assigned to people at an age that is astonishingly low when seen in the same chronological perspective in which life expectancies are established. When citizens are considered to be aged at the chronological age of 55, which has become customary in Europe since the lowering of pre-retirement ages in the 1990s (Walker, 2004), this status will remain with them for several decades (possibly another 55 years), during which they may continue to change and to "fan out," becoming even more different from other members of their birth cohorts, because they tend to follow their specific interests without being tied down by the institutional regularities of education, work, or raising children. It has even become customary to speak of "older workers" for people with ages over 40; not only in Europe, but also in the United States (cf. Henretta, 2001). Therefore, it makes sense to repeat basic gerontological insights: even if people have the same chronological age, there is an important intra-age variability (Dannefer, 1988): the differences *within* age groups may be more important than the differences *between* age groups.

This situation gives birth to unnecessary conflicts, as the abilities and needs of numerous people clash with informal and formal regulations by which they are in a generalizing way treated as aged and consequently excluded from important societal domains and activities. As populations age and break through life-course structures that may have made sense in bygone days, these structures are lagging behind differentiated processes of population aging (structural lag); a problem that plays a central role in the later work of Mathilda Riley (cf. Riley, Kahn, & Foner, 1994). A clear example of such asynchrony is the *acceleration of ascribed aging* in the labor markets of most Western countries, which suddenly emerged and culminated during the 1980s (cf. Kohli, Rein, Guillemard, & van Gunsteren, 1991), in stark contrast to the rising life expectancy (Oeppen & Vaupel, 2002), which can be interpreted as a *slowing down* of aging processes. This asynchrony may offer attractive perspectives of "golden years" to persons who can afford them, but excludes many aging people in Western Europe from important possibilities of gaining a decent income (Baars, 2002b; Walker & Maltby, 1997). Women who want to return to the labor market after having raised their children are particularly disadvantaged as they are right from the start labeled as older workers (Baars, Beck, & Graveland, 1997; Ginn, Street, & Arber, 2001). Finally, this acceleration of ascribed aging has increased the pressure on the lives of normal adults (25–45 years of age) to combine family life with a short and intense career during which the income of a long life must be gathered. When such long-term overburdening eventually leads to health problems, these are too often explained by referring to the ages of the persons concerned, offering another superficial argument to legitimate an early exit from the labor market.

Given these circumstances, knowing the chronological age of persons in such contexts can be quite informative because ages can easily be related to certain characteristics. If we take, for example, European women above age 55, we can predict that an overwhelming majority of them will not be formally working, which leads to other hypotheses with high probability. The point is, however, that this has nothing to do with aging as such, but everything with the way the labor market has been organized. This should qualify findings, for instance, that European males age 60 and higher are more strongly retrospectively oriented than prospectively (Van Praag & Ferreri-Carbonell, 2004). Given the importance of work for the articulation of personal identities and the exclusion of these people from the labor market, it is clear that such empirical characteristics are to a large degree constituted by the *chronological structuring* of the life course instead of being caused by aging processes per se. The labor market position of people above a certain age has, at least in the European Union, become an artifact of the budgetary strategies of large enterprises, governments, and labor unions (Walker & Maltby, 1997). For aging studies to focus on chronological age without analyzing the processes that constitute many of the characteristics associated with these ages merely because chronological age has been institutionalized in the societies in which people live, enforces the chronological regimes of these societies.

The paradoxical acceleration of ascribed aging in a situation of rising life expectancies presents another example of a general acceleration of the social change that characterizes contemporary societies. Modernity has been defined by a constant modernization and Late Modernity can be seen as its intensification in which "all that is solid melts into air" (cf. Baars, 2005; Giddens, 1990, 1991). An important part of the recent discussion on globalization focuses on this tendency to speed up change as part of the struggle to survive the global competition (cf. Baars, Dannefer, Phillipson, & Walker, 2005; Hardt & Negri, 2000). This acceleration of change cannot only be seen in the domains of production and consumption, but also affects other areas of daily life. People who have lived for many years in the same house will often not only discover that the areas where they used to play and the factories where they went to work have all disappeared, but that their own house suddenly gets another address. The frames of reference and orientation may change so drastically that these people become disoriented.

Metaphorically speaking, in terms of a changing relationship between time and space, we could say that there is less support for aging identities from identical space than before, resulting in a much more direct and subjective confrontation with the abstract nature of chronological time (Baars, 2000). Even 50 years ago, the specific historical space in which one was born (country, region, village, class, family, etc.) used to support or even determine much more strongly how a person should live. The late-modern acceleration of change tends to undermine the external support of identities, which also used to exist in the form of a clear and continuous profession or continuous customs and morals (Deats & Lenker, 1999; Peace, Holland, & Kellahar, 2005). This protean nature of late modernity has contributed to the many differences that have emerged in empirical research on aging and the aged. Small wonder that there is an extensive contemporary debate about the construction of identity and self (e.g., Holstein & Gubrium, 2000).

Chronological time plays an increasingly important role because it is typically used to measure all kinds of events or processes to see whether they can be more efficiently (better) organized: smoother or faster and less "time consuming." Such a restructuring of processes and situations from the perspective of chronological measurements may have several important consequences for the aged. We can think of the phenomenon of "time budgets" in institutions for care. There is a crucial transition from measuring the times of particular conversations or acts of care, establishing that these activities take five or nine minutes on the average, to regulations that a conversation or a specific act of care *may not exceed a precise amount of time*. But we can also think of the organization of leisure activities, culture, or entertainment in sophisticated time formats. We can observe the proliferation of chronologically structured events in which an "optimal abundance" of sensations is presented to the public, which encourages the late modern tendency to hurry from one sensation to the next and to pack life with as many events as possible. Some aspects of these processes have been well described by Paul Virilio (1998) and put in a historical context of changing perspectives on the human life course by Marianne Gronemeyer (1993), as she explored the genesis of the paradox that people have attained longer lives but are confronted with a chronic "shortage of time." There is too much that should be experienced, or rather *undergone*. The experience of a time shortage for people who live, historically speaking, longer than ever before, refers to the problem of *integrating* or digesting the many heterogeneous events and sensations. As several studies of cognitive aging have demonstrated, aging does not harmonize well with acceleration (Salthouse, 1996; van der Meer, this volume). All activities take time, which can be measured chronologically, but this does not add anything meaningful; nor does acceleration.

However, even if all barriers in terms of chronological age are removed and aged people are not any longer excluded from certain societal domains or separated from people with other ages, this would not mean that aging has become meaningfully integrated into society. The paradox is that the instrumental culture that has added years to life is not capable of giving aging a new inspiring meaning; although it embraces in sheer number of years a more important part of life than ever before. The quantitative perspective of chronological time remains completely abstract and offers in itself no possibilities to develop a meaningful understanding of human aging.

AT HOME IN THE CHRONOLOGICAL UNIVERSE?

The search for a new meaningful positioning of aging as living in time has also become necessary as the understanding of time has changed. Concepts of time have for ages been based on the assumption of an *eternal repetition* of nature's movements, which only had to be refined (going from celestial bodies to cesium atoms) to serve the needs for more precise measurements. This is still the basic idea of chronological time, which has become empty, however, of all meanings that were traditionally bestowed on the temporal movements of the cosmos.

From Greek philosophy in its classical form (Parmenides, Plato, and Aristotle) until around 1800, the basic idea was that the Ultimate Being, reality written in capitals, would be eternal. Change and time were regarded as misleading impressions of cyclically returning processes in the minds of human mortals, who had difficulty understanding and accepting the Eternal Truth of Reality. Viewed from this metaphysical idea of an unchanging reality, aging can be no more than a transition from one clearly identified and fixed life phase to the next, remaining essentially and eternally the same cyclical process for humanity as such. This is the basic model of aging that can be seen in the traditional images of clearly distinguished seasons, phases, or "Ages of Man," the title that, significantly, the authors of two different studies about medieval interpretations of the life cycle (Burrow, 1986; Sears, 1986) chose independently of each other.

This idea of an eternally identical reality became more and more strongly challenged during the nineteenth century, when scientists such as Buffon, Darwin, and many others started to systematically organize the accumulating evidence that the species we find in nature are the result of a long process of change, that the earth itself is a product of a long and ongoing evolution, and that the same is true for our bodies and brains (cf. Hayflick, 1990; Kirkwood, 1999; Toulmin & Goodfield, 1965).

During the last decades of the twentieth century, the Darwinian ideas about evolution have been further radicalized (Dennett, 1996), leading to new conceptions of spontaneously originating order and self-organizing complexity (Holland, 1999; Kauffman 1993, 2002; Waldrop 1992). However, the evolutionary origin in an environment in which the solar system imposes 24-hour-long rhythms on life cannot be easily escaped as it has led to so-called biological clocks, which regulate the circadian rhythms found in most physiological processes such as body temperature, blood pressure, and hormone secretion (Albrecht, 2002). But these new perspectives may contribute to understanding the phenomenon that biological entities such as animals and humans, within the limits of their species and their contexts, organize their own rhythms of living and aging. The tendency to conceptualize this in terms of biological *clocks* shows again the tendency to relate all temporal processes to metric time, as if this were the ultimate goal of our knowledge of time.

Many of these explorations throw a fascinating new light on the understanding of time, although some of their claims harmonize well with everyday intuitions. An example is the irreversibility of time, grounded in the increasing entropy in closed energetic systems (Nicolis & Prigogine, 1989; Prigogine, 1997), which fits the experience of human beings who are living in time. Surprisingly, these ideas argue the fundamental importance of gerontology as they claim that aging is not just a marginal experience in a reality that does not change, but that *change, aging, and emergent becoming* can be seen as *core processes of the universe.* However, these developments pose many new questions as the positioning of human beings in the universe (Kaufmann, 1996) requires new narratives that may guide both human aging and its study.

The Abstract Chronological Universe and the Short Breath of Humans

Whereas most traditional calendars were accompanied by cultural narratives that offered humans a central place in a universe that could be seen as *essentially related* to one's own life (for instance in the Judeo-Christian idea of being a personal part of a universal creation), the temporal and spatial dimensions of the expanding Big-Bang universe are in themselves meaningless and defy human imagination (Hawking, 1998). It seems an illusion that, in the face of such immense proportions, even a long human life could mean anything at all. The short breath of human life seems to get lost as the scissors of cosmological time open, a conflict that fascinated the German philosopher Hans Blumenberg (1986) toward the end of his life. The rational subject that could be associated with this chrono-logical universe is completely lost in its dimensions. The anthropological paradox is, however, that the chronological subject may be *theoretically* completely detached but remains *practically* necessarily *involved* in a time that tends to become meaningless space. Although *Homo sapiens* may seem nothing more than a short egocentric breath in a huge cosmic wind, it is only in the short breaths of human life that all meaningful questions arise and can be explored.

This poses challenges to develop cultural narratives that give meaning or rather, *articulate, reflect, and enrich* the temporal perspectives through which human beings try to grasp a meaningful understanding of their lives. Such needed cultural narratives cannot just be taken from the different traditional sources, but have to be reinterpreted and newly developed. As narratives appear to be a necessary ingredient in metatheoretical perspectives (Nash, 1990), gerontology also needs inspiring narratives that can meaningfully guide its explorations. This does not, however, imply that narratives can replace exact measurements as have been developed in the tradition of chronological time. Narrative practices have a strong appeal because they represent a way of paying attention and tribute to the uniqueness of persons, their experiences and histories (Birren & Cochran, 2001; Kenyon, Clark, & De Vries, 2001; Randall, 1997). But narratives in themselves are formal structures that offer no guarantee that they are meaningful or respectful of individuals. Before turning to narratives, we have, therefore, to reinterpret and revitalize an important traditional alternative to the chronological, "objective" or "objectifying" perspective: the subjective time perspective.

THE EMERGENCE OF A SUBJECTIVE TIME PERSPECTIVE

Is it possible to strengthen the personal experience of aging as living in time in such a way that the person would be able to understand all temporal dimensions of human lives *without* using chronological time? This has been the ambition of a long tradition in Western thinking about time that arose in opposition to a view of time that is grounded in the more or less regular movements of nature. This subjective time perspective offers possibilities to articulate the *personal* experience of time and has been developed gradually, with much effort, from within the traditional ontology of an unchanging reality. This struggle begins in full force with the work of the fifth-century thinker Augustine, who attempts to derive an understanding of time *as such* from his own experience. He struggles with the question that he, or *his living in finite time*, has become for himself, thus reframing the Socratic self-questioning in a *temporal* horizon. This influential work was elaborated much later by two important twentieth-century neo-Augustinians: Edmund Husserl and Martin Heidegger.

From the confrontation between these theoretical positions, which are still basic for contemporary thinking about concepts of time, it follows that *both* objective and subjective time are necessary. The ambitions of both traditions to constitute time *as such* must be seen as a failure; they cannot constitute each other's perspectives. Moreover, it becomes clear that a third temporal perspective is presupposed and must be acknowledged in its own right to allow a more adequate understanding of aging as living in time: narrative articulations of shared meaning.

As the Augustinian perspective is elaborated in a discussion with Aristotle, I shall begin with a short comment on Aristotle's concept of time. Of course, there are many other aspects in the confrontation of Augustine and Aristotle, which it would be relevant to discuss, as it represents a clash between two major sources of Western tradition: Greek philosophy and Judeo-Christian spirituality.

ARISTOTLE: FOUNDATIONS OF CHRONOLOGICAL TIME

Aristotle's *Physics* includes a text that is, in a certain sense, still basic to modern thinking about chronological time. He starts his analysis with change in general, including the movements of (unchanging) nature. This does not mean that time is identified with movement, because whereas movements are always specific and can stop, time necessarily goes on. This is Aristotle's main argument for the oneness of time. However, this nonidentity of time and movements does not lead to an *independence* of time from the movements of nature: "It is evident, then, that time is neither movement nor independent of movement" (*Physics,* 219a2). The nonidentity of time with what is regarded as its basis, the movements of nature, becomes more precisely articulated in relation to the concepts of continuity and magnitude. As a complex result of these three elements, the concept of measurable "objective" time emerges: "time is just this—number of movement in respect of 'before' and 'after'" (*Physics,* 219b1). This persistent emphasis on numbers and measurement that we still encounter in "chronological age" already had a long history in Aristotle's day, dating back to Babylonian and Egyptian cosmology (Wendorf, 1985) and can also be found in Plato's *Timaeus*: ". . . as He set in order the Heaven, of that Eternity which abides in unity He made an eternal image, moving according to number, even that which we have named Time" (37d).

The time of nature's movements, as Aristotle acknowledges in passing, requires a *soul* to distinguish the instants and count the intervals. He admits that the question whether time would exist if the soul did not exist "may fairly be asked" (*Physics,* 223a21-22). But his systematic emphasis is on countable numbers instead of numbers that are actually counted by a human soul. The human experience of time cannot be understood from Aristotle's physical definition of time; it remains largely hidden and unclearly presupposed. This residual role of a presupposed subjective experience of time has remained characteristic of the tradition of scientifically objectified time, which bases itself on the movements of nature, in spite of the important changes this tradition has undergone since Galileo and Newton.

AUGUSTINE: TIME AS A THREEFOLD PRESENT

Around 750 years later, Augustine presented a notion of time that can be regarded, in the context of Western thought on time, as the other major position. The Greek idea of a timeless reality however, can still be found in the work of Augustine, who was the first to explore the subjective experience of time, but for whom the ultimate reality was identified with an eternally unchanging God. Time and change were, also in Augustine's religious theory, just the experiences of a human creature caught up in his sinful existence; but he is overwhelmed by the problems that they present for his personal existence. In his *Confessions,* he starts to question his own personal experience of time. This is a fascinating new beginning, inspiring many thinkers after Augustine, because time is so common, and its forms of measurement are so much taken for granted that we seem to need a radically new perspective once we really start to think about it. Augustine's initial puzzlement is expressed in his remark that he knows what time is when nobody asks him, but if asked, he does not know. This has become a famous quotation because in thinking about time we go through the same astonishment as soon as we leave the seeming self-evidence of time behind.

For Augustine, this quest was more than a mere academic issue: "I have become a problem to myself. For I am not now investigating the tracts of the heavens, or measuring the distance of the stars, or trying to discover how the earth hangs in space. I am investigating myself, my memory, my mind" (*Confessions,* p. 223).

Within the context of the Christian faith, he only has his personal experience and its intellectual clarification to rely on.

The existence of time was doubtful according to traditional skeptical arguments, maintaining that time could not exist, because the past is no more, the future is not yet, and the present does not remain. Augustine, however, tried to show that the human soul makes the existence of time possible, because the past exists in *memory*, the future exists in *anticipation,* and the present in *attention*. This idea of a threefold present is Augustine's major contribution to notions of time, still inspiring twentieth-century philosophers like Husserl, Heidegger, and Merleau-Ponty. Augustine's *Confessions*, dating from around the year 400, strikes us as astonishingly modern, as his arguments on time are presented in the context of a frank autobiography. Time, for Augustine, is the extension of the human soul (*distentio animi*) ranging from memory to anticipation: "It is in my own mind, then, that I measure time . . ." (*Confessions,* p. 276). Time is something that is typical of the limited, finite status of the human creature, who longs for a unification with his creator: a God who lives in eternity, for whom time does not exist.

Augustine's Judeo-Christian faith in God the Creator separates him fundamentally from Aristotle's view of nature and his physical perspective on time. For Augustine, time is based on the movements of the soul, not on the movements of the celestial bodies (cf. *Confessions,* p. 273). According to the Holy Scriptures, the God who created these celestial bodies was also able to stop their movements, therefore these natural movements could not be fundamental. Augustine concluded that God had created the time of nature when he created heaven and earth: "You are the Maker of all time. . . ."; "No moment of time passes except by your will" (*Confessions,* pp. 263, 254).

Although the idea that a God would regulate the movements of stars and planets has become strange to a secularized mind, we may even in a modern cosmology still accept the idea that the origin of a (particular form of) time is connected with the origin of a (particular) universe. But Augustine's conclusion that God created the time of nature conflicts with his other conclusion, that time could be nothing else than the extension of the human soul. His contribution, in opposition to Aristotle's position, leaves us with the same basic problem: what is the relationship between the (conceptualizations of the) temporal dimensions of nature and time as a personally experienced phenomenon? They again appear to exclude or at least occlude each other.

Husserl's Phenomenology: A Longitudinal Present

Husserl's phenomenological approach developed from a need to introduce concrete, direct experience into philosophy in reaction to a neo-Kantianism, which invested its intellectual energy in endless conceptual formalization. Husserl saw this as an ongoing sharpening of the knives of analysis until there was no blade left to cut with. Therefore he proclaimed a new, "phenomenological" approach to philosophical problems with an emphasis on direct experience of phenomena: "To the things themselves" (*Zu den Sachen selbst*). In accordance with this adage, he also wanted to clarify how the *essence* of time (time "as such") could be directly experienced, instead of constructing time in a Kantian way as a presupposition. Within the general program of Husserl's phenomenology, his *Phenomenology of Internal Time-Consciousness* (1964) is characterized by an even stronger rigor, since he wanted to break away from what he gradually came to see as a rigid dominance of *perception* in phenomenology. He wanted a more direct experiential ("hyletic") relationship to the phenomena, especially to time, in order to lay the foundation for a definitive and truly absolute phenomenology.

Husserl's inspiration in his approach to time is, of course, Augustine, who is mentioned explicitly in the preface of the *Phenomenology of Internal Time-Consciousness*. His most important contributions to the theory of time can easily be seen as further refinements of Augustine's theory of a threefold present. More precisely, Husserl shows how the experience of something with temporal extension, for instance a long sound, not only contains actual listening, but also a "retention" of the part that has already sounded and a "protention" of the part to come and its ending as a sound. This configuration of retention, direct experience and protention can easily be understood when we realize that in listening to a song or to a speech, we do not hear isolated sounds. The listener, as well as the singer or speaker, composes melodies, words, and sentences: understandable wholes that are spoken "now." This "now" has the broad temporal extension that can be called the "present." It is a *longitudinal* present in which we hear a speech, instead of experiencing a long series of instants during which there are sounds, produced by a voice. Such an experience of the present cannot be obtained from the chronometer (cf. Hendricks, 2001; Hendricks & Peters, 1986). The human experience of the present, of a now in the full sense, is lost in a blur of rapidly running microseconds. Analogous processes of interpretation had been explored earlier, but Husserl sheds new light on its prereflective character and the temporal extension that goes with it.

Not only the results, but also the problems that are part and parcel of Husserl's approach can be compared to those of Augustine. It remains problematic to accept that the past, especially if it is centuries ago, can be reproduced on the basis of the prereflective experience of retentions that are added to each other. A long bygone historical past cannot be remembered by an individual consciousness, but has to be reconstructed on the basis of documents or other traces of the past. Many analogous questions arise with regard to the temporal dimensions of nature (such as evolutionary processes). Husserl's phenomenology of internal time consciousness remains bound to a situation of direct experience, not unlike the perception he wanted to distance himself from. But even at this level, it is apparently impossible to communicate a direct ("hyletic") experience of time without language or concepts, which not only interfere with, but also give shape to experience.

Therefore, we must conclude that Husserl's pretension to constitute time *as such* from an internal time consciousness has failed. He has to presuppose the structure of objective time, which may be an example of a more general problem concerning the phenomenological reduction (*Einklammerung*): what has been put in parentheses may remain presupposed and even guide the phenomenological analysis. Husserl leaves us again with an implicit dichotomy of objectively measured time versus subjectively experienced time, which becomes extreme in Heidegger's work.

HEIDEGGER: AUTHENTIC TEMPORAL BEING IN THE FACE OF DEATH

The dichotomy of objective time versus subjectively experienced time becomes sharper as the emphasis on the experiential dimensions of time gets stronger. Heidegger's reflective engagement with time in his *Being and Time* (B&T), originally published in 1927, is intensely personal. He is fully occupied by the Augustinian *question that I am for myself* and stresses that it is impossible to think adequately or truthfully about life and living from a perspective that would allow us to study objects outside ourselves: "*Dasein* is an entity which does not just occur among other entities. Rather it is ontically distinguished by the fact that in its very Being, that Being is an *issue* for it" (B&T, p. 32). Heidegger manages in his own specific way to break away from the theoretical perspective that had already irritated Husserl, who had, however, not been able to really leave behind the restrictions he ascribed to perception. However, Heidegger shares the same fundamental pretension of constituting time *as such*.

Heidegger's criticism of the "ordinary" (*vulgäre*) concept of time does not distinguish between everyday time and scientific concepts of time. This ordinary or scientific time has validity only as a derivation of authentic temporality. As the "end" of Being-in-the-world is death, dying is seen as "constitutive for *Dasein's* totality" (B&T, p. 284). This Being-towards-death becomes the seal of authentic temporality in Heidegger's work, which is dominated by a hierarchy of levels of (in)authenticity (Ricoeur, 1988). Infinite time is, according to Heidegger, just a "derived" product of "inauthentic temporality," resulting from an inability to recognize the finitude of Being-towards-death (B&T, p. 378f). In much the same way, the popular saying that "time flies," would actually mean that we are fleeing from ourselves in the face of death (B&T, p. 478; cf. Blattner, 1992, 1999; Dahlstrom, 1995; Fleischer, 1991; Ricoeur, 1988).

Heidegger makes a distinction between his existential (*existenziale*) analysis of the structure of Being and his personal "existentiell" (*existenzielle*) commitment to a concrete way of Being-in-the-world. The personal nature of temporality demands that the existential analysis must be verified by his own commitment. We can guess from his expressions that the importance of the "world" is acknowledged in the central importance attached to Being-in-the-world, but

Heidegger's emphasis on his own, almost exclusive authenticity distorts the world in its social and historical dimensions. The struggle for authentic Being-in-the-world is situated in a negatively evaluated social context in which other people mainly enter his perspective as inauthentic. Social life, or in Heidegger's terms "Being-with" (*Mitsein*) is practically identified with the prototype of inauthenticity: "They" ("*Das Man*").

We find a basic contradiction here: according to Heidegger, the existential analysis must be verified by the concreteness of everyday life, but this is also a sphere of inauthenticity. His preoccupation with Being-towards-death prohibits an adequate understanding of the social horizon, which makes Heidegger's analysis (which leans heavily on language, an eminently social phenomenon) possible. This criticism of Heidegger has been voiced at an early moment (not loudly but clearly), by his student Karl Löwith (1928) and has been elaborated by philosophers such as Emmanuel Levinas (1969, 1987) and Michael Theunissen (1986).

Heidegger's analysis of authentic temporality denies that objective concepts of time, related to nature's rhythms, have their own relative autonomy, which is the basic assertion of the Aristotelian tradition. He explicitly places his work in opposition to Aristotle, who inaugurated a tradition of thinking about time which, according to Heidegger, has dominated and darkened Western philosophy until his own work revealed the truth about temporality (B&T, p. 473; cf. Derrida, 1982).

INTERTWINING AND CONFLICTING DIMENSIONS OF TIME

What are we to conclude from this short confrontation between Aristotle's *Physics* on one side, Augustine, Husserl, and Heidegger on the other, which is representative of a major debate in Western thinking about time? It appears that the extension of physical time—the time of nature, its movements and rhythms—cannot be derived from the extension of the soul. Chronological measurement has nowadays reached dimensions where millions of light years can be measured in a theoretical continuum with nanoseconds. Even if we can imagine what aging processes in Red Dwarfs, mitochondria, or telomeres may look like, they presuppose complex theoretical constructions, and it would be farfetched to derive them from personal temporal experience. Therefore we can conclude that Aristotle was right and Augustine and his followers wrong.

But the chronological constructions and investigations cannot answer all questions that may be posed by human aging. The chronological time perspective has little to offer, apart from determining *when* something occurred, *how long* it lasted, and whether it was *earlier or later* relative to other phenomena. It serves as an important instrument, even for human memory, although this is far from a chronological data recorder that would just accumulate any amount of data (Kotre, 1995; van der Meer, this volume). What we tend to think of as our *selves* has a lot to do with the ability to situate our lives in the interrelated temporal dimensions of past, present, and future; and if this ability fails, these *selves* are endangered. This experience of the lived present, enriched with a remembered past and an anticipated future, cannot be derived from the movements of nature; so in this respect we can conclude that Augustine was right and Aristotle wrong.

The personal nature of subjective temporal perspectives makes them very different from each other, but it makes no sense to say that these differences are an indication or even proof that these experiences are *less precise* than chronological measurement, because they refer to different temporal perspectives. Human aging takes place in different dimensions. It is part of the human condition that we are corporeal beings and as such take part in the many cycles and rhythms of nature that form the material ground for chronological measurements. But human beings are not in the same blind way a part of nature as plants or fish, which are also aging. Human reproduction, growing up, aging, and eventual death are perceived in ways that are infused with meaning. The study of human aging involves more than aging processes in anonymous bodies; therefore, we need a broader understanding of time than just the chronological perspective, and at this point we can still learn from the philosophers who tried to explicate the subjective experience of time. But a next step, in which chronological measurement and personal experience are joined by a third temporal perspective appears to be necessary.

TIME, NARRATIVES, AND THE CONSTITUTIVE LIFE WORLD

During the last decades of the twentieth century, the debate about the ways knowledge is acquired and organized has profoundly changed. The main focus of criticism has been directed against the traditional (early modern) idea that reliable knowledge is acquired by an isolated rational subject, according to a stringent logic of his consciousness which would, in splendid isolation, direct the accumulation of certain knowledge. As I have discussed elsewhere (Baars, 1991), this idea has been thoroughly questioned in the history, sociology, and philosophy of science (cf. Kuhn, Lakatos, Bourdieu, Latour, Feyerabend, and many others). Contemporary philosophers such as Habermas, Foucault, Lyotard, and Derrida differ mainly in the way they articulate this criticism. In a way, it is the gradually developing impact of thinkers such as Marx, Nietzsche, and Freud, the nineteenth-century "masters of suspicion" as Levinas has called them, who already emphasized the constitutive role of "external" factors in the formation of rationality. In the analytical tradition of the twentieth century, the Cartesian idea of a subjective consciousness, which was supposed to arrive at eternally certain and pure knowledge by strictly rational methods, was mainly undermined through the work of Wittgenstein (1953). As a result, social forces in a broad sense (including language, cultural codes, etc.) have gradually been acknowledged as co-constitutive of rationality. These developments also have important implications for gerontology. Not only do processes of aging differ according to historical or social context and personal fate, but gerontology as well can be seen as socially constituted (Baars, 1991). This calls for a kind of reflexivity and responsibility that cannot be dealt with by the usual methodological textbooks. The articulation of this new reflexivity has led to an extended discussion about the constitutive importance of narratives (Hinchman & Hinchman, 1997; Kreiswirth, 1992; Nash, 1990).

Taking the constitutive social world seriously implies that we must avoid, even in thinking about the *personal experience* of time, the illusionary self-evidence of a purely original inner experience of time by some isolated subject. It appears to be impossible to experience time directly, without any culturally mediated constitution. Experiencing time presupposes a culture that has interpreted and organized time in specific ways; and as they grow up, children acquire temporal distinctions (cf. Dittmann-Kohli, this volume) enabling them to experience and articulate their living in time autonomously. Such subjective experience does not deny the importance of social contexts in which temporal perspectives have been and are being developed. In everyday life we do not live the present in isolation, but in relation to others. In this sense, lived time in the present is also a *social* and *communicative* process.

If we reflect from the perspective of a constitutive social world on the philosophical tradition of the subjective time perspective, a next step is desirable as this tradition appears to have a *subjectivist* tendency. Heidegger's existential analysis as well as Husserl's differentiations of Augustine's reflections about a lived present with its memories (retentions) and anticipations (protentions) remain highly monological constructs. We have discussed this already in the case of Heidegger's work; but also in Husserl's phenomenological analysis of temporal experience, the focus is on the individual subject, who hears a sound in its temporal extension or remembers experiences from the past. Although Husserl wanted to stay as close as possible to direct human experiences, he still clung to the Cartesian idea of the autonomous rational subject. The temporal deepening that took place in Husserl's analysis of the present must therefore be combined with its *social extension*. Not only is our experience of the present charged with references to our own (very close or remote) past and future, as in remembering our plans, we are also confronted with the remembered past and anticipated future of other people around us. Interestingly, Husserl's monological analysis of temporal experience contrasts strongly with an important innovation in his late thought, which came from his persistent radical questioning: the constitutive *life world*. However, the implications of this idea of a constitutive social life world were not elaborated by Husserl, but by his student Alfred Schütz. In Schütz's conception, social being and temporal being are interrelated because living together means that "we are growing old together" (1967 p. 163).

Action and the Narrative Constitution of Human Time

As soon as we acknowledge the constitutive importance of the social life world (putting the complex problems associated with the history of this term aside), we are introducing the basic relevance of *human action*. Especially if we extend our investigation of aging and time from anonymous physical or biological processes such as aging cells, to historical, social, or psychological subjects, we have to take into account that human action plays a major role (Baars, 1997). Human action is a special process compared with other temporal processes, because action not only takes time (which can be measured), but also *constitutes* time. We might be able to arrive at a more rewarding and more meaningful understanding of human time in gerontology if we would also approach time from the perspective of constitutive action, instead of only measuring time chronologically (cf. Mittelstrass, 1992). If we go swimming, go for a walk, or take care of somebody's needs, these actions constitute their *own* temporal order. We can distinguish, for instance, preparation, beginning, rhythm of walking and resting, turning back, and coming home. Of course, a walk may take one hour, twenty-one minutes, or five seconds; but who goes for a walk of that length of time? Every "good" walk has its own time. The same is true of having a conversation or taking care of a person in need: these activities create their own order and are complete and rounded off at a certain moment, not earlier or later. Such a sensitivity to the temporal implications of actions cannot be developed if one is caught up in chronological time. From a managerial standpoint, from which time budgets have been implemented in care, it may be suggested that it is not possible to control the time of workers in such a way. This may be a problem, but it may also be asked whether such a managerial approach is always adequate (even in the organization of care) and whether this approach can claim any normative status for *everyday life*.

To profit more fully from the philosophical tradition of subjective time experience, it is useful to connect this with the discussion about *narrative action*. In Augustine's *Confessions* such a connection has already been anticipated. His philosophical analysis of time was embedded in an autobiographical narrative, in which we can read how different configurations of the present, past, and future evolved as subsequent phases of his life. He tells about his success, failure, despair, and happiness; and by this narrative an integrated story emerges, in this case organized by the theme of conversion. This picture of human life as a profound *discordance*, a heterogeneous complex of unexpected complications, ambitions, failures, unintended results, circumstances, terrible and sad events, error and insight, was a classical theme of Greek tragedy. According to Aristotle's poetic theory, the *mythos* or plot of such a tragedy was a way of somehow integrating the plethora of human events, actions, and experiences, thus making sense of situations and events. According to Ricoeur (1988), this classically poetic way of composing meaningful wholes out of the chaotic complexity of human life is a way of constituting *human* time through narratives. This means that not only Aristotle's *Physics,* but also his *Poetics* belong to the classical sources of our thinking about time.

Alasdair MacIntyre exclaims that "Man is in his actions and practice, as well as in his fictions, essentially a story-telling animal" (1984, p. 216; cf. Sandel, 1996; Taylor, 1989). Many new questions arise as soon as the importance of narratives is introduced: how important are narratives and in what way? Can they fully or partly replace theories and if so, how can a good narrative be distinguished from a bad one (Carr, 1991; Danto, 1985)? Will, indeed "Everyman" become or have "his or her own annalist" (Mink, 1992)? With narratives, we inevitably introduce literary or textual elements, but can we grant a "life story" the same amount of textual freedom as we appreciate in literary fiction, or should it at least try to respect the basic facts? (Hardy, 1968; Mink, 1987). Are persons only what narratives make of them? Do narratives presuppose persons or must persons presuppose narratives, for instance about personhood? Does an acknowledgment of the importance of narratives only aim at fuller or more adequate descriptions or is there also a normative or even anthropological (ontological) conviction attached, as in MacIntyre's statement (Flanagan, 1991)? Are there limits to stories (Nelson, 1997)?

It may not be possible to answer all these questions, and it is certainly impossible to deal with them here. But sharing experiences by storytelling appears to be universal among human beings. If there are cultural universals at all, one of them might be communicating temporal experiences in the form of a story (Brown, 1991). If we were to ask somebody what a visit or a long period of work is like, it would be surprising if this person would give us a chronologically exact report. Actually, chronological measurement does not give a clue about what we should report, because we might measure anything. We would not know what to measure and report if there were no stories or theories to select from the immense universe of abstract possibilities.

Usually, memories of the past and visions of the future are expressed and communicated in narratives. Stories seem to grow so directly out of our actions and experiences that it can sometimes appear as if we are part of a developing story. We also know that people can have a strong need to communicate their experiences to others, to be able to tell their story and be heard. This strong connection between human activity and stories was already observed by Aristotle when he stated that narrative is the imitation of action (*mimesis praxeos*). Through stories, we communicate to others and clarify for them and to ourselves what it is to age and whom we have been or are in the process of becoming.

One of the remarkable aspects of a narrative is its ability to integrate in a loose, but potentially meaningful way the most diverse events and actions as well as their evaluations. According to Ricoeur, a central role in composing loosely integrative configurations is played by the act of *emplotment.* Hereby, unrelated incidents are integrated into a meaningful whole, making it part of a story that progresses, with a beginning and an end. Through the plot, events and story are connected reciprocally so that the story changes when other events or interpretations are introduced and vice versa. This implies that the same events can be integrated into different stories, where the elements are arranged differently, with other emphases or from other points of view. Such differences are not due to a lack of precision, as it may appear from the point of view of methodically controlled intersubjectivity. Different stories may express other experiences, other evaluations, or different points of view very precisely.

Another important achievement of emplotment is the integration of the *configurational* dimension of the narrative (where the emphasis falls on the meaningful pattern) with its *chronological* dimension (where the emphasis falls on the timing and succession of events). In every story there is a succession of events (we cannot fly somewhere without going to an airport first), and their exact timing may be important as well. So narrative time does not exclude chronological time. But what is emphasized and told in the story depends on the meaningful configuration. Chronological exactness is not important per se, but for reasons following from the plot. A narrative can run parallel to clock time, which may suddenly surface when the story tells that a person came too late or too early; but the narrative does not adhere to clock time. Chronological measurement may become important in a story when somebody did not show up at the agreed time (for reasons that may be told subsequently) or to emphasize a certain characteristic of the person ("he is always late" or "always punctual"). This integrative capacity of narratives, however, does not imply that it can replace chronological time. Even Roland Barthes, who wanted as part of his semiological adventures to free narratives completely from the "chronological illusion," had to admit that this is not entirely possible (cf. Barthes, 1985).

Narratives and the (Dis)Continuities of Personal Identity

In studying adult aging, gerontology focuses on the changes that take place when somebody has lived relatively long in terms of a given life expectancy. Such changes are investigated empirically, trying to grasp the process of *living* in terms of *life* (cf. Eldridge, 1989; Wollheim, 1982). In these cases, the characteristics for which changes are investigated, searching for (causal) explanations, are distinguished from the *identity* of the research subjects. This is done because, if we speak of the changes that go with aging, we presuppose a continuous person who goes through these changes and only appears to be a different person at different moments in time (otherwise we would not speak of change, but of two different persons). Such a continuous identity must be a mixture of constancy and change, of continuity and discontinuity (cf. Baars, 2002a; Holstein & Gubrium, 2000). Usually however, such identities are assumed to be continuous and an unproblematic *background* of the search for specific changes in biological, psychological, or social variables. But from the body of accumulated empirical research, we can learn that the sheer amount of changes in a biological, psychological, or social sense, taking place over a lifetime, is impressive and disturbing for someone who would still like to cling to the idea of a clear continuous identity. This problem is often evaded in constructions in which the changes that persons go through over the life course are classified according to age categories.

In modern society, this problem of changing identities is "solved" by strategies of identification and registration, which are used to determine the identity of a person within a supervised territory, which is also structured according to age. Even when individuals change their name or sex, such changes are documented carefully in the official registers on which the control of a population is based. Large-scale empirical research draws from such registers. In this sense, the continuity of identity seems to be safeguarded. But such a concept of identity aims at control over anonymous, but technically identifiable bodies (fingerprints, DNA), not at personal identity. These practices do not represent the end but the beginning of a more thorough questioning of what an aging identity might be (Gadamer, 1987).

The concept of *narrative* identity sheds another light on the meaning of personal identity. We can start from everyday experience: if we ask what kind of person somebody is or has been, what kind of life they lead or have led, the answers come in the form of stories (Arendt, 1958). Although there are several ways to understand human lives, stories form an important part of them. We can say that a person's life cannot be understood without stories. Even if we know that somebody has been a clerk or a sailor for 40 years, this does not give us a clue as to how this person has fulfilled this role, even if we limit our interest in his or her life to this particular role. The question of personal identity can only be answered fragmentarily by giving information about what a person (in the sense of same/*idem*) is. It has to be completed by telling stories about who (in the sense of self/*ipse*) he or she is (Ricoeur, 1992). These stories contribute especially to narrative identity if the meaningful pattern of a narrative can be caught in a theme that runs through it. This pattern and the underlying theme can be reflected and reshaped: Is this what happened? Should it be interpreted like this? Once such stories have been formed, it is even possible to follow them backwards, to *read time backwards* as it were—from the known ending to earlier phases that led to the results—and to learn from the consequences of earlier events or decisions.

Out of this narrative questioning, meaningful *phases* in somebody's life may emerge, which are colored by a dominant theme: a journey to Russia, the career as a clerk, suffering loss, becoming a grandparent, etc. Such phases do more justice to individuals than phases that are constructed according to chronological schemes or developmental trajectories that are based on averages and are assumed in an ambiguous sense (where statistical scores gain normative status) to represent "normal" aging (cf. Dannefer, 1984). Through narrative understanding of meaningful themes and phases, some light can be shed on the complex and manifold identities of persons, which may be more informative than age-related concepts of identity, such as young old, old, oldest old, etc.

Calendars: Different Cultural Narratives of Time

The calendar shows that chronological time is embedded in cultural narratives. A calendar is a dating system that is numerically structured around a zero point representing an event that is regarded within a specific cultural tradition as so important that it inaugurates a new era. The event is generally grounded in traditional belief in a decisive manifestation of the absolute into the finite human world. In this way, dating in the Christian calendar starts with the birth of Christ; but in the Muslim calendar it starts with the *Hedshra*, the flight of Mohammed to Medina; and in the Jewish tradition with God's creation of the world. All calendars necessarily share such a zero point, but they localize it differently along the time continuum, so years that could roughly be regarded as "the same year" can have a different number. The common chronological units (years, months) make it possible to transpose age-related calculations from one calendar to another. The year 2005 can be transposed into the Jewish year 5765 or the Muslim year 1426, and ages of people can be counted in much the same way within and beyond the different calendars.

However, this does not mean that the differences between calendars can be eliminated by arithmetic. This is a point of increasing importance as globalization implies migration of people through different cultural environments (Phillipson, 2005; Torres, 2005), which are embedded in different calendars. Neither time nor age are only a matter of arithmetic. Even if the religious origin of the zero point may have sunk into the background, such a secularization does not necessarily mean that *cultural* differences, in a broad sense, that are related to different calendars have also become unimportant. Living within the horizon of such a culturally specific calendar also has consequences for the understanding of aging as living in time. Moreover, the temporal horizons that we find in different cultural interpretations of aging are not static but changing over time. This may once more imply that gerontological generalizations can collide with specific cultural contexts and must be reinterpreted or abandoned.

Cultural Narratives and Aging

Narratives do not constitute only periods in lives and (aspects of) the identity of a person or a life; stories that are shared in a life world also constitute the cultural codes that shape collective processes and their experiences. Traditional narratives, which play an important role in the transmission of cultural motives or ideals, such as the stories of Oedipus, Ulysses, Croesus, or Don Juan, embody a form of practical intelligence, warning, or wisdom about intergenerational conflicts, adventures, wealth, or sexuality. They can open a horizon of possible experiences and present challenges to reinterpret the meaning they might still have for us (Cole, 1992). In this sense, these configurations can function as *refigurations* of life (Ricoeur, 1988). In the same way, cultural narratives about aging constitute or open up different meaningful perspectives on aging. We can observe, however, that the modern Western tradition of the last four centuries harbors few inspiring narratives about aging, apart from hopes for more technological control of aging processes. It seems we have almost completely lost forms of practical wisdom concerning aging that may have been present in certain elite circles in classical Rome, as witnessed by the writings of Cicero and Seneca (De Luce, 1993; Parkin, 2003). Recently there have been attempts to reinterpret traditional Jewish, Christian, and other sources to harvest inspiring and meaningful narratives for aging in the late- or postmodern world (MacKinlay, 2001; McFadden & Atchley, 2001; cf. Moody & Carroll, 1997).

But the most dominating cultural narratives are communicated through the media. Here we can observe a cultural ambivalence regarding aging, corresponding with two expanding markets. One market, through commercially designed narratives, advertises a successful battle against the decay of human nature in the form of wrinkles as well as loss of energy and memory (Hall, 2003; Overall, 2003; Stock, 2003). The ammunition for this battle can be bought in the form of expensive lifts, suctions, creams, or pills. Another market concentrates on providing care for the elderly, who are losing the battle to stay young forever. As these costs can put a certain pressure on collective finances, political narratives about aging are dominated by costs of care required by the aging society. These political narratives constitute an image of profoundly problematic aging as a real burden for society (Estes, 2005). Present-day grand narratives about aging are inspired by a mixture of huge market interests, budgetary strategies, and generalizations about the aged, who are often categorized according to their chronological age. Such approaches also exploit and transform narrative activity when stories of aging people are used to market anti-aging products (Calasanti & King, 2005), or when elderly persons in institutions are treated in a generic way as persons who should reminisce and tell stories about their past (cf. Coleman, 1986; Hendricks, 1995; Lamme & Baars, 1993). In such situations, narratives are not intended to be listened to and possibly to (ex)change ideas about what aging may be like, but as a way to keep older people buying and busy, thus expressing more interest in manipulative strategies than in personal experiences of aging. We can agree with Ricoeur that it is not just the narrative itself, but especially the act of reading or listening that carries and embodies the capacity of the narrative to refigure or transfigure the experience of aging. We need inspiring narratives about aging as living in time, in which the *realities* of aging are acknowledged, but also the *personal* experience and meaning are acknowledged in their own right, without reducing them to mere manifestations of bodily aging or to examples of narrative formats.

CONCLUSION

Concepts of time refer to a fundamental level in aging studies where questions abound and easy answers are not available. Temporal concepts can always be seen as mere conventions because there are no definite representations of time as such. This does not imply, however, that their specific form and content are arbitrary, as they make a decisive contribution to the ways we understand aging processes. Although aging is not a conceptual process, we cannot understand or study it without concepts, and they must be adequate to clarify the many-layered interacting processes of aging. Human aging presupposes the existence of a specific *person* with a unique life history, who is and has a specific *body* and lives within a *context* with natural, social, and cultural characteristics. Moreover, these three domains are not only very complex in themselves, leading to different scientific disciplines that are subject to further differentiation and specialization, but they constantly influence and change processes in the other domains.

An important step toward the development of interdisciplinary conceptual clarification of temporality would be to acknowledge this complexity and the threefold nature of its representations, which flow from three constitutive sources: natural rhythms (the foundation of chronological time), personal experiences or perspectives, and sociocultural contexts (including narratives). In this way, an overemphasis on one of these three temporal perspectives can be evaded. In the triple temporality of aging chronological measurement, personal experiences, and narrative articulations, each must play their own interactive role.

REFERENCES

Albrecht, U. (2002) Invited review: Regulation of mammalian circadian clock genes. *Journal of Applied Physiology, 92,* 1348-1355.

Arber, S., Davidson, K., & Ginn, J. (Eds.). (2003). *Gender and ageing. Changing roles and relationships*. Buckingham: Open University Press.

Arendt, H. (1958). *The human condition.* Chicago: University of Chicago Press.

Aristotle. (1984). *The complete works of Aristotle. The revised Oxford translation* (2 Volumes), J. Barnes (Ed.). Princeton: Princeton University Press.

Augustine. (1961). *Confessions.* R. S. Pine-Coffin (Trans.). London: Pinguin.

Avineri, S., & De Shalit, A. (Eds.). (1992). *Communitarianism and individualism.* Oxford: Oxford University Press.

Baars, J. (1991). The challenge of critical gerontology: The problem of social constitution. *Journal of Aging Studies, 5,* 219-243.

Baars, J. (1997). Concepts of time and narrative temporality in the study of aging. *Journal of Aging Studies, 11,* 283-296.

Baars, J. (2000). Time, age and autonomy. *European Journal of Social Quality, 2,* 9-27.

Baars, J. (2002a). *Ouder worden en de Fragiliteit van de Intermenselijke Conditie* [Aging and the fragility of the interhuman condition]. Utrecht: Universiteit voor Humanistiek.

Baars, J. (2002b). West Europe. In D. J. Ekerdt (Ed.), *Encyclopedia of aging*. New York: Macmillan Reference.

Baars, J. (2005). Beyond neo-modernism, anti-modernism and post-modernism. Basic categories for contemporary critical gerontology. In J. Baars, D. Dannefer, C. Phillipson, & A. Walker (Eds.), *Aging, Globalization and Inequality: The New Critical Gerontology* (pp. 17-42). Amityville, NY: Baywood.

Baars, J., Beck, W., & Graveland, I. (1997). *De verjonging van de ouderdom in een vergrijzende samenleving* [A young old age in a graying society]. Amsterdam: SISWO.

Baars, J., Dannefer, D., Phillipson, C., & Walker, A. (Eds.). (2005). *Aging, globalization and inequality: The new critical gerontology*. Amityville, NY: Baywood.

Baars, J., & Thomése, F. (1994). Communes of elderly people: Between independence and colonization. *Journal of Aging Studies, 8,* 341-356.

Baltes, P., & Mayer, K. U. (1999). *The Berlin Aging Study: Aging from 70 to 100.* New York: Cambridge University Press.

Barthes, R. (1985). *L'Aventure sémiologique* [The semiological adventure]. Paris: Seuil.

Birren, J. E., & Cochran, K. N. (2001). *Telling the stories of life though guided autobiography groups.* Baltimore: Johns Hopkins.

Blattner, W. D. (1992). Existential temporality in "being and time." In H. Dreyfus & H. Hall (Eds.), *Heidegger: A critical reader.* Cambridge: Cambridge University Press.

Blattner, W. D. (1999). *Heidegger's temporal idealism.* Cambridge: Cambridge University Press.

Blumenberg, H. (1986). *Lebenszeit und Weltzeit.* Frankfurt: Suhrkamp.

Brown, D. E. (1991). *Human universals.* New York: McGraw-Hill.

Burrow, J. A. (1986). *The ages of man. A study in medieval writing and thought.* Oxford: Clarendon Press.

Calasanti, T., & King, N. (2005). Empowering the old: Critical gerontology and anti-aging in a global context. In J. Baars, D. Dannefer, C. Phillipson, & A. Walker (Eds.), *Aging, globalization and inequality: The new critical gerontology.* Amityville, NY: Baywood.

Carr, D. (1991). *Time, narrative and history.* Bloomington: Indiana University Press.

Cole, T. (1992). *The journey of life: A cultural history of aging in America.* New York: Cambridge University Press.

Coleman, P. G. (1986). *Ageing and reminiscence processes. Social and clinical implications.* Chichester: John Wiley.

Dahlstrom, D. O. (1995). Heidegger's concept of temporality: Reflections on a recent criticism. *Review of Metaphysics, 49,* 95-115.

Dannefer, D. (1984). Adult development and social theory: A paradigmatic reappraisal. *American Sociological Review, 49,* 100-116.

Dannefer, D. (1988). What's in a name? An account of the neglect of variability in the study of aging. In J. E. Birren & V. L. Bengtson (Eds.), *Emerging theories of aging* (pp. 356-384). New York: Springer.

Danto, A. C. (1985). *Narration and knowledge.* New York: Columbia University Press.

Deats, S. M., & Lenker, L. T. (1999). *Aging and identity: A humanities perspective* Westport: Praeger.

De Luce, J. (Ed.). (1993). Continuity and change: Four disciplinary perspectives on reading Cicero's "De Senectute." *Journal of Aging Studies, 7,* 335-381.

Dennett, D. C. (1996). *Darwin's dangerous idea: Evolution and the meanings of life.* London: Simon & Schuster.

Derrida, J. (1982). Ousia and Gramme: Note on a note from "being and time." In *Margins of philosophy.* Chicago: University of Chicago Press.

Eldridge, R. (1989). *On moral personhood. Philosophy, literature, criticism and self-understanding.* Chicago: University of Chicago Press.

Estes, C. (2005). Critical feminist perspectives, aging and social policy. In J. Baars, D. Dannefer, C. Phillipson, & A. Walker (Eds.), *Aging, globalization and inequality: The new critical gerontology*. Amityville, NY: Baywood.

Flanagan, O. (1991). *Varieties of moral personality*. Cambridge: Harvard University Press.

Fleischer, M. (1991). *Die Zeitanalysen in Heideggers "Sein und Zeit." Aporien, Probleme und ein Ausblick* [The analysis of time in Heideggers "Being and Time." Aporias, problems, and a perspective]. Königshausen & Neumann: Würzburg.

Gadamer, H. (1987). *Ueber leere und erfüllte Zeit, Gesammelte Schriften* [About empty and fulfilled time] (pp. 137-152). Bd. 4. Mohr: Tübingen .

Giddens, A. (1990). *The consequences of modernity*. Cambridge: Polity Press.

Giddens, A. (1991). Modernity and self-identity. Self and society in the late modern age. Cambridge: Polity Press.

Ginn, J., Street, D., & Arber, S. (Eds.). (2001). *Women, work and pensions. International issues and prospects*. Buckingham: Open University Press.

Gronemeyer, M. (1993). *Das Leben als Letzte Gelegenheit. Sicherheitsbedürfnisse und Zeitknappheit* [Life as last opportunity. The needs for security and a shortage of time]. Darmstadt: WBG.

Hall, S. S. (2003). *Merchants of immortality: Chasing the dream of human life extension*. Boston: Houghton Mifflin.

Hardt, M., & Negri, A. (2000). *Empire*. Cambridge: Harvard University Press.

Hardy, B. (1968). Towards a poetics of fiction: An approach through narrative. *Novel, 2,* 5-14.

Hayflick, L. (1990). *How and why we age*. New York: Ballantine.

Hawking, S. W. (1998). *A brief history of time*. London: Bantam.

Heidegger, M. (1962). *Being and time*. New York: Harper and Row.

Hendricks, J. (Ed.). (1995). *The meaning of reminiscence and life review*. Amityville, NY: Baywood.

Hendricks, J. (2001). It's about time. In S. McFadden & R. Atchley (Eds.), *Aging and the meaning of time* (pp. 21-50). New York: Springer.

Hendricks, J., & Peters, C. B. (1986). The times of our lives. In J. Hendricks & M. M. Seltzer (Eds.), *Aging and time. American Behavioral Scientist, 29*(6), 662-678.

Hendricks, J., & Seltzer, M. M. (Eds.). (1986). Aging and time. *American Behavioral Scientist, 29*(6).

Henretta, J. C. (2001). Work and retirement. In R. B. Binstock & L. George (Eds.), *Handbook of aging and the social sciences* (pp. 255-272). San Diego: Academic Press.

Hinchman, L. P., & Hinchman, S. K. (Eds.). (1997). *Memory, identity, community. The idea of narrative in the human sciences*. Albany: SUNY.

Holland, J. H. (1999). *Emergence: From chaos to order*. Oxford: Perseus.

Holstein J. A, & Gubrium, J. (2000). *The self we live by: Narrative identity in a postmodern world.* New York: Oxford University Press.

Husserl, E. (1964). *The phenomenology of internal time-consciousness*. Bloomington: Indiana University Press.

Kauffman, S. (1993). *The origins of order: Self-organization and selection in evolution.* New York: Oxford University Press.

Kauffman, S. (1996). *At home in the universe: The search for the laws of self-organization and complexity.* New York: Oxford University Press.

Kauffman, S. (2002). *Investigations.* Oxford: Oxford University Press.

Kenyon, G., Clark, P., & De Vries, B. (Eds.). (2001). *Narrative gerontology: Theory, research, practice.* New York: Springer.

Kirkwood, T. (1999). *Time of our lives. The science of human ageing.* London: Phoenix.

Kohli, M. (1986). The world we forgot: A historical review of the life course. In V. Marshall (Ed.), *Later life. The social psychology of aging.* London: Sage.

Kohli, M., Rein, M., Guillemard, A.-M., & van Gunsteren, H. (1991). *Time for retirement. comparative studies of early exit from the labor force.* Cambridge: Cambridge University Press.

Kotre, J. (1996). *White gloves. How we create ourselves through memory.* New York: Norton.

Kreiswirth, M. (1992). Trusting the tale: The narrative turn in the human sciences. *New Literary History, 23,* 629-657.

Lamme, S., & Baars, J. (1993). Including social factors in the analysis of reminiscence in elderly individuals. *International Journal of Aging and Human Development, 37,* 297-311.

Leisering L., & Leibfried, S. (1999). *Time and poverty in western welfare states.* Cambridge: Cambridge University Press.

Levinas, E. (1987). *Time and the other.* Pittsburgh: Duquesne University Press.

Levinas, E. (1969). *Totality and infinity. An essay on exteriority.* Pittsburgh: Duquesne University Press.

Löwith, K. (1928). *Das Individuum in der Rolle des Mitmenschen. Ein Beitrag zur anthropologischen Grundlegung der ethischen Probleme* [The individual in the role of a fellow human being. A contribution to Anthropological Foundation of Ethical Problems]. Munich: Drei Masken Verlag in München.

MacIntyre, A. (1984). *After virtue.* Notre Dame: University of Notre Dame.

MacKinlay, E. (2001). *The spiritual dimension of ageing.* London: Kingsley.

Mayer, K. U., & Müller, W. (1986). The state and the structure of the life course. In A. B. Sorensen, F. E. Weinert, & L. R. Sherrod (Eds.), *Human development and the life course. Multidisciplinary perspectives* (pp. 217-245). Lawrence Erlbaum: Hillsdale and London.

McFadden, S., & Atchley, R. (Eds.). (2001). *Aging and the meaning of time.* New York: Springer.

Mink, L. O. (1987). *Historical understanding.* London: Cornell UO.

Mink, L. O. (1992). Everyman his or her own annalist. *Critical Inquiry, 9,* 777-784.

Mittelstrass, J. (1992). Zeitformen des Lebens: Philosophische Unterscheidungen [Temporal forms of life: Philosophical distinctions]. In P. Baltes & J. Mittelstrass (Her.). (1992). *Zukunft des Alterns und gesellschaftliche Entwicklung* [The future of aging and societal development] (pp. 386-407). Berlin/New York: De Gruyter.

Moody, H. R., & Carroll, D. (1997). *The five stages of the soul.* New York: Anchor.

Nash, C. (Ed.). (1990). *Narrative in culture. The uses of storytelling in the sciences, philosophy and literature.* London: Routledge.

Nelson, H. (1997). *Stories and their limits. Narrative approaches to bioethics.* New York: Routledge.

Nicolis, G., & Prigogine, I. (1989). *Exploring complexity: An introduction.* San Francisco: Freeman.

Oeppen, J., & Vaupel, J. (2002). Broken limits to life expectancy. *Science, 296.*

Overall. C. (2003). *Aging, death and human longevity*. Berkeley: University of California Press.

Parkin, T. G. (2003). *Old age in the Roman world*. Baltimore: Johns Hopkins.

Peace, S., Holland, C., & Kellahar, L. (2005). *Environment and identity in later life*. Buckingham: Open University Press.

Phillipson, C. (2005). Aging and globalization: Issues for critical gerontology and political economy. In J. Baars, D. Dannefer, C. Phillipson, & A. Walker (Eds.), *Aging, globalization and inequality: The new critical gerontology*. Amityville, NY: Baywood.

Plato (1975). Timaeus. In *Plato in twelve volumes* (Vol. IX). Cambridge: Harvard University Press.

Prigogine, I. (1997). *The end of certainty. Time, chaos and the new laws of nature*. Glencoe: Free Press.

Randall, W. L. (1997). *The stories we are. An essay on self-creation*. Toronto: University of Toronto Press.

Ricoeur, P. (1988). *Time and narrative* (3 volumes). Chicago: University of Chicago Press.

Ricoeur, P. (1992). *Oneself as another*. Chicago: University of Chicago Press.

Riley, M. W., Kahn, R. L., & Foner, A. (1944). *Age and structural lag*. New York: Wiley.

Rosenblum, N. (Ed.). (1989). *Liberalism and the moral life*. Cambridge: Harvard University Press.

Salthouse, T. A. (1996). The processing-speed theory of adult age differences in cognition. *Psychological Review, 103*, 403-428.

Sandel, M. J. (1996). *Democracy's discontent. America in search of a public philosophy*. Cambridge: Harvard University Press.

Schütz, A. (1967). *Phenomenology of the social world*. Chicago: University of Chicago Press.

Sears, E. (1986). *The ages of man. Medieval interpretations of the life cycle*. Princeton: Princeton University Press.

Settersten, R. A. (2002). *Invitation to the life-course: Toward new understandings of later life*. Amityville, NY: Baywood.

Stock, G. (2003). *Redesigning humans: Choosing our genes, changing our future*. Boston: Houghton Mifflin.

Taylor, C. (1989). *Sources of the self. The making of modern identity*. Cambridge: Cambridge University Press.

Theunissen, M. (1986). *The other. Studies in the social ontology of Husserl, Heidegger, Sartre and Buber*. Cambridge: The MIT Press.

Torres, S. (2005). *Culture, migration, inequality and 'periphery' in a globalized world*. In J. Baars, D. Dannefer, C. Phillipson, & A. Walker (Eds.), *Aging, globalization and inequality: The new critical gerontology*. Amityville, NY: Baywood.

Toulmin, S., & Goodfield, J. (1965). *The discovery of time*. Chicago: University of Chicago Press.

Van Praag, B. M. S., & Ferreri-Carbonell, A. (2004). *Happiness quantified: A satisfaction calculus approach*. Oxford: Oxford University Press.

Virilio, P. (1998). *The Virilio reader*. Oxford: Blackwell.

Waldrop, M. M. (1992). *Complexity: The emerging science at the edge of order and chaos*. London: Simon and Schuster.

Walker, A,. & Maltby, T. (1997). *Ageing Europe.* Buckingham: Open University Press.
Walker, A. (Ed.). (2004). *Growing older in Europe.* Buckingham: Open University Press.
Wendorf, R. (1985). *Zeit und Kultur. Geschichte des Zeitbewusstseins in Europa* [Time and culture. A history of time-consciousness in Europe]. Opladen: Westdeutscher Verlag.
Wittgenstein, L. (1953). *Philosophical investigations.* Oxford: Blackwell.
Wollheim, R. (1982). *The thread of life.* Cambridge University Press.
Zerubavel, E. (1981). *Hidden rhythms: Schedules and calendars in social life.* Berkeley, CA: University of California Press.

CHAPTER 3

Psychological Time: Empirical Evidence, Theories, and Aging-Related Effects

Elke van der Meer

INTRODUCTION

Time is basic to the conception of the universe in natural sciences. Furthermore, time is one of the most central and familiar aspects of human life. We ourselves are creatures in time. This is reflected in the many ways of behaving in the world as well as in thinking and talking about time and the temporal aspects of reality. Despite its familiarity, time remains profoundly puzzling. It puzzles contemporary physicists, philosophers, and also psychologists, who spend a lot of time thinking about it and analyzing its manifold influences in search of a deeper understanding.

The basic patterns structuring time in the way it is conceptualized develop with age. In addition, the ways in which time is represented, as far as these are open to the human mind, depend on the general scientific level of a society. Referring to this, Grüsser (1989) distinguished five concepts of time: (1) the prescientific (theological/mythological) time, (2) time in philosophy, (3) the time in theories of the physical world (physical time), (4) historical time, and (5) the subjective or psychological time as a specific part of historical time.

As Sklar (1995) argues, the time that is given in our theory of the physical world (physical time) must be the same as the time given in our experience (psychological time). However, the different concepts of time imply different formal properties (Denbigh, 1981).

This chapter focuses on psychological time. It summarizes major theories and bodies of evidence concerning fundamental experiences and concepts of psychological time, linking aging-related changes to their underlying cognitive and (more elementary) neural substrates. Because the coverage is broad in scope, the scientific review must be selective. I begin with a neuropsychological framework, introducing relevant terminology. The three fundamental concepts of psychological time (succession or temporal order, duration, perspective) are addressed in detail. Then, I will illustrate aging-related changes (losses and gains) in temporal information processing. Different views of mechanisms hypothesized to account for these cognitive aging-related effects will be discussed.

TAXONOMY OF SUBJECTIVE TEMPORAL PHENOMENA

More than a century ago, the physicist Mach started some classic experimental studies on the sense of time. He looked for Weber's law in temporal perception (1865) and argued later on that "time is an abstraction, at which we arrive by means of the changes of things" (Mach, 1886, p. 209). Indeed, no sense or sense organ is known by which time can be perceived directly. Based on this evidence, Wundt (1911, p. 172) suggested that the psychological background of the time sense is more general in nature rather than determined by specific characteristics of sense organs.

Researchers have been trying to disclose the secret of information processing responsible for the sense of time. The studies reveal that the psychology of time is extremely complex. No simple theory can adequately describe the multifaceted pattern of temporal experiences and behaviors. According to Block (1990), psychological time consists of three fundamental aspects: (1) succession, (2) duration, and (3) perspective. Succession refers to the sequential occurrence of events (i.e., changes in the world) as reflected by the temporal order. Duration expresses the persistence of events or the interval between events or time periods. Temporal perspective relates to the experiences and conceptions of a person concerning past, present, and future time. Obviously, these fundamental aspects of psychological time refer to different concepts of psychological time.

A very similar classification of subjective temporal phenomena is proposed by Pöppel (1985, 1997). He distinguishes five hierarchically ordered elementary experiences: (1) simultaneity, (2) nonsimultaneity (asynchrony), (3) succession, (4) the subjective present (now), and (5) duration. Due to the fact that the perception of simultaneity or asynchrony of events must precede the perception of temporal order, these phenomena can be considered together. In addition, I agree with Block (1990) that beside the subjective present, emphasized by Pöppel, the subjective past and future are fundamental components of temporal perspective and should be considered separately.

In the cognitive realm, the elementary temporal experience and its representation in long-term memory (LTM) may be related, but are indeed different aspects. The same is true for the singular temporal experience and the classification of temporal experiences. A temporal concept is a classification of temporal experiences or temporal phenomena based on common, relevant properties of these experiences or phenomena.

THEORETICAL FRAMEWORK

Memory Models

Cognitive psychologists typically agree that all major experiences and conceptions of psychological time are mediated by memory structures, procedures, and processes. There is a variety of sophisticated models describing the structure and functioning of human memory. The information processing model proposed by Cowan (1995) provides a good descriptive framework within which some main assumptions may be illustrated. A brief sensory store is assumed that contains literal, unanalyzed information on incoming stimuli. Further, a short-term memory (STM) is proposed. This is not a separate store, but rather a part of LTM that is in a temporarily heightened state of activation. Finally, a central executive directs attention and controls voluntary processing. The focus of attention comprises only a subset of information that is currently activated and in consciousness. Engle, Tuholsky, Laughlin, and Conway (1999) unite STM and controlled attention to the construct of working memory (WM) (Baddeley, 1995; Baddeley & Hitch, 1974). The notions "attention-independent" and "attention-dependent" are used synonymously for automatic and controlled processes. Automatic processing is viewed as a fast process that does not require any resources or attention. Automatic processes are considered to be resistant to deliberate suppression. They are always completed and work parallel or simultaneously. Controlled processes are regarded as elementary operations that can be serially combined and executed depending on actual requirements. They require resources and attention. Both types of processes are poles on a continuum. Frequently, they are combined and embedded, for example, in deliberate actions.

LTM can further be divided on the basis of psychological as well as neurobiological evidence. Currently, the established models of LTM are multiple memory system models (cf. Ryan & Cohen, 2003). These authors distinguish between one memory component based on the hippocampus, and a second memory component based on a composite of other brain structures. Cohen and Squire (1981), Cohen and Eichenbaum (1993), and Squire (1987, 1992) have suggested a distinction between a hippocampal-dependent declarative memory and a nonhippocampal-dependent procedural memory (cf. Ryle, 1949). Declarative (relational) memory supports the encoding, retention, and retrieval of generalized facts (semantic memory) of singular events and personal episodes (episodic memory, cf. Tulving, 1972). The procedural memory supports the acquisition and expression of skilled performance, of priming, and simple conditioning. A similar distinction was suggested by Schacter (1987, explicit versus implicit memory). This account emphasizes the critical role of conscious recollection of a prior learning episode; that is, whether memory can be accessed explicitly and, thus, requires conscious recollection versus being accessed implicitly, without needing conscious recollection of any particular learning episode. Although the memory systems viewpoint has its critics, who stress processing-based views (see, e.g., Roediger III, Buckner, & McDermott, 1999), it undoubtedly provides a good descriptive framework within which the aging-related effects in temporal information processing may be explained.

Attribute Model of Kesner and DiMattia

However, memory is based on many neural systems and their interconnections, in addition to the hippocampus. Due to the fact that the psychology of time is extremely complex, the representation and processing of temporal information is assumed to be distributed across a network of neural regions. Kesner and DiMattia (1987) proposed a neuropsychologically based "attribute model" and argued that this attribute model is a well-differentiated frame for the representation and processing of temporal information. The attribute model is organized into a data-based and knowledge-based memory system (Kesner, 1998). Both systems contribute to information processing with a varying proportion of involvement, depending on the specific situation.

The *data-based memory system* mainly processes new and current information (facts, data, egocentric events) within specific external and internal contexts and provides for its temporary representation. The emphasis is on bottom-up processing. This memory system consists of different independently operating forms of memory (so-called attributes). The fundamental attributes are space, response, sensory perception, language, and affect. Based on extensive research with working-memory paradigms, it has been shown that damage to the hippocampus disrupts spatial, temporal, and language information; damage to the caudate impairs response attributes; damage to the amygdala influences affect; and damage to the extrastriate visual cortex impairs visual perception (Kesner, 1998).

The *knowledge-based memory system* is assumed to represent the abstract knowledge of the world of a person. It consists of the same set of attributes as the data-based memory system. It is assumed that these attributes are organized as interactions of cognitive maps or neural nets, which are specific for each memory form. Within this system, the emphasis is on top-down processing of information. Based on extensive research with paradigms that measure learning, executive functions, acquisition of skills etc., it has been shown that damage to the posterior parietal cortex impairs spatial attributes, damage to the prefrontal cortex influences temporal and response attributes, damage to the agranular insular and orbitofrontal cortex disrupts affect, and damage to the inferotemporal cortex interferes with sensory perception (Kesner, 1998).

According to Block (1990), Kesner (1998) distinguishes duration, succession (temporal order), and temporal perspective. These temporal aspects are mediated by memory attributes; that is, space, response, affect, sensory perception, and language (Figure 1).

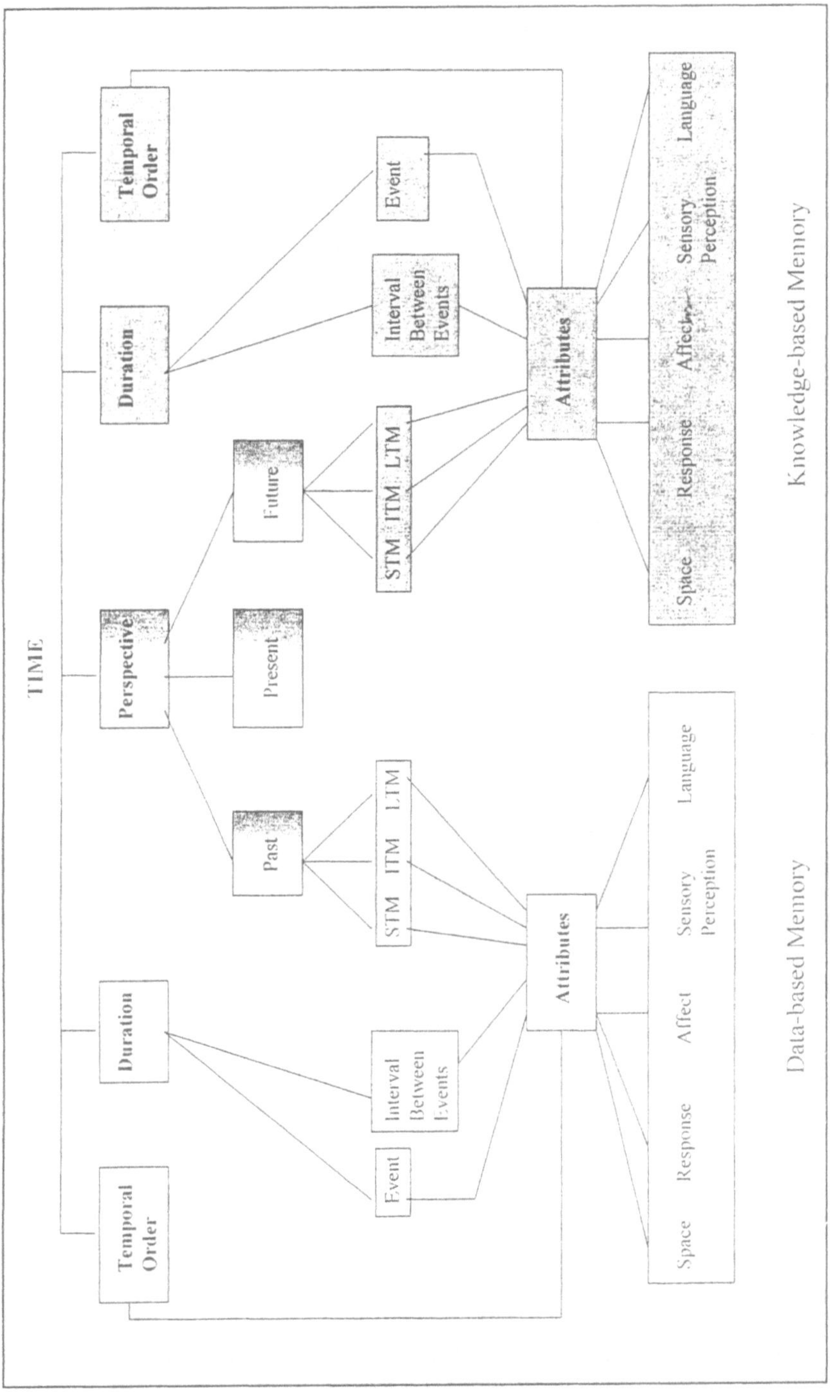

Figure 1. Illustration of the attribute model.

The most convincing evidence of the role of different brain structures in temporal processing comes from human neuropsychology.

Duration

Humans with hippocampal damage are impaired in representing short-term memory for object duration, but not short-term memory for a single object. On the other hand, humans with prefrontal cortex damage do not have any difficulties in short-term memory for object duration (Disterhoft, Carillo, Hopkins, Gabrieli, & Kesner, 1996; Hopkins & Kesner, 1994).

Temporal Order

Patients with hippocampal damage have difficulties in remembering the order in which new information has been experienced and in remembering the item information per se. In contrast, frontal-lobe damaged patients have only problems with remembering the order in which new information has been presented (Kesner, Hopkins, & Fineman, 1994). If the information is well known or a structured rule can be applied, only patients with prefrontal cortex damage show impaired performance (Hopkins, Kesner, & Goldstein, 1995).

Time Perspective

The medial prefrontal cortex as well as the dorsolateral prefrontal cortex seem to mediate future time perspective within the knowledge-based system (Fuster, 1985; Kametani & Kesner, 1989). There is evidence that the prefrontal cortex is also involved in the use of strategic retrieval processes; that is, in representing the past (Nadel & Moscovitch, 1997).

In conclusion, the hippocampus and interconnected neural circuits are mainly involved in mediating the temporal information within the data-based memory system, while the prefrontal cortex and interconnected neural circuits are mainly involved in mediating the temporal information within the knowledge-based memory system. Kesner (1998) argued that future research is needed to further differentiate these findings and to uncover the critical interconnected neural circuits that subserve the temporal features (see, e.g., Harrington, Lee, Boyd, Rapcsak, & Knight, 2004; Ivry & Spencer, 2004; Lewis & Miall, 2003a,b).

PROCESSING OF TEMPORAL INFORMATION

In the following, I will describe in more detail the fundamental experiences and concepts of psychological time: succession or temporal order, duration, and perspective. First presenting theoretical considerations and empirical findings. Then characterizing aging-related changes in memory for time and address mechanisms hypothesized to account for these effects.

Succession or Temporal Order

Simultaneity and Asynchrony

If two acoustic stimuli are binaurally presented with a stimulus-onset asynchrony (SOA) of 1 or 2 ms, and the participant is asked whether one or two stimuli had been perceived, only one stimulus is experienced. If the temporal difference between two brief auditory events is at least 3 ms, the participant hears a separate tone in each ear. The transition from simultaneity to asynchrony depends on the modality and on the complexity of stimuli. The fusion threshold is about 10 ms in the tactile system and about 20–30 ms in the visual system (Pöppel, 1997). These differences are due to transduction processes that differ between sense organs (Grüsser, 1989). Transduction refers to the transformation of physical events (e.g., acoustic stimuli) into electric brain potentials.

The Perception of Temporal Order: Elementary Mechanisms

However, if the participant has to indicate which stimulus came first and which second, the picture changes: relatively accurate temporal-order judgments require an interval between two events of approximately 30 ms to 50 ms, regardless of the modality of events (Hirsh & Sherrick, 1961). Obviously, temporal-order judgments are based on only one cerebral processing mechanism (Pöppel, 1989).

Under conditions in which events are to be placed in a temporal order, it is necessary to identify the individual events. The minimal time required to identify events consciously was analyzed in different studies. Studies of the intrahemispheric reaction times in decision making (stimuli are presented only to one hemisphere) provide evidence that it requires about 30–50 ms to make a decision between stimuli. Possibly, sensory stimuli trigger oscillatory processes in the various sensory systems, creating a temporal framework that enables a person to differentiate whether events are correlated or bound (cf. Pöppel, 1989, 1997) and temporally distinct (temporal order). This explanation corresponds with the assumption that there is a cortical pacemaker or a clock in the brain that determines a fundamental rhythm characterizing all mental activities. The corresponding models are called psychological-moment models or perceptual-moment models. The notion of a perceptual moment was introduced by von Baer (1860), suggesting that different durations of such moments produce a different flow of subjective time. Stroud (1955) proposed that the incoming information is processed in temporally discrete scans. The temporal order of stimuli within a scan is not preserved (discrete-moment model). Allport (1968) postulated in his travelling-moment model that information processing takes place according to a continuously moving window of a specific temporal size. Concerning the duration of this hypothetical moment, there is varying evidence from about 50 ms to 200 ms (cf. Block, 1990).

Another framework, the Taxonomic Quantum Model (TQM), was proposed by Geissler (1987; Geissler & Kompass, 2003). Derived through comparative evaluation of critical time periods from various research domains and tasks, this model assumes that mental processing is organized in finite ranges of discrete periods, which in turn are multiples of the smallest quantal period of about 4.5 ms. Of course, the psychological moment could be represented as integer multiples of the quantal period. Obviously, there is a clear need for more research on the relationship between both constructs and on the neural implementation of quantal units and psychological moments.

The Representation of Temporal Order in LTM

The perceived (or inferred) temporal order of stimuli or events can be represented in memory, either temporarily or more permanently. In the following, I will restrict myself to the representation of temporal information in LTM.

There is a variety of methods that have been used for the study of memory for the time of past events. A first distinction is between laboratory studies and studies of real life memories. Studies of real life memories involve judging the time of public events or personal events. In laboratory studies, participants are presented with a seriès of stimuli (e.g., words, pictures, numbers). They have to judge when some of the stimuli occurred during the session. Experimenters can control the number and the nature of items, whether they are semantically related or repeated. Participants are asked to make their judgments after this presentation.

A second distinction of methods is based on the types of questions used. For example, in studies of real-life memories, participants have to give locations in time (the calendar date of the event), distances in time (how long ago the event occurred), or judgments of relative recency (which of two events is more recent).

There is a variety of theoretical positions that address the memory for the time of past events. Friedman (1993, 2001) has presented a detailed evaluation of these theories based on empirical findings. In particular, two separate processes subserve memory for the times of past events: distance-based processes and location-based processes. Neither of these processes assigns temporal codes to individual memories. Instead, events are placed in time by cognitive processes. Distance-based processes depend on the amount of time that has elapsed between the past event and the present. Distance-based theories of memory for time are based on the assumption that strength-like qualities of memory decline as the memory grows older. Friedman and deWinstanley (1998) asked students to rate their memory of the Thanksgiving holiday at various times within a six month period after the event. The vividness of participants' memories decreased with the passage of time. The time course resembled the function of subjective recency.

Information used to infer distances appeared to be directly available. Location-based processes depend mainly on the relatively automatic encoding of events in a rich cognitive context. The information used to judge the time that has passed between events is assumed to be in the ordinary content of memory. When participants remember an event especially well, they are also highly correct in judging the time when it occurred (e.g., Fozard & Weinert, 1972). This finding stresses the reconstructive nature of our memory for the times of past events: the greater the amount of information available about an event, the better we can infer the time when the event occurred. Contextual information enables people to locate events on a relative scale of psychological time. For example, Friedman and Wilkins (1985) asked participants to recall the times of 10 news events from the preceding 20 years. The participants were asked to make separate judgments on the following time scales: hour of the day, day of the week, day of the month, month, and year. Participants were able to locate these events in time with some accuracy. However, systematic errors, called scale effects, appeared as well. For example, an event may be accurately remembered as having occurred during a particular hour of the day, but inaccurately remembered as to the day, month, or year. Scale effects support the notion that people use temporal locations (contextual landmarks) to judge the time of past events.

There is a third way in which one can know the time of past events. We often remember the order of a pair of events. The order code theory (cf. Tzeng & Cotton, 1980) states that a perceived event activates a related event in memory. Both events are linked to each other. This old/new or before/after relation is stored in memory and can later be activated automatically. Order codes play an important role in our memory for the times of routine events. Routine events have a preferred chronological orientation. In the following, let me elaborate this crucial point in more detail.

Time's Arrow

The temporal order relations of our experience are asymmetric relations: everyone has experienced a glass slipping out of our hand, falling on the floor, and breaking, but no one has experienced this in the reverse order. This temporal irreversibility of event sequences is known as temporal anisotropy or "time's arrow" (Eddington, 1928). In the microscopic world of atomic particles, laws of nature make no difference between forward and backward direction. However, in the macroscopic world, we always experience the arrow of time. Therefore, the question arises whether and how this preferred temporal orientation is mentally coded. It is readily apparent why this question points to one relevant feature of the temporal order concept.

Freyd (1987, 1992) has proposed the theory of "dynamic mental representations." She argues that the environment is complex and dynamic. Therefore, mental representations of the environment, including concepts, should also be dynamic. A dynamic mental representation is characterized by two criteria. First, the temporal dimension is inextricably embedded in the representation. Second, the internal temporal dimension is like external time, directional (goes forward) and continuous.

Grafman (1995) proposed an association strength account. The more frequent a special event order is carried out in real life, the more established time's arrow is in LTM and the lower the threshold for its activation. Consequently, Grafman (1995) argued that time's arrow is mentally coded by means of association strengths between events represented in memory. Higher association strengths between events are assumed to cause higher activation levels, and, in consequence, a faster access. However, these assumptions raise further questions. First, is time's arrow exclusively coded in links between mentally represented events? Second, if the temporal order of events has to be reconstructed by inferential processes, do these processes lead to a preferred temporal orientation?

To investigate these questions, a relation-recognition paradigm was used. Participants were presented pairs of verbs (e.g., *burn, extinguish*). They had to decide as quickly as possible whether there was an immediately recognizable meaningful relationship between both words. We manipulated relatedness (related or unrelated), SOA between the presentation of the first and the second word (200 ms and 1000 ms), and temporal orientation for related items (chronological or reverse). The word materials were collected in a preliminary controlled association experiment. They consisted of highly typical temporally related items. The association frequency for chronological items was higher compared with reverse items. This corresponds with Grafman's (1995) view of temporal order coding in LTM. The reaction times are displayed in Figure 2.

Results showed that chronological items were processed significantly faster than reverse items. This was found for both SOA intervals (van der Meer & Schmidt, 1992). Automatic activation processes are assumed with a SOA of 200 ms and controlled, strategy-driven activation processes with a SOA of 1000 ms (cf. Till, Mross, & Kintsch, 1988). Thus, time's arrow seems to be mentally coded. It is made available by automatic activation processes. This corresponds with Grafman's (1995) assumptions.

But what about the mental representation of time's arrow, if chronological and reverse items do not differ in their association strength? A second experiment addressed this question. The results are indicated in Figure 3. A significant interaction effect between SOA and temporal orientation was found for reaction times. Chronological items were processed faster than reverse items with a SOA of 1000 ms, whereas with a SOA of 200 ms there was no difference between both item groups (van der Meer, Krüger, & Nuthmann, 1999).

The memory model proposed by Cowan (1995) can help to explain this finding. Consider, for example, the highly typical event sequence *fatten, slaughter, sell:* the presentation of *slaughter* is assumed to activate related concepts in memory. *Fatten* and *sell,* both are assumed to be activated due to identical association

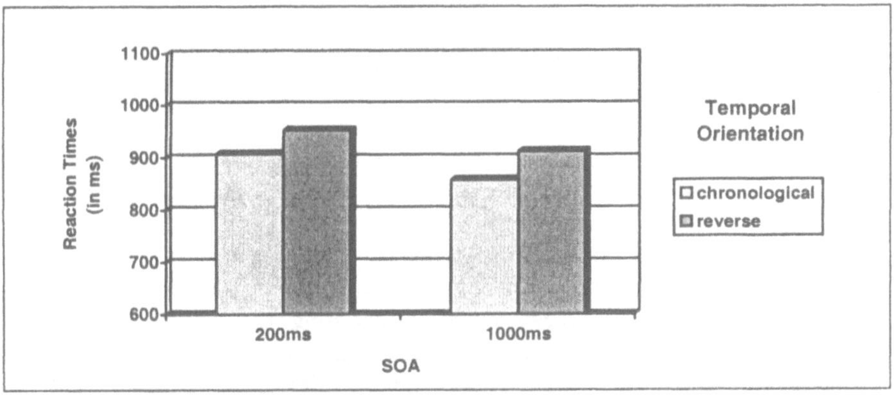

Figure 2. Reaction times (in milliseconds) required to accept meaningfully related items depending on temporal orientation and stimulus onset asynchrony (SOA); (Experiment 1: Chronological items are stronger associated than reverse items).

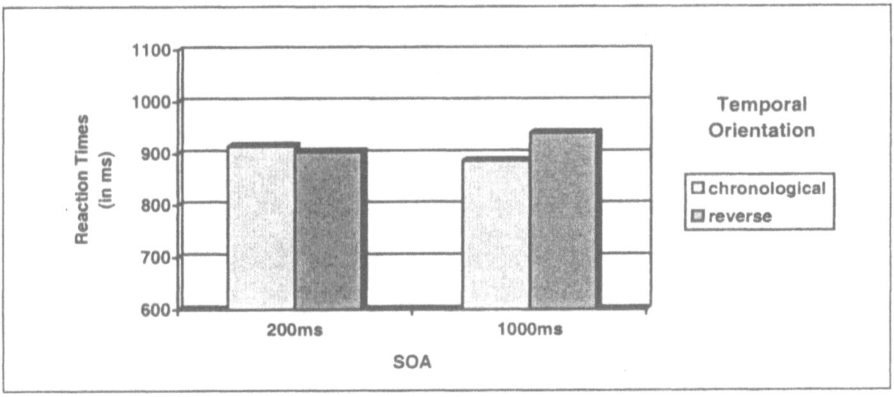

Figure 3. Reaction times (in milliseconds) required to accept meaningfully related items depending on temporal orientation and stimulus onset asynchrony (SOA); (Experiment 2: Chronological items and reverse items have the same association strength).

strength. A subset of activated items can enter the focus of attention. With an item presentation frequency of 50% in chronological and 50% in reverse order, odds for the event concepts are the same in both temporal orientations. The central executive is assumed to choose the simplest solution that enhances survival in a competitive environment: it directs the attention to processing of the chronological order. The underlying mechanism can be compared to the expectancy-based priming mechanism (Neely, Keefe, & Ross, 1989).

A third experiment focused on the question whether time's arrow is not only coded in the connection between events, but also in single everyday events. The participants were presented with word pairs and had to decide whether they were meaningfully related (e.g., *heating warm*) or not (e.g., *heating high*). Again, the temporal orientation was varied (chronological order, e.g., *heating warm* or reverse order, e.g., *heating cold*). Figure 4 indicates the results (van der Meer, 1999).

Reaction times for chronological items were significantly faster than for reverse items. Obviously, the natural, chronological order is also mentally coded in single everyday events. According to Freyd (1987, 1992), mental representations have an inherent time component, making them dynamic representations. This internal temporal dimension is directional, like external time.

The experiments presented so far indicate that time's arrow is not restricted to routine event sequences, but seems to be a more general phenomenon in event-related knowledge structures (van der Meer, Beyer, Heinze, & Badel, 2002). The preferred chronological orientation of events is coded in LTM in different ways: by higher association strengths between events and by expectancy-based selection processes (van der Meer, Krüger, & Nuthmann, 1999; van der Meer, Beyer, Hagendorf, Strauch, & Kolbe, 2003). The multiple coding of time's arrow in LTM stresses the significance of temporal information about the immediate future. For routine event sequences, it points to the relevance of time's arrow for characterizing the temporal order concept.

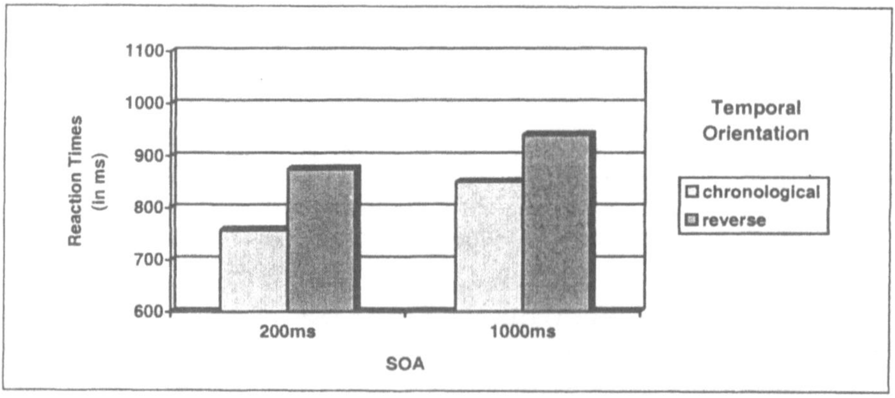

Figure 4. Reaction times (in milliseconds) required to accept meaningfully related items depending on temporal orientation and stimulus onset asynchrony (SOA); (Experiment 3).

Temporal Order: Aging-Related Effects

Given these general findings concerning the temporal order, I will now turn to aging-related changes in memory for temporal order. Change in quantity and quality is a premise of both gains and losses. A change may be evaluated as a gain if it involves movement from a "lower" (worse) to a "higher" (better) state or a loss if it involves the opposite movement. If there is no change in a system it is said to be in a period of stability (Dixon, 2000). In the following, I will present empirical evidence illustrating aging-related changes in memory for temporal order. The focus here is on addressing the specific mechanisms certain authors hypothesized to account for the aging-related variability in performance. At the end of the chapter I will summarize the different cognitive mechanisms that seem to be sensitive to aging-related changes and will discuss how they might be interrelated.

Neuropsychologists typically observe that aging brings widespread changes in cognitive functions. Some cognitive changes may stem from global alterations in brain functions; others may result from a localized decline of specific neural structures. At present, the evidence for aging-related alterations of frontal and medial lobe functions is the most compelling (Reuter-Lorenz, 2000). Moscovitch and Winocur (1995) argue that patterns of impaired and preserved memory functions for temporal information in the elderly correspond closely to those observed in patients with lesions to the hippocampal and frontal systems as well as to anatomically related structures in the limbic system and diencephalon. Memory of temporal order is worse in old than in young adults. Old adults have greater difficulty than young adults in judging the relative recency of two items (McCormack, 1982). They also have problems in reproducing the order of a recently presented list of words or pictures (Kinsbourne, 1973; Naveh-Benjamin, 1990). Parkin, Walter, and Hunkin (1995) found aging-related deficits in tests of temporal order that are more akin to list differentiation. The degree of impairment was significantly correlated with performance on frontal lobe tests measuring spontaneous flexibility (fluency tests), but not with performance on tests measuring reactive flexibility (e.g., Wisconsin Card Sorting Test). Moscovitch and Winocur (1995) argue that these findings suggest an association of aging-related decline in memory for temporal order with deterioration of some functions of the prefrontal cortex, but not of others.

Contrary, Perlmutter, Metzger, Nezworski, and Miller (1981) reported aging-related impairment in retrieving spatial context information, but no aging-dependent impairment in retrieving temporal context information. A contrary result was reported by McIntyre and Craik (1987). They found that older people remembered new facts quite well, but forgot when they had learned them. Johnson and Chalfonte (1994) as well as Craik (2000) have begun making explicit theoretical connections between the aging-related forgetting of contextual details and binding mechanisms. That is, older people may have special problems in forming and using associative connections among mental events. Additional research with different tasks is needed before this interesting conclusion can be accepted with confidence.

Correspondingly, it should be stressed that in the studies mentioned above in which aging-related decline in memory for temporal order was found, participants were asked to make judgments mainly by using the data-based memory system (new temporal order information). However, if the temporal order information presented was well known (prior knowledge), only quantitative aging-related impairments were found. Dörnberg (1998) has analyzed the comprehension of sentences in younger (mean age, 23 years) and older healthy adults (mean age, 73 years). The participants were presented with sentences (e.g., *The boy soils his shorts* or *The clothes dry in the sun.*). After each sentence, a test word was presented (e.g., *wash*). The participants were asked to decide as soon as possible whether there was a meaningful relationship between the sentence and the test word. The temporal orientation between sentence and test word (chronological vs. reverse order) and the answering condition (meaningful vs. nonmeaningful relationship between sentence and testword) were manipulated. It was assumed that sentence processing requires the activation of prior knowledge represented in long-term memory. The activation refers to knowledge that is mentioned explicitly in the sentence as well as to knowledge that is not mentioned explicitly, but associated with the presented information. If time's arrow is mentally coded in long-term memory, then sentence/test-word pairs with chronological orientation (e.g., *The boy soils his shorts – wash*) should be processed significantly faster than sentence/test-word pairs with a reverse temporal orientation (e.g., *The clothes dry in the sun – wash*). The results showed a significant aging-related increase in reaction times. This finding is consistent with the speed-of-processing construct of cognitive aging (Salthouse, 1996). Salthouse (1996) argued that the fundamental mechanism responsible for aging-related effects in performance is due to decreased speed of performing mental operations.

Furthermore, and quite importantly, both young and old participants have shown significantly shorter reaction times and much more accurate decisions for chronological items compared with reverse items. These results suggest that the processes participants engage in when trying to recognize a temporal order relation are quite the same in young and older age. Further, they also seem to be using the same knowledge structures (cf., Radvansky, Copeland, Berish, & Dijkstra, 2003). However, older participants have shown a superior effect of time's arrow than younger participants (Dörnberg, 1998). This finding is consistent with the assumption that older participants activate prior knowledge to a greater extent (McKay & Burke, 1990). In different contexts, this seems to be a very useful compensation strategy for reducing or closing the gap between currently accessible means of performing a cognitive task and environmental demands. However, the finding is also consistent with another construct in the cognitive aging literature; namely, a decrease of inhibitory control in the elderly.

Hasher and Zacks (1988) have proposed that, with age, we have greater problems focusing on target information and inhibiting attention to irrelevant material. Shimamura (1995) as well as Miller and Cohen (2001) claimed that initiation and maintenance of inhibitory processes are a crucial function of the prefrontal cortex. Corresponding with this view, the deficits associated with prefrontal cortex deterioration might be attributed to a decrease or loss of inhibitory control necessary for selecting relevant or correct information and suppressing irrelevant or incorrect information. This inhibitory hypothesis can explain the superior time's arrow effect in the elderly (Dörnberg, 1998). However, the other aging-related deficits in memory for temporal order are difficult to reconcile with the loss-of-inhibition concept (cf. Moscovitch & Winocur, 1995).

Duration

The second major concept of psychological time is duration. The perception of duration is found at a higher hierarchical level than the perception of simultaneity, asynchrony, and temporal order (Pöppel, 1997). Duration timing is essential for representing the current external environment. Much progress has been made in uncovering the nature of the processes underlying duration estimation.

Duration Judgments: Influencing Factors

In studying duration timing, investigators often present participants with tasks differing in length. They are then asked to estimate the duration of each task. Such duration judgments are influenced by different factors (cf., Block, 1989).

The characteristics of the time period which a person experiences and judges are one major factor. There are two kinds of duration judgments: judging the duration of a single stimulus (or the relative duration of two stimuli), and judging the interval between two stimuli. In addition, the characteristics of the time period include the absolute duration of the time period (short vs. long durations), as well as various contents. These contents consist of events, external or purely cognitive ones, which occur during the critical time period. For example, a time period may be empty; that is, it does not contain any stimuli or other tasks. On the other hand, the time period may be filled with a second temporal or nontemporal task. Characteristics of events include their number, their complexity, their modality, their difficulty, etc.

A second factor would be the activities during the time period. Activities are mainly influenced by the events occurring during a time period, by instructions given by the experimenter, by previous knowledge, and by obtained strategies of information processing. A participant can be engaged in effortful information-processing strategies or in effortless nonattending.

A third factor is made up of the characteristics of the person making the judgment. The variables included here are fixed (as sex), mildly changeable (such as personality) or highly variable (such as age, previous knowledge).

A fourth factor is the kind of method used to study the duration judgment: methods can either demand a verbal estimation, a temporal production or reproduction, or a comparison of two duration periods. A verbal estimation would require a translation of the experienced time into clock units after the time period (a second, a minute, etc.). Verbal estimates are more variable than estimates obtained by other methods (Zakay & Block, 1997). A duration may be estimated by absolute or comparison methods. With the comparison method, a standard duration is presented, and the participants have to estimate the target duration by comparing it to the standard duration. With the absolute estimation methods (production, reproduction), only the target duration is judged. In the method of reproduction, the participants experience the critical time period (e.g., by performing a specific task). Subsequently, they are asked to perform another task (e.g., to press a button) for the same duration of time as they experienced for the critical time period (e.g., the time it took them to perform the task). When producing a duration, a specific duration is presented verbally. The participants are asked to time the duration of a time interval corresponding to the verbally presented duration.

A further, most crucial factor is whether the duration judgment is prospective or retrospective. In a prospective design, the participant is aware that she or he has to estimate a forthcoming duration and is assumed to direct her or his attention to the "flow of time." In a retrospective design, the participant does not know beforehand that she or he will have to judge a duration. Only after its termination, perhaps a long time after, will the pertinent instruction be given to the participant.

Prospective Interval Timing

The majority of experiments has examined prospective interval timing. Thus far, the dominant theoretical model of interval timing has been the scalar expectancy theory, or SET (see Figure 5).

This model has been successfully adapted to the wide variety of temporal behaviors expressed by both animals and humans (Waerden, 2003). Scalar-timing researchers have proposed three distinct stages: a clock stage (composed of a pacemaker, a gate, and an accumulator), a memory stage (reference memory), and a decision stage (comparator). The construct of the pacemaker is fundamental: it is considered to be an endogenous process that provides basic temporal units. This endogenous process is often conceptualized as a neural oscillatory process with high frequency that emits pulses at a mean rate, but with variability that is multiplicative and consistent with Weber's Law (Mangels & Ivry, 2001). There is evidence that processing of brief durations below approximately 500 ms appears to be based on processes that are automatic (cf., Fraisse, 1984; Michon, 1985a) and primarily mediated by dopaminergic activity in the basal ganglia (Rammsayer, 2003). An alternative form of temporal representation is the interval timer.

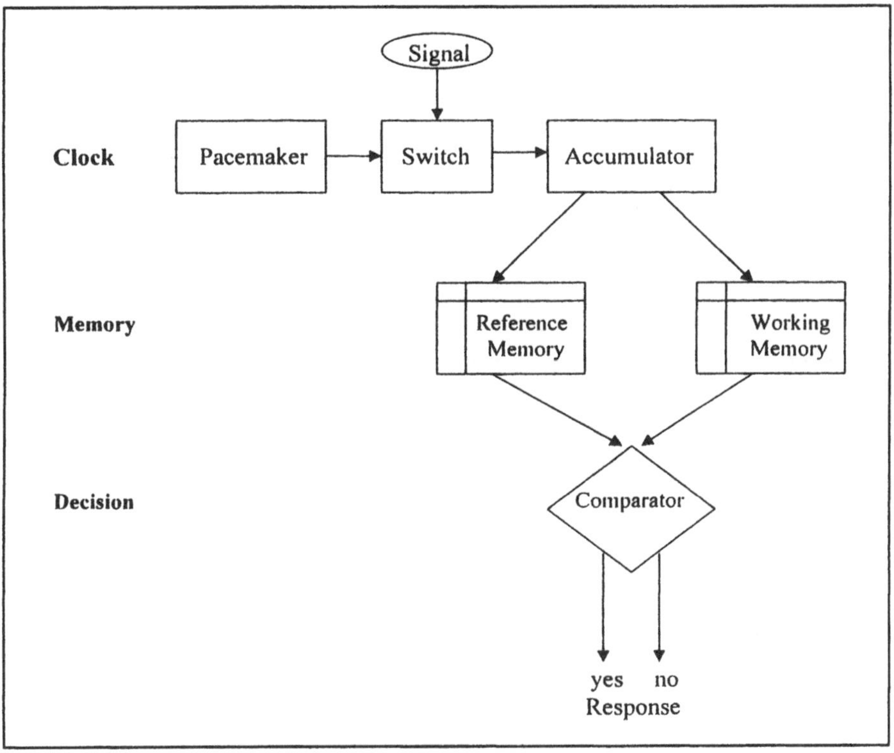

Figure 5. Illustration of the scalar-expectancy model of interval timing.

According to this account, different intervals are represented by distinct elements, each corresponding to a specific duration (Ivry, 1996). It is hypothesized that the cerebellum might provide interval-based representations.

In contrast, temporal processing of intervals in the range of seconds or more is cognitively mediated. For example, if participants are asked to divide their attention between temporal and nontemporal information (e.g., 75% to duration, 25% to words), the duration judgments vary according to the specific division of attention (Macar, Grondin, & Casini, 1994). Obviously, attending to time as well as attending to nontemporal information depends on access to limited attentional resources. Zakay, Nitzan, and Glicksohn (1983) have analyzed attention to time in more detail. They presented either an empty-time condition in which no task was performed or a verbal task of varying difficulty (easy task, reading words; intermediate task, naming objects shown in pictures; difficult task, giving associations to low-frequency words). In addition, the external pace was varied (a bulb was flickering with either 0.5 or 2 flashes per second for each 14 seconds duration). Participants were aware before each time period started that its length had to be reproduced. Generally, reproductions were shorter than the presented durations. However, they were longest in the empty-time condition and decreased with increasing task difficulty. A slow external pace caused shorter reproductions compared with a fast external tempo. The attentional-gate model proposed by Zakay and Block (1996) was developed to account for these and similar results (Figure 6).

The attentional-gate model contains scalar-timing properties, but goes further. It assumes that the attentional resources can be divided between nontemporal components of external events and temporal information. The model consists of different components. The pacemaker produces pulses, influenced only by circadian and stimulus-induced arousal. The attentional gate opens when the person attends to temporal information. In this case, the pulses trigger a switch allowing them to pass through to a cognitive counter. The summed pulses are transferred to a working-memory store. A reference-memory store contains records of numbers of pulses accumulated in the past, before a certain time interval

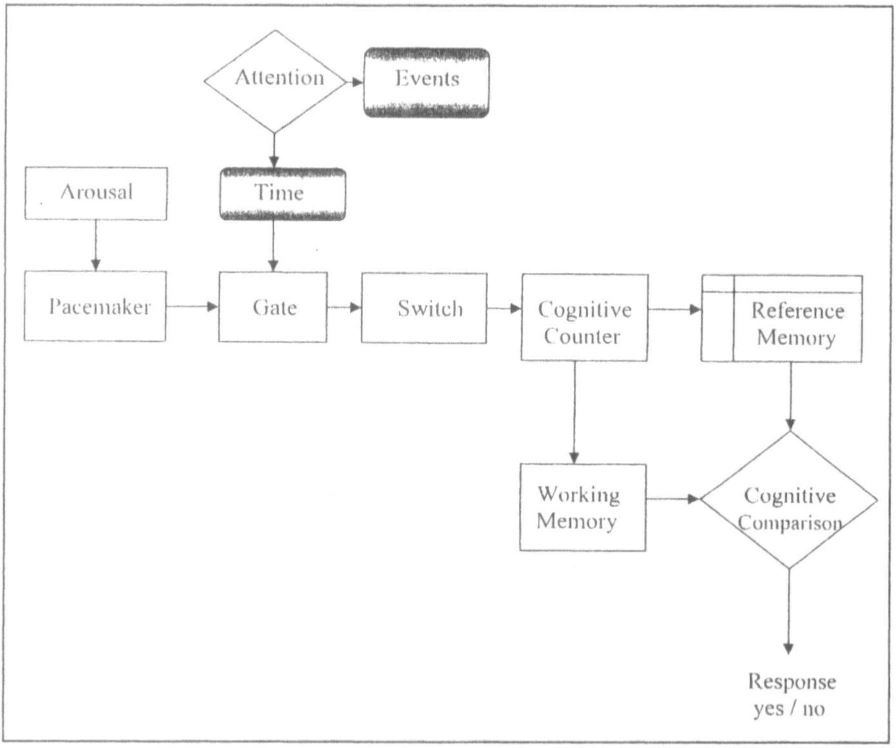

Figure 6. Illustration of the attentional-gate model of prospective duration judgment.

was complete. In addition, it contains learned correspondences between number of pulses and verbal labels for temporal units. If the pulse count in working memory approximates the pulse count in reference memory, a cognitive comparison is initiated indicating the end of the required time interval or resulting in some other duration-based behavior.

As Zakay and Block (1997) argue, the model can explain the following empirical findings: first, in prospective timing, increasing arousal causes a higher pulse rate per time unit; therefore reproduced durations lengthen if the external pace becomes faster. Second, difficult nontemporal tasks require more attentional resources than easy tasks. The amount of attention left for temporal attributes is smaller, causing a smaller attentional gate and fewer pulses can pass through the gate. This leads to shorter verbal estimates and reproductions for difficult tasks than for easy tasks. Third, in case of duration productions the result changes: again, less attention can be focused on temporal attributes due to the difficulty of the task. Consequently, more clock time is needed in order to reach the target time as compared with easy tasks.

Retrospective Timing

Retrospective duration judgments are not greatly influenced by attention allocation. In contrast to prospective judgments, retrospective judgments do not depend on task difficulty (Block, 1992). This finding suggests that different processes subserve duration judgment in the prospective and retrospective paradigms. A contextual-change model was proposed to explain the findings. The model assumes that duration judgments are based on the amount of encoded contextual changes available in memory. The encoding of stimulus information is accompanied by changes in contextual elements. Contextual changes include external and internal changes (e.g., changes in environmental conditions, in type of processing, in mood). The greater the changes in the contextual information are, the greater is the contextual information available in memory. At the time the duration is judged, the participant retrieves and estimates these contextual changes encoded in association with (nontemporal) stimulus information. The remembered duration of a time interval lengthens with the increasing amount of encoded contextual changes. Therefore, a period filled with complex stimuli is remembered as being longer than a period filled with simple stimuli. The same holds for a time period spent with different types of processing compared with a time period spent performing a uniform type of processing (Zakay & Block, 1997).

The main assumption is that the prospective and retrospective paradigms differ in the amount of various types of encoded contextual information. In the prospective paradigm, the participant is aware that she or he has to estimate a forthcoming duration and is assumed to direct her or his attention to the flow of time; that is, the participant mainly encodes temporal information. In the retrospective paradigm, the participant mainly encodes nontemporal information.

For example, you are engaged in prospective timing when waiting for a friend who is expected to arrive in one hour, and your attention is focused on temporal attributes of stimuli. As a result, the one-hour time period is experienced to pass slowly. However, when writing an interesting paper, your attention is not focused on temporal attributes and the one-hour time period is experienced to pass very fast. Retrospectively, the duration of this time interval can be judged by means of the number of contextual changes retrieved from memory. At present, the results of many studies support these explanatory models. Of course, there is a need for more research on how the assumed mechanisms work and whether they are intertwined (cf. Schulze-Kissing, van der Meer, & Urbas, 2004).

Duration Judgments: Aging-Related Effects

Aging-related effects on duration judgments have been evaluated using many different types of experimental tests. A meta-analysis (prospective paradigm, empty durations, three age groups with mean ages of 25, 43, and 71 years) showed interesting age differences in human duration judgments (Block, Zakay, & Hancock, 1995). The duration judgments of older adults were more variable compared with those of younger adults. However, the slope of the psychophysical or regression function relating judged duration to target duration did not vary as a function of age. Older adults produced greater duration periods when estimating verbally and made shorter productions of duration than younger adults, but they made fairly comparable reproductions. This was the case regardless of the duration length used. These findings oppose the prediction made by the model of a biological pacemaker, which runs slower with increasing age.

Block, Zakay, and Hancock (1998) argue that the attentional-gate model mentioned above can explain these patterns of results. The analyzed experiments tended to lack attentional demands caused by processing nontemporal information. Therefore, the older adults could have had a large amount of resources to attend to time. This should increase their verbal estimates and shorten their productions, just as the findings indicate.

McCormack, Brown, Maylor, Darby, and Green (1999) were interested in examining whether there are developmental changes in the estimation of very short time intervals across the life span and whether developmental differences in timing behavior in childhood are qualitatively similar to developmental differences in old age. Participants from ages 5 to 99 were presented with two time estimation tasks: a temporal generalization task and a temporal bisection task. In the temporal generalization task, participants were exposed to a standard stimulus of a fixed duration. They were asked to judge whether subsequently presented stimuli (125, 250, 375, 625, and 875 ms) had the same duration as the standard stimulus (500 ms). In the temporal bisection task, participants were exposed to two standard durations (800 ms, 200 ms). They had to judge whether presented durations (300, 400, 500, 600, and 700 ms) were more similar to the short or to the long standard. Both tasks measure the timing of short, empty time intervals. The used stimulus durations prevent chronometric counting. Both tasks require simple comparative duration judgments (same/different or more similar to). Therefore, differences on such tasks could not be due to changes in the ability to use a scale. The findings supported developmental differences in overall levels of performance. The differences were only significant in the generalization task, consistent with the findings of Waerden, Waerden, and Rabbitt (1997). The results of temporal generalization in adults pointed to a significant right asymmetry in the generalization gradient (i.e., more positive responses to stimulus durations longer than the standard than to those shorter than the standard but at an equal distance from it). There was an overall decline in performance with old age (percentage of correct responses). This finding is consistent with the reduced-processing-speed theory of cognitive aging (Salthouse, 1996).

All groups of children produced a general trend for left asymmetry; that is, their performance differed qualitatively from adult human performance including old age. McCormack et al. (1999) propose a general model of perceptual identification fitted to the data. Generally speaking, it is based on the neural noise hypothesis (Welford, 1980), assuming that the signal-to-noise ratio in the human brain decreases with increasing chronological age.

Rammsayer (1992) recently presented some findings that contradict the results of McCormack et al. (1999). Just as McCormack et al. (1999), he analyzed the estimation of very short, empty time intervals in young and old adults. Three groups of participants (mean age 25, 46, 65 years) were exposed to a standard stimulus of fixed duration (50 ms) and a target stimulus of varied duration (starting with 98 ms, subsequently diminished in steps of 6 ms). The participants were asked to judge which of the two sequentially presented acoustic stimuli was the longest. Reaction times as well as duration discrimination performances did not show an aging-related decline. Rammsayer (1992) argues that very short time intervals are processed without cognitive control (cf., Michon, 1985a). Instead, its estimation seems to be based on a fundamental biological function, which is not influenced by chronological age. These results suggest that there might be a lack of aging-related differences in the assumed internal clock or neuronal pacemaker.

A further phenomenon in psychological duration research is that we frequently experience an acceleration of the passage of time as we grow older. However, this is a difficult notion to examine experimentally. The supporting evidence comes from questionnaires in which participants indicate that time passes more quickly now than when they were younger. Sometimes, the slowing of specific physiological processes was hypothesized to account for this cognitive aging effect. According to the timing-with-a-timer models, the pacemaker, a part of the internal clock, reduces its pulse rate resulting in the impression that external time is passing faster. Due to the contradictory results presented earlier (McCormick et al., 1999; Rammsayer, 1992), this assumption remains unconfirmed. In addition, the acceleration could also be attributed to cognitive components. Friedman (1990) argues that the experiences in childhood are distinct and diverse. Due to the dominance of routines in older age, these years appear to be briefer. Thus, at this point, the cognitive mechanism underlying the aging-related acceleration of the passage of time is not clear.

Temporal Perspective: Past, Present, Future

The third major concept of psychological time is the concept of "temporal perspective." It traces back to Frank (1939), a pupil of Kurt Lewin. It is regarded to be a fundamental cognition referring to how a person tackles the knowledge-mediated past, the current present, and the anticipated future. Of course, the conceptualization of past, present, and future is not only a matter of psychology. Especially philosophers spent large amounts of time thinking about it. McTaggart's (1908) now standard distinction between A-series (past, present, future) and B-series (earlier than, later than), as well as Mellor's (1998) sophisticated discussion of the concept of time can illustrate this nicely. In the following, however, I will elaborate the concept of temporal perspective from a psychological point of view. This involves viewing one's own person, one's own life within a temporal dimension instead of simply considering it as it presents itself here and now. The past holds everything we have seen and done (i.e., the past is remembered). The future holds everything that has not yet happened or not yet been done (i.e., the future is planned). And the present holds all our immediate experiences, actions, and thoughts (i.e., the present is perceived). The present is seen as one moment within an evolving process. It can be explained, at least in part, by reference to what has occurred in previous stages or in the light of its predicted future development (Montangero, 1996, p. 2). This diachronic approach greatly enhances people's understanding of reality.

Studies about representations and processes that underlie temporal perspective have mainly emphasized the experiences and conceptions of persons about future time. In the following, I will briefly discuss the three subconcepts of temporal perspective and the methods of research used. I then review the existing literature according to these subconcepts, describing some main phenomena that have been discovered. Finally, I address aging-related effects.

Subjective Present

The concept of subjective present (now) or immediate consciousness refers to the integration of single events into unified concepts or bounded sequences. Michon (1978, p. 89) argues that the psychological present "is a highly flexible tuning process that is dynamically fitting the temporal width of the field of attention . . . to the sequential structure of the pattern of events." In the literature, there is much controversy concerning the duration of psychological present and the underlying mechanism in the brain. Michon (1978) assumed a variable width of the psychological present, but an upper limit of about 7 or 8 seconds. Fraisse (1984) proposed an upper limit of about 5 seconds and an average of 2 to 3 seconds. Pöppel (1989) argued that the subjective present can last only about 3 seconds. For example, verbal units in spontaneous speech are limited to about 3 seconds. Verse lines of poems in different languages preferably take 3 seconds when spoken aloud. Ceremonial gestures and many other types of intentional behavior in different cultures (Europeans, Yanomami Indians, Kalahari Bushmen, and Trobriand Islanders) have a temporal limit of about 3 seconds. In addition, musical themes (e.g., from Beethoven's Fifth Symphony) support the 3 seconds phenomenon. Pöppel (1989) assumes the integration of sequential elements of our consciousness (temporal windows of about 3 seconds) to be the basis of the subjective continuity; that is, the subjective impression of a "temporal flow."

Subjective Past

The concept of the subjective past is closely related to autobiographical memory. In general, memory plays a crucial role in keeping our experiences temporally organized so that we are able to remember the past more or less reliably at a later time. Besides chronological ordering, the temporal order of past reality can also be made by causal ordering. This follows simply from the fact that causes generally precede their effects. Autobiographical memory is regarded to be a subset of episodic memory involving the events in one's life. In a recent review, Thompson, Skowronski, Larsen, and Betz (1996) described the results of their long-lasting diary research. Let me briefly elaborate the major findings.

The autobiographical memory is assumed to be connected with remembering "what" and remembering "when." Initially, it is highly reproductive based on the retrieval of a detailed memory trace. However, the participants' ability to date events exactly decreases extremely at middle and long retention intervals (more than one year ago). The exact dating measure shows Ebbinghaus-like tendencies with lengthening retention intervals (see also p. 50, distance-based processes). There is significant evidence of time expansion for events that occurred recently. Participants' estimates of dates of events tend to be earlier than the actual occurrence of the event. In addition, there is also evidence of significant telescoping for the oldest events. Participants' estimates of dates appear to be more recent than the actual date of occurrence for the event. Both tendencies limit the direction of error near a certain time boundary, for example, anchor dates (i.e., near temporal landmarks).

The decrease in dating performance seems to be due to at least two factors: forgetting the actual date of the event (event-related information) and forgetting information that could be used to reconstruct the dates (time-related information; see also p. 50, location-based processes). Thompson et al. (1996) reported that infrequent, emotion-producing, frequently rehearsed, and mentally involving events were associated with better event dating. The mechanisms underlying dating of self-events and other events seem to be very similar. However, self-event dating produces a higher level of accuracy.

At longer retention intervals the autobiographical memory is largely reconstructive (Thompson et al., 1996). Direct-date associations are only available for a minority of events (less than 10%). There is no coding of temporal trace in autobiographical memory. Instead, when individuals attempt to locate an event in time, they try to infer the exact time of the event. In doing so they rely on (a) temporal information contained in the event (e.g., snow around), (b) temporal information about the class of events (e.g., specific day-of-the-week knowledge as church on Sunday), ©) categories with temporal boundaries (e.g., during college or other life periods), (d) related chains of events to put the events in the appropriate order (e.g., *fatten, slaughter, sell* . . .), and (e) recurrent (cyclic) or specific (linear) landmarks to infer temporal location (e.g., Challenger disaster).

Autobiographical memories appear to our present consciousness as representing, more or less completely, a chronologically ordered, continuous, past reality. However, the experience of continuity does not require that life events should be mapped onto a mental time scale with equidistant units. Personal history includes marked events, lengthenings, and shortenings. It includes the embedding and overlapping of events. Thus, the past can be conceptualized in a number of ways. Michon (1985b) argues that the required structures could perhaps be expressed most adequately in terms of either temporal logic (Allen, 1985; van Benthem, 1985) or measurement theory (Campbell, 1928; Stevens, 1951), as long as the functions of temporal processing in everyday life are not lost from sight.

Subjective Future

The concept of future is the third component of the temporal perspective. It comprises everything that will happen in the actual world, as well as a realm of indeterminate possibilities. Given that everyday life activities are directed, implicitly and explicitly, toward the achievement of goals, it is assumed that the temporal perspective contains these intentions and plans for future attempts to achieve goals. We plan for the future because we might affect it. In addition, the temporal perspective contains personal wishes, expectations, and anticipations focused on the unfolding of actions and events in time.

Participants develop planning strategies and infer possible future events by utilizing information that is mainly stored in semantic and episodic memory, but that is also given in the environment. Two categories of processes are associated with planning. The first category consists of generation, selection, and coordination of goals. The second category includes strategies for goal-directed decisions and action sequences (Smith, 1996).

There are different criteria to quantify and characterize cognitively the subjectively inferred future (cf. Plattner, 1990). Wallace and Rabin (1960) proposed the criteria "extension" and "coherence." Extension (in years) refers to the space of time a person is anticipating; coherence refers to the number of relations between anticipated events. There are various methods used to measure the extension of the subjective future. Using the "life-space-sample," participants are asked to anticipate 10 events that they expect to happen in their future life. LeShan (1952) proposed the method of story completion. Participants are given the beginning of a story, either temporally prestructured or not. They are asked to continue and complete the story. The produced time span is assumed to reflect the future perspective of a person. Kastenbaum (1961) has added the criteria "density" and "directionality." Density refers to the number of anticipated events; directionality addresses whether a person prefers a static or a dynamic conception of time. Taken together, today the subjective future is generally described by five dimensions: extension, density, coherence, directionality, and intrinsic pleasantness (cf. Wittkowski, 1990). However, this conception does not cover content-dependent aspects.

Ideas about the present and future time can also be found in questionnaire research. Zimbardo and Gonzales (1984) applied this method and identified the following main dimensions: future-task perseverance (delaying rewards for later gain), future planning (goal setting), present hedonism (current pleasures), present fatalism (the future cannot be influenced), and time pressure (importance of punctuality in oneself and others). These dimensions cover content-dependent and emotional aspects. There is evidence that people differ on these dimensions due to sex, chronological age, social class, and success in school.

So far, we have assumed a linear structure of time. However, it should be stressed that important changes in the environment are of a cyclic nature: the seasons, the rising and setting of the sun. Undoubtedly, cyclic processes in the macroscopic world are relevant to the life of human beings and exert a strong influence on their behavior. These cyclic processes are also used to measure time (e.g., clocks, calendars). Here I will not discuss in detail the philosophical question whether the structure of time is linear or cyclic. Newton's theory of physics and Darwin's theory of evolution finally established the linear view of time in the macroscopic world. While it seems manifest in our experience that time flows from the past over the present moment and into the future, there are a number of philosophical as well physical considerations and objections to this commonsense view of dynamic, linear time (Price, 1996; Savitt, 1995). In any case, we are able to experience and remember time on different scales and in different cycles and to relate these memories to conventional linear time by means of inferential processes. This supports the claim that we possess many representations of time patterns including different kinds of temporal information.

Temporal Perspective: Aging-Related Effects

Given these findings and theoretical considerations, I will now address aging-related changes in various aspects of temporal perspective. There is empirical evidence regarding the description of losses, gains, and maintenance in the underlying cognitive abilities with aging.

Dimensions of Temporal Perspective

As described earlier, Zimbardo and Gonzales (1984) identified basic dimensions of people's attitudes toward the present and future. They analyzed some factors underlying these differences. One of the influencing factors was chronological age. Young participants (under 19) had lower levels of future task perseverance, future planning and time pressure, but higher levels of present hedonism compared with older age groups. Old participants (over 60) and young participants showed the highest levels on present fatalism.

Brandtstädter and Wentura (1994) reported similar results. Participants from ages 54 to 78 were asked to answer questions. Seven different components of temporal perspective were explored: concreteness, openness, controllability, affective quality of future perspective, preoccupation with the past, experiences of obsolescence, and acceptance of life's finitude. Brandtstädter and Wentura (1994) found interesting aging-related effects on these components of temporal perspective. Older adults reported a stronger preoccupation with the past. The perspectives of the personal future in old age were less concrete, less open, and less controllable.

Some authors reported findings that contradict the results of Zimbardo and Gonzales (1984) and Brandtstädter and Wentura (1994). In a number of studies, the temporal perspective of people aged between 9 and 69 (Eson & Greenfield, 1962), between 21 and 60 (Lehr, 1961), and between 45 and 55 (Wittkowski, 1990) was analyzed. The results suggested that people from early and middle adulthood into old age had high levels of future planning. However, older participants reported more frequently thoughts of "waiting for the end" than younger participants. These findings point to an aging-related gain in time memory: the extension of the temporal perspective increases with increasing age due to the growth of prior experiences and the growing goal complexity (Bühler, 1933; Plattner, 1990). Thomae (1989) also argues that there seems to be a remarkable consistency in the temporal perspective of the elderly.

In the light of these inconsistent patterns, it is reasonable to ask what is responsible for the discrepancies in the effects of chronological age on temporal perspective. First, Lehr (1961) and Wittkowski (1990) have not considered old adults. Second, there is a variety of methods and contents used in analyzing the temporal perspective. It is necessary to look for confounding or mediating factors. For example, Brandtstädter and Wentura (1994) argued that some aging-related differences were more pronounced when the subjective residual life expectancy instead of chronological age was taken into account. Therefore, the findings reported so far stress the need for more research.

Linear versus Cyclic Concepts of Time

A further point refers to the general conceptions of time people have. The degree to which people use linear versus cyclic concepts of time has been studied by Häder (1996). He analyzed concepts of time depending on chronological age, sex, social class, and success in school. Young participants aged between 18 and 24 had higher levels of linear open concepts of time compared with older age groups. Old participants (60 and older) showed the highest level of cyclic concepts of time. However, the effects are also mediated by success in school and social class. Higher educated members of the upper class tended to prefer linear concepts of time. The concept of time was not influenced by sex.

Planning

A further crucial aspect of temporal perspective refers to planning. It is mainly connected with establishing the future time. There is a long history of research into planning skills in old age. Laboratory studies typically show that older participants are not as proficient as young participants (Chalmers & Lawrence, 1993). The picture changes if planning tasks are presented that require the use of personal experiences. The accumulated experiences of a lifetime across extended periods of time and various life contexts provide older participants with resources for dealing with life problems that are beyond the reach of young participants. "Elderly people think in terms of a long time span in which the trajectory of various kinds of events is well mapped" (Cole, 1996, p. 82). Smith and Baltes (1990) were interested in aging-related effects on life-planning tasks. They analyzed comments from older adults about life dilemmas of late adulthood. The findings suggested that older adults showed greater wisdom-related knowledge than young adults. Wisdom has been defined as an expert knowledge system in the fundamental pragmatics of life. The core features of wisdom-related knowledge and heuristics are a rich factual and procedural knowledge about life, life-span contextualism, value relativism, awareness, and management of uncertainty. Obviously, old participants have benefits in life-planning tasks due to domain-specific experiences and well-established heuristics. This knowledge is stored in LTM and can be activated if needed.

Prospective Memory

The success of planning in everyday life is connected with the ability to remember to perform intended future actions (prospective memory). The literature is sparse on aging-related differences in prospective memory. There is some current debate as to whether aging-related differences in prospective memory exist at all. In prospective-memory research, participants are engaged in an ongoing task and are asked to perform an action in the future. If there is an external cue that is associated with the to-be-remembered action (e.g., remembering to ask a person for something when meeting the person), this is called an event-based prospective-memory task. It is called a time-based prospective-memory task if an activity is to be done at a particular time (e.g., remembering to visit a friend at home tomorrow). Einstein and McDaniel (1996) found no aging-related differences on event-based tasks, but aging-related differences on time-based tasks. The authors argue that time-based tasks are more dependent on self-initiated retrieval than event-based tasks. Just as Craik (1986) they suggest that there are aging-related impairments in self-initiated processes.

On the other hand, d'Ydewalle, Luwel, and Brunfaut (1999) found superior time-based prospective-memory performance among elderly as compared with their event-based prospective-memory performance. The experimental conditions used by Einstein and McDaniel (1996) and d'Ydewalle et al. (1999) differed in timing constraints in the procedure. Therefore, d'Ydewalle et al. (1999) argued that the hypothesis of aging-related slowing down of mental activities (Salthouse, 1996) might provide a better explanation for the findings than the decline in self-initiated activities by the elderly. Future research on aging-related effects in prospective memory should analyze in more detail the resources that are used for the ongoing tasks.

The findings reported by Maylor (1990) support this notion. She found a positive correlation between remembering to perform future actions and chronological age in those participants who made active use of external cues. In the case of those participants who attempted to remember "by themselves" to perform future actions, correlation with chronological age was negative. Craik and Jennings (1992) argued that external mnemonic aids might compensate for the decline in prospective-memory abilities in the elderly. They further assumed that aging-related effects in prospective memory depend, first, on the level of forward strategic planning participants implement; second, on the salience of the reminding event; and third, on the ability of participants to perform self-initiated mnemonic activities.

Autobiographical Memory

Since the autobiographical memory is an important component in establishing the temporal perspective, a few studies have examined aging-related differences in autobiographical memories. It is difficult to study age-dependent changes in autobiographical memory experimentally because factors such as initial learning as well as subsequent retrieval and transfer cannot be controlled. Bahrick (1979) analyzed real-life memories over periods of up to 50 years (spatial layout of a city that participants once had lived in). Memory for this knowledge declined exponentially for 3 to 6 years and remained relatively stable over the period of 6 to 25 years, whereas a decline was observed after 25 years.

Rubin, Wetzler, and Nebes (1986) analyzed autobiographical memories by means of the memory evocation method. Participants were given a single word and asked to describe a personal memory the word triggered. Subsequently, they were asked to date the memory. The authors reported a similar retention curve for younger (20-year-olds) and older (70-year-olds) participants, which can be described as a power function.

Alongside the similarities between young and old participants concerning the autobiographical memory, some differences should be expected. Context information is one source for inferring the date of events (Thompson et al., 1996; Friedman, 1993, 2001). In general, older adults are more deficient in identifying the source of the events they have experienced than younger adults. They have difficulties in source monitoring and context attribution in laboratory experiments. Craik, Morris, Morris, and Loewen (1990) showed that performance on the source or context attribution test in old people is correlated with the number of perseverative errors on the Wisconsin Card Sorting Test, a test of frontal function. This finding is supported by studies of Schacter, Kaszniak, Kihlstrom, and Valdiserri (1991), and Spencer and Raz (1994). Source memory failure is assumed to be caused by an impairment in frontal lobe function (Moscovitch & Winocur, 1995). These difficulties in context attribution in the elderly may hamper reconstructive strategies in dating events.

Taken together, the findings indicate a pattern of impaired, maintained, and improved temporal perspective functions in the elderly. As is clear from this overview, the temporal perspective is not a unitary phenomenon. A number of separable components have been identified at both the functional and structural level. Aging-related impairments are mainly found in controlled processes, whereas performance based on automatic processing or using prior knowledge appears to be mainly unimpaired or even improved.

GENERAL MECHANISMS OF GAINS AND LOSSES IN COGNITIVE AGING

The aim of this chapter was to review recent research concerning psychological time and aging-related effects in processing temporal information. Taking into account the variety of findings and theoretical considerations addressed, a more general question arises: What happens to the cognitive system as we get older? Generally, studies have indicated a changing balance between losses and gains across the lifespan. There are aging-related declines in memory tasks that require complex self-initiated processing, but aging-related stability on less effortful memory tasks. Other effects of cognitive aging are small or nonexistent on tasks that rely more on prior knowledge rather than on controlled cognitive processing. The aging-related variance that occurs on processing temporal information supports this statement. Taking into account the variety of experimental findings, four mechanisms have been hypothesized to account for the variability in performance that is due to aging (Park, 2000).

Speed of Information Processing (Salthouse, 1996)

Aging-related variance in performance is assumed to be caused by a generally decreased speed of performing mental operations. Due to this slowdown the results of earlier operations are lost. Therefore, older adults are impaired in reaching later processing stages.

Sensory Function (Lindenberger & Baltes, 1994)

The aging-related cognitive decline is mediated by sensory functioning as measured by simple tests of visual and auditory acuity. The sensory measures are assumed to provide an index of neural integrity, which in turn mediates cognitive function. The aging-related cognitive decline is based on biological rather than social characteristics, as the slope of the decline gradient does not vary as a function of education, occupation, social class, and income. The findings from the Berlin Aging Study (Baltes & Lindenberger, 1997; Baltes & Smith, 1997) suggest that individuals age at the same rate and show age-related decline regardless of the initial level of ability. Consequently, "being highly educated, affluent, or of high cognitive ability does not protect an individual from age-related decline" (Park, 2000, p. 17). However, an individual who initially has many cognitive resources available and experiences age-related decline will continue to possess enough cognitive resources to perform everyday tasks successfully. In contrast, an individual who starts out with a low amount of cognitive resources might be expected to fall below some critical threshold of resources needed to successfully manage tasks of daily living (cf. Park, 2000).

Working Memory (Craik & Byrd, 1982)

Older adults are deficient in the ability to engage in self-initiated processing. There is an aging-related decrease in the processing resources; that is, in the amount of online cognitive resources available to process information. Therefore, the contents of working memory decrease with age.

Inhibition (Hasher & Zacks, 1988)

There is an aging-related decline in the efficiency of inhibitory processes. The inability of older adults to stay focused on relevant information and to inhibit attention to irrelevant information affects subsequent cognitive performance.

Each of these mechanisms is conceptualized as a specific type of processing resource. It is, of course, possible that combinations of these mechanisms may provide a better estimate of processing resources. Park (2000) argues that sensory function and processing speed might be elementary indicators of the overall neural integrity of the individual's nervous system. Working memory is directly related to speed of processing. However, the use of structural-equation modeling and path analysis demonstrates that it is an important construct in its own right. At present, the role of inhibition for understanding effects of cognitive aging is less well understood. Thus, further research is needed to specify the relationship between these mechanisms and to link the behavioral constructs to their underlying neural substrates.

Although more is known about the losses associated with cognitive aging, there is also evidence that aging-related increase in knowledge and experience might produce gains in late life. Many researchers consider the possibility of gains in cognitive aging (Baltes, 1987). Dixon (2000) has developed a taxonomy representing how the concept of gains is used in cognitive aging.

Gains Qua Gains

Cognitive aging undergoes continued or renewed growth throughout adulthood (increased knowledge, expertise). Examples include research on metacognitive characteristics and wisdom.

Gains as Losses of a Lesser Magnitude

Some consolidation may be taken in selected features of certain cognitive losses. As a result, the losses occur later, less uniformly, or less universally than expected. Examples include rearranging priorities to manage resources efficiently and providing forgiving environments.

Gains as a Function of Losses

Cognitive deficits are an inevitable fact of aging. However, there are conditions under which older persons perform effectively and at effective levels of achievement. Examples include compensatory substitution of losses (e.g., new pathways in the brain for performing a function occurring as a result of stroke) and adaptive uses of collaborative contexts to overcome a specific aging-related loss.

This overview of the general mechanisms of gains and losses in cognitive aging illustrates that cognitive aging is very complex. "The phenomena of cognitive aging actually are characterized by multiple determinants, multiple directions, and multiple aspects" (Dixon, 2000, p. 38). The multitude is reflected in a variety of findings, perspectives, and theories on cognitive aging. However, there is still a lack of theoretical coherence in the psychology of cognitive aging.

The human brain is a biological organ like the heart and the kidneys. All biological organs lose efficiency with increasing age. Therefore, the neuropsychology of aging has looked for crucial sources of aging-related changes in the brain. Given the brain's structural diversity, it is not surprising that some regions seem to age faster than others. "In this light, accounts attributing cognitive aging to such global mechanisms as a generalized slowing or loss of resources are incomplete" (Reuter-Lorenz, 2000, p. 110). Structural imaging studies reveal the greatest atrophy in the hippocampus, dorsolateral prefrontal cortex, and portions of the cerebellum. These changes seem to be responsible for aging-related decline of cognitive functions, including the encoding and retrieval of time-related information.

Over the past years, considerable progress has been made on the analysis and characterization of the mental structures and mechanisms underlying the memory for time and aging-related changes in psychological time. In particular, there now exist a number of detailed neuropsychological and psychological models of brain structures and cognitive processes underlying the temporal ordering of events, the timing of duration, and the establishing of a temporal perspective. First attempts have been made to link cognitive research with brain-based research. There is strong support for the assumption that the prefrontal cortex and its interconnected neural circuits are mainly involved in mediating the temporal information in the knowledge-based memory system. There is also good evidence that the hippocampus and cerebellum appear to be directly involved in processing temporal information. Thus, the found aging-related atrophy in the prefrontal cortex, hippocampus, and cerebellum should affect memory for time. As I have tried to show in this chapter, this is the case.

However, the correspondence between structure and function is not perfect. Reorganization, compensation, and strategy changes can help overcome a regional dysfunction. Correspondingly, Moscovitch and Winocur (1995) emphasize that cognitive function does not decline in a one-to-one fashion with chronological age. Different factors influence cognitive abilities. Environmental and psychological factors significantly influence cognitive performance in the elderly. Changes in psychosocial well-being (e.g., activity level, perceived control over life-affecting conditions) correlate with changes in cognition (Moscovitch & Winocur, 1995). In addition, decline in cognitive performances with chronological age is not irreversible. The exciting clues about plasticity and compensation in aging encourage new research lines and new approaches to optimizing cognitive functioning across the life span. This is also true for time-related memory functions.

ACKNOWLEDGMENT

This research was supported by research grants (ME 1362/2-1 and ME 1362/2-2) from the German Research Foundation.

REFERENCES

Allen, J. F. (1985). Maintaining knowledge about temporal intervals. In R. J. Brachmann & H. J. Levesque (Eds.), *Readings in knowledge representation.* Los Altos, CA: Kaufmann.

Allport, D. A. (1968). Phenomenal simultaneity and the perceptual moment hypothesis. *British Journal of Psychology, 59,* 395-406.

Baddeley, A. D. (1995). Working memory. In M. S. Gazzaniga (Ed.), *The cognitive neurosciences* (pp. 755-764). Cambridge, MA: The MIT Press.

Baddeley, A. D., & Hitch, G. (1974). Working memory. In G. A. Bower (Ed.), *The psychology of learning and motivation* (Vol. 8, pp. 47-89). New York: Academic Press.

Bahrick, H. P. (1979). Maintenance of knowledge: Questions about memory we forgot to ask. *Journal of Experimental Psychology: General, 108,* 296-308.

Baltes, P. B. (1987). Theoretical propositions of life-span developmental psychology: On the dynamics between growth and decline. *Developmental Psychology, 23,* 611-626.

Baltes, P. B., & Lindenberger, U. (1997). Emergence of powerful connection between sensory and cognitive functions across the adult life span: A new window to the study of cognitive aging? *Psychology and Aging, 12,* 12-21.

Baltes, P. B., & Smith, J. (1997). A systemic-wholistic view of psychological functioning in very old age: Introduction to a collection of articles from the Berlin Aging Study. *Psychology and Aging, 12,* 395-409.

Block, R. A. (1989). Experiencing and remembering time: Affordances, context, and cognition. In I. Levin & D. Zakay (Ed.), *Time and human cognition* (pp. 333-363). Amsterdam: Elsevier.

Block, R. A. (1990). Models of psychological time. In R. Block (Ed.), *Cognitive models of psychological time* (pp. 1-35). Hillsdale, NJ: Erlbaum.

Block, R. A. (1992). Prospective and retrospective duration judgment: The role of information processing and memory. In F. Macar, V. Pouthas, & W. J. Friedman (Eds.), *Time, action and cognition: Toward bridging the gap* (pp. 141-152). Dordrecht: Kluwer.

Block, R. A., Zakay, D., & Hancock, P. A. (1995). *Human duration judgment: Age- and sex-related differences.* Poster presented at the triennial meeting of the International Society for the Study of Time, Sainte-Adele, Quebec, Canada.

Block, R. A., Zakay, D., & Hancock, P. A. (1998). Human aging and duration judgments: A meta-analytic review. *Psychology and Aging, 13,* 584-596.

Brandtstädter, J., & Wentura, D. (1994). Veränderungen der Zeit- und Zukunftsperspektive im Übergang zum höheren Erwachsenenalter: entwicklungspsychologische und differentielle Aspekte [Changes in time perspectives and attitudes toward the future during the transition to later adulthood: Developmental and differential aspects]. *Zeitschrift für Entwicklungspsychologie und Pädagogische Psychologie, 26,* 2-21.

Bühler, Ch. (1933). *Der menschliche Lebenslauf als psychologisches Problem* [Human life course: A psychological problem]. Leipzig: Hirzel.

Campbell, N. R. (1928). *An account of the principles of measurement and calculation.* London: Longmans Green.

Chalmers, D., & Lawrence, J. A. (1993). Investigating the effects of planning aids in adults' and adolescents' organization of a complex task. *International Journal of Behavioral Development, 16,* 191-214.

Cohen, N. J., & Eichenbaum, H. (1993). *Memory, amnesia, and the hippocampal system.* Cambridge, MA: The MIT Press.

Cohen, N. J., & Squire, L. R. (1981). Preserved learning and retention of pattern-analyzing skill in amnesia: Dissociation of knowing how and knowing that. *Science, 210,* 207-210.

Cole, M. (1996). Interacting minds in a life-span perspective: A cultural-historical approach to culture and cognitive development. In P. B. Baltes & U. Staudinger (Eds.), *Interactive minds* (pp. 59-87). Cambridge, NY: Cambridge University Press.

Cowan, N. (1995). *Attention and memory. An integrated framework.* Oxford: Oxford University Press.

Craik, F. I. M. (1986). A functional account of age differences in memory. In F. Klix & H. Hagendorf (Eds.), *Human memory and cognitive capabilities: Mechanisms and performance* (Part A, pp. 409-422.) Amsterdam: North-Holland.

Craik, F. I. M. (2000). Age-related changes in human memory. In D. Park, & N. Schwarz (Eds.), *Cognitive aging* (pp. 75-92). Philadelphia, PA: Psychology Press.

Craik, F. I. M., & Byrd, M. (1982). Aging and cognitive deficits: The role of attentional resources. In F. I. M. Craik & S. Trehub (Eds.), *Aging and cognitive processes* (pp. 191-211). New York: Plenum Press.

Craik, F. I. M., & Jennings, J. M. (1992). Human memory. In F. I. M. Craik, & T. A. Salthouse (Eds.), *The handbook of aging and cognition* (pp. 51-110). Hillsdale, NJ: Erlbaum.

Craik, F. I. M., Morris, L. W., Morris, R. G., & Loewen, E. R. (1990). Relations between source amnesia and frontal lobe functioning in older adults. *Psychology & Aging, 9,* 149-156.

Denbigh, K. G. (1981). *Three concepts of time.* Berlin/Heidelberg/New York: Springer.

Disterhoft, J. F., Carrillo, M. C., Hopkins, R. O., Gabrieli, J. D. E., & Kesner, R. P. (1996). Impaired trace eyeblink conditioning in severe medial temporal lobe amnesics. *Society for Neuroscience Abstracts, 22,* 1866.

Dixon, R. A. (2000). Concepts and mechanisms of gains in cognitive aging. In D. Park & N. Schwarz (Eds.), *Cognitive aging* (pp. 23-41). Philadelphia, PA: Psychology Press.

Dörnberg, K. (1998). *Zeitliche Organisation von Vorwissen beim Sprachverstehen in Abhängigkeit vom Lebensalter* [Temporal organisation of prior knowledge in language comprehension depending on age]. Master thesis, Humboldt University Berlin, (unpublished).

d'Ydewalle, G., Luwel, K., & Brunfaut, E. (1999). The importance of on-going concurrent activities as a function of age in time- and event-based prospective memory. *European Journal of Cognitive Psychology, 11*(2), 219-237.

Eddington, A. S. (1928). *The nature of the physical world.* Cambridge: Cambridge University Press.

Einstein, G. O., & McDaniel, M. A. (1996). Remembering to do things: Remembering a forgotten topic. In D. J. Herrmann, C. McEvoy, C. Hertzog, P. Hertel, & M. K. Johnson (Eds.), *Basic and applied memory research, practical applications* (Vol. 2, pp. 79-94). Mahwah: NJ: Erlbaum.

Engle, R. W., Tuholsky, S. W., Laughlin, J. E., & Conway, A. R. A. (1999). Working memory, short-term memory, and general fluid intelligence: A latent-variable approach. *Journal of Experimental Psychology: General, 128*(3), 309-331.

Eson, M. E., & Greenfield, N. (1962). Life space: Its content and temporal dimensions. *Journal of Genetic Psychology, 100,* 113-128.

Fozard, J. L., & Weinert, J. R. (1972). Absolute judgments of recency for pictures and nouns after various numbers of intervening items. *Journal of Experimental Psychology, 95,* 472-504.

Fraisse, P. (1984). Perception and estimation of time. *Annual Review of Psychology, 35*, 1-36.

Frank, L. K. (1939). Time perspective. *Journal of Social Psychology, 4*, 239-312.

Freyd, J. J. (1987). Dynamic mental representations. *Psychological Review, 94*, 427-438.

Freyd, J. J. (1992). Dynamic representations guiding adaptive behavior. In F. Macar, V. Pouthas, & W. Friedman (Eds.), *Time, action and cognition* (pp. 309-324). Dordrecht: Kluwer.

Friedman, W. J. (1990). *About time*. Cambridge, MA: The MIT Press.

Friedman, W. J. (1993). Memory for the time of past events. *Psychological Bulletin, 113*(1), 44-66.

Friedman, W. J. (2001). Memory processes underlying humans' chronological sense of the past. In C. Hoerl & T. McCormack (Eds.), *Time and memory* (pp. 139-167). Oxford: Clarendon Press.

Friedman, W. J., & deWinstanley, P. A. (1998). Changes in the subjective properties of autobiographical memories with the passage of time, *Memory, 6*, 367-381.

Friedman, W. J., & Wilkins, A. J. (1985). Scale effects in memory for the time of events. *Memory and Cognition, 13*, 168-175.

Fuster, J. M. (1985). The prefrontal cortex, mediator of cross-temporal contingencies. *Human Neurobiology, 4*, 169-179.

Geissler, H.-G. (1987). The temporal architecture of central information processing: Evidence for a tentative time-quantum model. *Psychological Research, 49*, 99-106.

Geissler, H.-G., & Kompass, R. (2003). Invariants of mental timing: From taxonomic relations to task-related modeling. In H. Helfrich (Ed.), *Time and mind II* (pp. 185-207). Göttingen: Hogrefe & Huber.

Grafman, J. (1995). Similarities and distinctions among current models of prefrontal cortical functions. In J. Grafman, K. J. Holyoak, & F. Boller (Eds.), Structure and Functions of the Human Prefrontal Cortex. *Annals of the New York Academy of Science, 769*, 337-368.

Grüsser, O.-J. (1989). Zeit und Gehirn [Time and brain]. In H. Gumin & H. Meier (Eds.), *Die Zeit. Dauer und Augenblick* (pp. 79-132). [Time. Duration and moment]. München: Piper.

Häder, M. (1996). Linear, zyklisch oder okkasional? Ein Indikator zur Ermittlung der individuell präferierten Form des Zeitbewußtseins [Linear, cyclic or occasional? A new indicator for identifying a person's individual view of time]. *ZUMA-Nachrichten, 39*, 17-44.

Harrington, D. L., Lee, R. R., Boyd, L. A., Rapcsak, S. Z., & Knight, R. T. (2004). Does the representation of time depend on cerebellum? Effect of cerebellar stroke. *Brain, 127*, 561-574.

Hasher, L., & Zacks, R. T. (1988). Working memory, comprehension, and aging: A review and a new review. In G. H. Bower (Ed.), *The psychology of learning and motivation* (Vol. 22, pp. 193-225). New York: Academic Press.

Hirsh, J. I., & Sherrick, C. E. J. (1961). Perceived order in different sense modalities. *Journal of Experimental Psychology, 62*, 423-432.

Hopkins, R. O., & Kesner, R. P. (1994). Short-term memory for duration in hypoxic subjects. *Society for Neuroscience Abstracts, 20*, 1075.

Hopkins, R. O., Kesner, R. P., & Goldstein, M. (1995). Memory for novel and familiar spatial and linguistic temporal distance information in hypoxic subjects. *Journal of the International Neuropsychological Society, 1,* 454-468.

Ivry, R. B. (1996). The representation of temporal information in perception and motor control. *Current Opinion in Neurobiology, 6,* 851-857.

Ivry, R. B., & Spencer, R. M. C. (2004). The neural representation of time. *Current Opinion in Neurobiology, 14,* 225-232.

Johnson, M. K., & Chalfonte, B. L. (1994). Binding complex memories: The role of reactivation and the hippocampus. In D. L. Schacter & E. Tulving (Eds.), *Memory systems 1994* (pp. 311-350). Cambridge, MA: The MIT Press.

Kametani, H., & Kesner, R. P. (1989). Retrospective and prospective coding of information: Dissociation of parietal cortex and hippocampal formation. *Behavioral Neuroscience, 103,* 84-89.

Kastenbaum, R. (1961). The dimensions of future time perspective, an experimental analysis. *The Journal of General Psychology, 65,* 203-218.

Kesner, R. P. (1998). Neural mediation of memory for time: Role of the hippocampus and medial prefrontal cortex. *Psychonomic Bulletin & Review, 5*(4), 585-596.

Kesner, R. P., & DiMattia, B. V. (1987). Neurobiology of an attribute model of memory. In *Progress in psychobiology and physiological psychology* (pp. 207-277). New York: Academic Press.

Kesner, R. P., Hopkins, R. O., & Fineman, B. (1994). Item and order dissociation in humans with prefrontal cortex damage. *Neuropsychologia, 32,* 881-891.

Kinsbourne, M. (1973). Age effects on letter span related to rate and sequential dependency. *Journal of Gerontology, 28,* 317-319.

Lehr, U. (1961). Veränderungen der Daseinsthematik der Frau im Erwachsenenalter [Changes in Life Themes of Women in Adulthood]. *Vita hum. 4,* 193-228.

LeShan, L. L. (1952). Time orientation and social class. *Journal of Abnormal and Social Psychology, 47,* 589-592.

Lewis, P. A., & Miall, R. C. (2003a). Brain activation patterns during measurement of sub- and supra-second intervals. *Neuropsychologia, 41,* 1583-1592.

Lewis, P. A., & Miall, R. C. (2003b). Distinct systems for automatic and cognitively controlled time measurement: Evidence from neuroimaging. *Current Opinion in Neurobiology, 13,* 250-255.

Lindenberger, U., & Baltes, P. B. (1994). Sensory functioning and intelligence in old age: A strong connection. *Psychology and Aging, 9,* 339-355.

Mach, E. (1886). *Beiträge zur Analyse der Empfindungen* [Contributions to the analysis of perception]. Jena: Fischer.

Macar, F., Grondin, S., & Casini, L. (1994). Controlled attention sharing influences time estimation. *Memory and Cognition, 22*(6), 673-686.

Mangels, J. A., & Ivry, R. B. (2001). Time perception. In B. Rapp (Ed.), *The handbook of cognitive neuropsychology* (pp. 467-518). Hove: Psychology Press.

Maylor, E. A. (1990). Age and prospective memory. *Quarterly Journal of Experimental Psychology: Human Experimental Psychology, 42,* 471-493.

McCormack, P. D. (1982). Temporal coding and study-phase retrieval in young and elderly adults. *Bulletin of the Psychonomic Society, 20,* 242-244.

McCormack, T., Brown, G. D. A., Maylor, E. A., Darby, R. J., & Green, D. (1999). Developmental changes in time estimation: Comparing childhood and old age. *Developmental Psychology, 35*(4), 1143-1155.

McIntyre, J. S., & Craik, F. I. M. (1987). Age differences in memory for item and source information. *Canadian Journal of Psychology, 41,* 175-192.

McKay, D. G., & Burke, D. M. (1990). Cognition and aging. In T. M. Hess (Ed.), *Aging and cognition: Knowledge organization and utilization.* North-Holland: Amsterdam.

McTaggart, J. M. E. (1908). The unreality of time. *Mind, 18,* 457-484.

Mellor, D. H. (1998). *Real time II.* New York: Routledge.

Michon, J. A. (1978).The making of the present: A tutorial review. In J. Requin (Ed.), *Attention and performance* (Vol. VII, pp. 89-111). Hillsdale, NJ: Erlbaum.

Michon, J. A. (1985a). The compleat time experiencer. In J. A. Michon & J. L. Jackson (Eds.), *Time, mind, and behavior* (pp. 21-52). Berlin: Springer.

Michon, J. A. (1985b). Temporality and metaphor. In J. A. Michon & J. L. Jackson (Eds.), *Time, mind, and behavior* (pp. 288-296). Berlin: Springer.

Miller, E. K., & Cohen, J. D. (2001). An integrative theory of prefrontal cortex function. *Annual Reviews of Neuroscience, 24,* 167-202.

Montangero, J. (1996). *Understanding changes in time.* London: Taylor & Francis.

Moscovitch, M., & Winocur, G. (1995). Frontal lobes, memory, and aging. In J. Grafman, K. J. Holyoak, & F. Boller (Eds.), *Annals of the New York Academy of Sciences* (Structure and Functions of the Human Prefrontal Cortex), *769,* 119-150.

Nadel, L., & Moscovitch, M. (1997). Memory consolidation, retrograde amnesia and the hippocampal complex. *Current Opinion in Neurobiology, 7,* 217-227.

Naveh-Benjamin, M. (1990). Coding of temporal order information: An automatic process? *Journal of Experimental Psychology: Learning, Memory, and Cognition, 16,* 117-126.

Neely, J. H., Keefe, D. E., & Ross, K. L. (1989). Priming in the lexical decision task: Roles of prospective prime-generated expectancies and retrospective semantic matching. *Journal of Experimental Psychology: Learning, Memory, and Cognition, 15*(6), 1003-1019.

Park, D. C. (2000). The basic mechanisms accounting for age-related decline in cognitive function. In D. C. Park & N. Schwarz (Eds.), *Cognitive aging* (pp. 3-21). Philadelphia, PA: Psychology Press.

Parkin, A. J., Walter, B. M., & Hunkin, N. M. (1995). The relationship between normal aging, frontal lobe function, and memory for temporal and spatial information. *Neuropsychology, 9,* 304-312.

Perlmutter, M., Metzger, R., Nezworski, T., & Miller, K. (1981). Spatial and temporal memory in 20 and 60 years old. *Journal of Gerontology, 36,* 59-65.

Plattner, I. E. (1990). *Zeitbewußtsein und Lebensgeschichte* [Consciousness of time and biography]. Heidelberg: Asanger.

Pöppel, E. (1985). *Grenzen des Bewußtseins: Über Wirklichkeit und Welterfahrung* [Mindworks: Time and conscious experience]. Stuttgart: Deutsche Verlagsanstalt.

Pöppel, E. (1989). The measurement of music and the cerebral clock: A new theory. *Leonardo, 22*(1), 83-89.

Pöppel, E. (1997). A hierarchical model of temporal perception. *Trends in Cognitive Science, 1*(2), 56-61.

Price, H. (1996). *Time's arrow & Archimedes' point*. New York: Oxford University Press.

Radvansky, G. A., Copeland, D. E., Berish, D. E., & Dijkstra, K. (2003). Aging and situation model updating. *Aging Neuropsychology and Cognition, 10*(2), 158-166.

Rammsayer, T. (1992). *Die Wahrnehmung kurzer Zeitdauern* [The processing of very brief time intervals]. Münster: Waxmann.

Rammsayer, T. (2003). Sensory and cognitive mechanisms in temporal processing elucidated by a model system approach. In H. Helfrich (Ed.), *Time and mind II* (pp. 97-113). Göttingen: Hogrefe & Huber.

Reuter-Lorenz, P. A. (2000). Cognitive neuropsychology of the aging brain. In D. Park & N. Schwarz (Eds.), *Cognitive aging* (pp. 93-114). Philadelphia, PA: Psychology Press.

Roediger III, H. L., Buckner, R. L., & McDermott, K. B. (1999). Components of processing. In J. K. Foster & M. Jelicic (Eds.), *Memory: Systems, process, or function*? (pp. 66-103). New York: Oxford University Press.

Rubin, D. C., Wetzler, S. E., & Nebes, R. D. (1986). Autobiographical memory across the lifespan. In D. C. Rubin (Ed.), *Autobiographical memory* (pp. 202-221). Cambridge, England: Cambridge University Press.

Ryan, J. D., & Cohen, N. J. (2003). Evaluating the neuropsychological dissociation evidence for multiple memory systems. *Cognitive, Affective, & Behavioral Neuroscience, 3*(3), 168-185.

Ryle, G. (1949). *The concept of the mind.* London: Hutchinson.

Salthouse, T. A. (1996). The processing-speed theory of adult age differences in cognition. *Psychological Review, 103*, 403-428.

Savitt, S. F. (Ed.). (1995). *Time's arrow today.* Cambridge, NY: Cambridge University Press.

Schacter, D. L. (1987). Implicit memory: History and current status. *Journal of Experimental Psychology: Learning, Memory, and Cognition, 13,* 501-518.

Schacter, D. L., Kaszniak, A. W., Kihlstrom, J. F., & Valdiserri, M. (1991). On the relation between source memory and aging. *Psychology and Aging, 6*, 559-568.

Schulze-Kissing, D., van der Meer, E., & Urbas, L. (2004). A psychological analysis of temporal errors in human-machine systems. *IFAC-2004 Proceedings,* Atlanta.

Shimamura, A. P. (1995). Memory and frontal lobe function. In M. S. Gazzaniga (Ed.), *The cognitive neurosciences.* Cambridge, MA: The MIT Press.

Sklar, L. (1995). Time experience and the theoretical description of the world. In S. F. Savitt (Ed.), *Time's arrows today* (pp. 217-229). Cambridge, NY: Cambridge University Press.

Smith, J. (1996). Planning about life: Toward a social-interactive perspective. In P. B. Baltes & U. M. Staudinger (Eds.), *Interactive minds* (pp. 242-275). Cambridge, NY: Cambridge University Press.

Smith, J., & Baltes, P. B. (1990). Wisdom-related knowledge: Age/cohort differences in response to life-planning problems. *Developmental Psychology, 26*(3), 494-505.

Spencer, W., & Raz, N. (1994). Memory for facts, source and context: Can frontal lobe dysfunction explain age-related differences? *Psychology & Aging, 9,* 149-158.

Squire, L. R. (1987). *Memory and brain.* New York: Oxford University Press.

Squire, L. R. (1992). Memory and the hippocampus: A synthesis of findings with rats, monkeys, and humans. *Psychological Review, 99,* 195-231.

Stevens, S. S. (1951). Mathematics, measurement, and psychophysics. In S. S. Stevens (Ed.), *Handbook of experimental psychology* (pp. 1-49). New York: Wiley.

Stroud, J. M. (1955). The fine structure of psychological time. In H. Quastler (Ed.), *Information theory in psychology: Problems and methods* (pp. 174-205). Glencoe, IL: The Free Press.

Thomae, H. (1989). Veränderungen der Zeitperspektive im höheren Alter [Changes in temporal perspective in older age]. *Zeitschrift für Gerontologie, 22*, 58-66.

Thompson, C. P., Skowronski, J. J., Larsen, S. F., Betz, A. (1996). *Autobiographical memory: Remembering what and remembering when.* Mahwah, NJ: Erlbaum.

Till, R. E., Mross, E. F., & Kintsch, W. (1988). Time course of priming for associate and inference words in a discourse context. *Memory & Cognition, 16,* 283-298.

Tulving, E. (1972). Episodic and semantic memory. In E. Tulving & W. Donaldson (Eds.), *Organization of memory* (pp. 382-403). New York: Academic Press.

Tzeng, O. J. L., & Cotton, B. (1980). A study-phase retrieval model of temporal coding. *Journal of Experimental Psychology: Human Learning and Memory, 6*, 705-716.

van Benthem, J. (1985). Semantics of time. In J. A. Michon & J. L. Jackson (Eds.), *Time, mind, and behavior* (pp. 266-278). Berlin: Springer.

van der Meer, E. (1999). Zeitkodierung in Wissenskörpern [Coding of temporal information in semantic memory]. *Zeitschrift für Psychologie, 207*, 363-381.

van der Meer, E., Beyer, R., Hagendorf, H., Strauch, D., & Kolbe, M. (2003). Temporal relations between event concepts. In H. Härtl, & H. Tappe (Eds.), *Mediating between concepts and grammar* (pp. 225-254). Berlin/New York: Morton de Gruyter.

van der Meer, E., Beyer, R., Heinze, B., & Badel, I. (2002). Temporal order relations in language comprehension. *Journal of Experimental Psychology: Learning, Memory, and Cognition, 28*(4), 770-779.

van der Meer, E., & Kolbe, M. (1997). Zur Kodierung von Zeitbezügen in begrifflichen Wissensstrukturen [Coding of temporal information in conceptual knowledge structures]. In R. H. Kluwe (Ed.), *Strukturen und Prozesse intelligenter Systeme* [Structures and processes of intelligent systems] (pp. 107-132). Wiesbaden: Deutscher Universitätsverlag.

van der Meer, E., Krüger, F., & Nuthmann, A. (1999). Memory for temporal order. *Abstracts of the Psychonomic Society, 4*, 41.

van der Meer, E., & Schmidt, B. (1992). Finale, kausale und temporale Inferenzen—Analyse ihres kognitiven Hintergrundes [Final, causal, and temporal relations—Analysis of the cognitive background]. *Zeitschrift für Psychologie, 200*, 303-320.

Wallace, M., & Rabin, A. I. (1960). Temporal experience. *Psychological Bulletin, 57,* 213-236.

Waerden, J. H. (2003). Applying the scalar timing model to human time psychology: Progress and challenges. In H. Helfrich (Ed.), *Time and mind II* (pp. 21-39). Göttingen: Hogrefe & Huber.

Waerden, J. H., Waerden, A. J., & Rabbitt, P. M. A. (1997). Age and IQ effects on stimulus and response timing. *Journal of Experimental Psychology: Human Perception and Performance, 23*, 962-979.

Welford, A. T. (1980). Relations between reaction time and fatigue, stress, age and sex. In A. T. Welford (Ed.), *Reaction times* (pp. 321-354). London: Academic Press.

Wittkowski, J. (1990). Konstanz und Veränderung der Zukunftsperspektive im mittleren Erwachsenenalter [Stability and change of the time perspective in middle adulthood]. In E. Baumgartner, F. C. Sauter, H-P. Trolldenier (Eds.), *Ich und Gruppe* [Self and group] (pp. 61-71). Göttingen: Hogrefe.

Wundt, W. (1911). *Grundriss der Psychologie* [Compendium of psychology] (10.Aufl., 1. Aufl. 1896). Leipzig: Wilhelm Engelmann Verlag.

Zakay, D., & Block, R. A. (1996). The role of attention in time estimation processes. In M. A. Pastor & J. Artieda (Eds.), *Time, internal clocks and movement* (pp. 143-163). North-Holland: Elsevier.

Zakay, D., & Block, R. A. (1997). Temporal cognition. *Current Directions in Psychological Science, 6*(1), 12-16.

Zakay, D., Nitzan, D., & Glicksohn, J. (1983). The influence of task difficulty and external tempo on subjective time estimation. *Perception and Psychophysics, 34*, 451-456.

Zimbardo, P. G., & Gonzales, A. (1984). The times of your life. *Psychology Today, 18*, 53-54.

CHAPTER 4

Temporal References in the Construction of Self-Identity: A Life-Span Approach

Freya Dittmann-Kohli

INTRODUCTION: TIME FOR ALL VERSUS SUBJECTIVE TIME

Baars (1997a) and others (e.g., Hendricks, 2001) have argued that there is an important contrast between chronological, objective time in human lives on the one hand and subjective time on the other. Objective time and socially organized time are a sort of "time for all," but subjective time or the experience of temporality in human existence are part of self and life experience. Objective time may include cosmic change, socially organized and institutionalized time, and is usually instrumentally constructed, metric time.

The "socially organized time patterns" are internalized from early on in life through the acquisition of certain patterns of social organization and daily routines in the family (Gell, 1992). Somewhat later, during middle childhood, cognitive conceptualization of objective time is achieved through the emergence of a unifying, metric time concept in middle and later childhood (Piaget, 1970). Thus, both a generalized conception of objective time and the routines of the clock and the patterns of social time organization are acquired well before midlife.

During middle childhood, subjective time also emerges, in the sense that there is a growing personal time perspective linking the events of the past and the expected future to the autobiographical self. With the advent of adolescence and young adulthood, the future time perspective becomes more important as an extension of the present self, containing goals and expectations of future changes from the present state of affairs.

Around and after midlife, however, a qualitatively different sort of subjective temporal perspective emerges. The experience of the self as having limited duration and facing decline as a living human being in the here and now becomes more real. The abstract knowledge that living things die is acquired before that time. But around middle adulthood, this general knowledge becomes personalized: personal change, transience, and finitude become individually relevant as a part of identity and personal reality. The awareness of personal change related to aging and of diminishing time left to live is increasing throughout the second half of life.

Such awareness of a temporal identity implying finitude may, in some cases, develop well before midlife, for instance, in case of fatal illness (Merriam, Courtenay, & Reeves, 2001), war, and other imminently dangerous life conditions. Within the normal life course in present time (in Western countries), the subjective time perspective is constituted by a cognitive framework that is internalized and personalized on the basis of a certain type of cultural model of the life course.

Subjective time and its gradual change over the life span will be the main topic of my contribution. In contrast to traditional approaches to future time perspective, however, the emphasis will be on an "existential time perspective," an element of identity developing during the second half of life. In the following, I shall first discuss how subjective time is anchored in human neurophysiology and mental organization. Psychological approaches to the "temporally extended self," the emergence of an autobiographical self, and narrative identity will exemplify that subjective time is an important feature of human identity construction. This concerns a realm of theorizing and research on the psychology of time that is not included in the experimental study of short-term, sensory time perception.

In a later the part of this chapter, spontaneous self and life descriptions of young and elderly adults are analyzed to test whether the passage of time is indeed a more salient element of self-experience in later life, compared to young adulthood. I shall also present data on how this affects the meaning content of temporal identity in young and elderly adults. For the collection of these data, an open method for the study of identity and features of self-construction has been used to assure that unknown features of the temporal self can be discovered. This new method, with suitable properties for these objectives, will be described; it is based on a view of a person's self-construction presented earlier (i.e., the autobiographical self and narrative identity). The method is thus directly linked to the model of identity within my theoretical set-up.

Temporal Life Patterns and Temporal Identity

Biological processes have their own temporal organization. These processes have their genetically determined speed and form, and they are part of reality, measured in terms of the standard metric (objective) time concept. As all other organisms, human beings have built-in, genetically determined, and environmentally influenced "time schedules" as their constitutive parts and as organic wholes. Human death is thus the ultimate point in time that can be subjectively experienced as the end of one's own life. In childhood, on the other hand, the subjective feeling of having a temporally limited life span is still undeveloped.

To our scientific and evolutionary understanding, human organisms and all other living beings (including the world and the cosmos in general) are subjected to time in an objective way. Organisms are processes in time. Biological time patterns constitute life processes such as breathing, sleeping, and waking, and are characteristic of psychological processes and states as well (e.g., mood changes and activity levels). From childhood to old age there are biological time lines; aging is associated with a slowing down of mental and motor processes, as well as changes in the experience of the passing of time (Brockmeier, 1991; cf. Hendricks, 2001). Objective biological time (i.e., the speed of biological processes) may thus be related to a subjectively perceived speed of change.

Empirical researchers in psychology have a long tradition of investigating the subjective perception of duration and speed of stimuli; time perception is considered as a basic human capacity by experimentalists. Experiments on time perception are generally not intended to study time experience over long periods of life, but to understand the immediate, short-term time perception as one of the sensory capacities of the organism (such as the perception of short time units regarding duration, speed, temporal order, etc., see Dittmann, 1973; van der Meer, this volume; Wallace, 1956). Basic predispositions are assumed to exist, allowing human beings to perceive movement and duration in an outside event, as well as their own behaviors and internal events.

There is, however, also an indication of a basic capacity to apprehend or perceive one's own existence (a very extended, long-term event) as situated and limited in time. This type of time perception is different from elementary, short-term time perception that can be directed to discover movements and experienced duration (e.g., in pain). Long-term subjective time perception is always tied to cognitive structures and involves (cultural) ideas of phases of life. The individual life-span construct (Whitbourne, 1985) is such a cognitive construct (with age-normative expectations, subjective age, etc.). It is intimately connected with the development of self-understanding, identity, and selfhood. The understanding of one's own life trajectory, temporality, and finitude is dependent on the emergence of a complex, personalized understanding of selfhood. This, in turn, is dependent on a long biological selection and cultural/historical evolution. The temporally extended self-concept of our present time is an example of identity development and selfhood based on neurological and cultural evolution.

Regarding cultural evolution, Vroon (1978) has delineated the early human history of the gradual development of today's concept of individuality. Human beings did not always understand themselves as coherent persons in body and mind. Early inhabitants of Greece and Israel did not see the mind as an origin of one's own thoughts and feelings. The modern understanding of awareness, individuality, and self-reflection was only achieved in an epoch close to the beginning of Christianity (Vroon, 1978).

Time Perception as a Biological Given

Cultural evolution and transmission depend on biologically rooted neurological foundations in the brain that make the cognitive integration and complexity of self-understanding possible. Sedikides and Skowronski (1997) have traced the prehistoric evolution of a symbolic, individualized self-concept and its survival benefits. Other authors have also taken an evolutionary perspective on self-construction (e.g., Smith, 2002). Evolutionary evidence is, of course, difficult to find in this field. However, research into the biological structures and functions of the brain have brought an important addition to our understanding of the connection between the organism, foundations of identity, temporality, and the collective and individual development of the mind.

In the last few decades, neurophysiological and neuropsychological research has increasingly directed attention to the biological foundations of autobiographical identity and the identity-related aspects of time experience. In the clinical context, Damasio (1999) believes to have found sufficient evidence for a biological foundation of a so-called core self. The core self implies the ability to locate oneself in a here and now; that is, in a time located between past and future. We are able to do this as we are aware of our spatial position, our movements, and our posture. Roth (2001) presents corresponding conclusions from extensive brain studies. He postulates several basic, genetically determined elements and functions of self-perception; the significance of this research and conceptualization is that the self is not an indifferent and insignificant mental structure but is necessary for psychological functioning. Roth (2001) differentiates the following aspects:

1. The body self—a sense that my body is mine and that it is I who moves and controls it;
2. The sense of self-location—I know I am here now in this place and not in another place or time;
3. The sense of perspective—the perception and knowledge that I am the focal point of reality around me;
4. The self as experiencing subject—the knowledge and feeling that I am the one who has the perceptions, thoughts, feelings, and not somebody else (as perhaps in schizophrenia);
5. The self as author and agent—the sense of myself being the cause and the controlling agent of my thoughts and actions;
6. The autobiographical self—the belief that I am the one that I was yesterday, and that there is a certain continuity in the various sensations and experiences (to maintain a sense of continuity, verbal communication is important);

7. The self-reflective self—the possibility to think about myself (here too, language plays an important role);
8. The moral self—there is a source from which information and orders are issued on what to do and not to do on moral grounds.

These functions or capacities are the nuclei for the emergence of a later, temporally extended self-concept that is built up by memory, cognitions, and attached feelings. Autobiographical memories and cognitive schemata (and affective schemata) are accumulated and organized into a structure and a process that will finally make up the overall subjective sense of self and identity. Thus, from the perspective of brain research, there are biological preconditions for extending the core self into a complex self-concept that will include a "temporal identity," that is, an awareness and knowledge of being a person with a past and a future, as well as a developmental trajectory and (changing) present. Cultural evolution since at least Augustine's time (Baars, 2000) has developed the availability of a symbolic environment that allows individuals in modern countries to develop a temporally extended, complex self-concept and a subjective time experience that entails an existential identity of an aging, mortal individual. As already put forth, this time awareness grows with chronological age.

Based on clinical observation, the neurologist Damasio (1999) has for the last decade insisted on the distinction between a core self and an extended self as well. He understands the latter as a network of learned self-knowledge in which the present identity is tied to an understanding of having a personal past and a personal future. The core self is the nucleus for our autobiographical memory and our self-awareness. In the beginning of life, this biologically anchored core self is important as a nucleus for the accumulation of simple autobiographical memories (of episodes and events). Throughout adolescence and in the course of adulthood, this core self may expand and be reorganized to include a widening experience of a self as life, a deeper understanding, and more complex knowledge systems that make up mature self-awareness (Staudinger & Dittmann-Kohli, 1992).

In summary, it is nowadays considered an evolutionary fact that the human species has the potential for developing subjective time experience in which the individual is aware of her/himself and temporal existence. Under favorable sociocultural conditions, intentional and spontaneous perceptions as well as (extensive) reflections of the self are the rule, in addition to the self's relations to the world. Another specifically human potential is the ability to make language-based constructions of the self, resulting in a "narrative identity" which may contain complex lines of event sequences (see below). These are integrated with the experience of the living, self-aware person in the here and now, as well as with the projections of the self into a future. The next section will provide some further considerations on this topic.

Autonoetic Memory

There are additional examples of authors who connect biological, subjective, and cultural aspects of the temporally extended self-understanding. Welzer and Markowitsch (2001) have been studying human memory functions. They propose to integrate the perspectives of several disciplines and to use knowledge and insight from the social, cultural, and biological sciences. According to their integrative view, a coherent sense of identity and a continuing self-image are based on the capability for autonoetic memory. This memory allows us to construct a self that has existed in the past and that will be existing in the future on the basis of what is present. Brain research has underpinned in detail how different brain regions and periods of learning interact to produce the acquisition of facts and symbols with the help of language. The frontal lobes are necessary for a "theory of mind" (Stuss, Gallup, & Alexander, 2001), which is a "theory" where information is temporally connected into prospective and retrospective perspectives within the episodic autobiographical memory (Welzer & Markowitsch, 2001, p. 212).

Klein (2001) has made a cognitive neurophysiological contribution to the social/psychological construction of the self. He describes how self creates memory and memory creates self. He points to numerous former and present authors who hold the self to be a product of the personal past. At the same time, "remembering events of a personal past presupposes a self" (Klein, 2001, p. 26); the interdependence of self and memory is very complex. The natural sense of self contains experiences of continuity, agency, and knowledge of self; the constituents of self-continuity are self-reflection, personal agency, and personal ownership of knowledge and feelings (which can be disturbed in schizophrenia and depression, for instance). In brain-damaged patients, semantic and episodic self-knowledge can be dissociated, so that self-knowledge of traits (e.g., honest, old, ill) ". . . can be learned and remembered without access to episodic memory" (p. 37).

In the following section, we leave neurophysiology to focus on more psychological approaches to temporal identity. Some authors stress the temporal dimension of the self in a perspective of developmental cognitive constructionism, while others refer to a context of personal meaning of self and life.

THE TEMPORAL EXTENSION OF THE SELF-CONCEPT IN COGNITIVE AND CLINICAL PSYCHOLOGY

Neisser (1988) is a cognitive psychologist who has distinguished various types of self-knowledge, with basic domains such as the ecological and social self. He has also proposed a temporal self that was originally conceptualized as an "extended self" with knowledge and memories of one's own past and future. The temporal self and a conceptual self are thought to be based on cognitive development and abstract knowledge. Later he recast the temporal self as the "remembering self" (Neisser & Fivush, 1994) and included divergent scientific approaches such as the autobiographical self, research on self-narratives, on autonoetic memory, personal identity, etc. The remembering self is an integration of autobiographical memory and identity as a lifelong process (Neisser & Fivush, 1994). The development of our identity in relation to the world and our sense of personhood and continuity from past to future is a process that continues from childhood to old age. The remembered self was originally constructed in the context of traditional cognitive psychology, but has been extended to include more comprehensive approaches, as many of the contributions to the work on the remembered self show. The point that I want to stress again is that time-perception research has moved from a study of elementary functions to the attempted understanding of the individual as a unit complete with personal meanings, identity, emotion, and motivation. Psychological research on time has come to include personality, language, and (cultural) context.

For instance, Neimeyer and Metzler (1994, p. 128) represent a sort of clinical perspective on the overall personality. They comment that "personal memory and personal identity are interdependent processes, which are broadly consistent with a conceptualization of the self as a personal scientist or personal historian . . . whose efforts are directed toward the evolution and preservation of a meaningful sense of self" (p. 129). Referring to work by Epstein (1973) and Greenwald (1980), the authors state ". . . we regard the preservation of a meaningful sense of self-identity as an important factor in [the] reconstructive process. . ." and the authors assume ". . . that there are important differences in identity development that may carry implications for autobiographical recall" (Neimeyer & Metzler, 1994, p. 129). Thus, identity and identity development may influence what is said about the past.

NARRATIVE APPROACHES TO SELF-CONSTRUCTION, IDENTITY, AND TIME PERSPECTIVE

In recent years, an increasing number of publications on autobiographical self-construction have stressed its temporal dimension. Biographical self-construction implies the concepts of personal past, present, and future; research on identity and self-narratives has thus called special attention to representations of subjective time perspective. Cohler (1982) argues that "a personal narrative . . . represents the most internally consistent interpretation of presently understood past, experienced present, and anticipated future" (pp. 206-207).

The special emphasis of the psychology of narrative identity must be contrasted to the study of the development of an objective, metrical time concept in children and adolescents. Individual perception and understanding of objective time have been investigated by Piaget (1970) as a fundamental and quasi-universal aspect of development toward higher cognitive functioning; that is, intelligence. Once the abstract time concept is acquired, it is used throughout life.

Narrative psychology, on the other hand, aims at the constitution of identity along the temporal dimension of human self and life. Implicit in narrative identity is an experienced time dimension: who I was, who I am now, what I experienced, what I will have and be soon and later. Therefore, narrative identity related to aging research touches on issues like mortality, decline, stability, and well-being. Our modern construction of personhood necessarily includes a personal time perspective that orders past events, representing origin and development, and reaches into a future that will realize one of my possible selves. Thus, "existential time experience," comprehending my life and defining the different stages of existence as a person, is part of my identity and self-awareness. This temporal self-awareness will therefore be intimately linked to the stages of life already lived. The narrative identity of a young person will include a short life, and possibly an open future, whereas the autobiographical self-awareness of an older person will include many events and experiences. The future of an older person is usually constructed from self-knowledge of past and present in combination with knowledge about the further aging process.

These conceptualizations produced by narrative psychologists are in close correspondence with those underlying more traditional aging research. A particular feature of narrative psychology, however, is its direct connection between the construct and an empirical methodology. Narratives are assumed to be the natural medium of private and public self-construction. This also makes them a natural means of research on identity and subjective time perspective. In this chapter, it is of importance with respect to the methodology used to tap the temporal aspects of identity in the empirical data presented later.

Polkinghorne (1991) has stressed that identity as a concept and research program and concept is directly connected with a narrative and temporally extended structuring and ordering of the self. It is emphasized that identity is constructed by means of a cognitive framework that corresponds with a narrative structure or schema. Brockmeier (1991, 2000, 2001) has repeatedly presented a psychological and logical argument on the relations between narrative form, narrative and temporal conceptualization, and linguistic development. Baars (1997a) has stressed the interface between chronological time, aging, and a narrative time perspective. In his view, the important functions of chronological time as a "measure" for aging must be complemented by nonmetric time concepts. Individual aging takes place within a subjective time perspective that is reflected in narratives, which are used to construct narrative identities.

The inherent time dimension in the autobiographical self and its narrative cognitive structure is implied in the form of a "story" which has an author, the I, and a protagonist, the Me. The Me is the hero in the story, who may be seen as moving through environmental and developmental settings moving from one event to the other on a single time line. Not all self-theorists however comprehend self-construction as implying a single coherent knowledge structure. Narratives can accommodate that too. The self-report could also be a linguistic product in which the Me is constructed out of an interwoven set of different stories or authors. Different story lines can also be emanations of an author who is unable to construct one coherent story out of the contradicting experiences and cultural models providing metaphors for the self (cf. Hermans, 1996). Concepts of time and narrative approaches from the perspective of philosophy have been analyzed by Baars (1997b), who also linked them to the aging personal identity.

PSYCHOLOGICAL LIFE-SPAN CONCEPTS

In the everyday life of industrialized countries and in global communication, aging has become a focus of many social representations and cultural models. Thinking and talking about the aging process, staying young, and the management of later life and continued growth has become widespread. It has been intensified during the last decades by influences from science, the media, the experience of longevity, and the increasing numbers of elderly people. This indicates that public, media-based social representations about aging and the life course go hand in hand with personal life-span constructs (Whitbourne, 1985) and life stories that can serve as cognitive frameworks in organizing everyday talk as well as private information processing. Whitbourne (1985) has presented the concept of life-span construct as a personal version of a temporal organization of one's life in connection with coping and adaptation.

The life-span construct is necessarily rooted in social representations and cultural models of the life course. As a personalized framework it also acts as a dynamic model that integrates autobiographical events and developmental goals and expectations. Heckhausen's (1999) conceptualization of the life course and developmental regulation and action is an example of a more modern version of adaptation over the life course which is in turn related to the selection, optimization, compensation model (SOC) of Baltes and his colleagues. The experience of one's present condition and life situation and its shifting location on the life span as well as the shifting future time perspective is the focus of the next section; it is conceptually in line with our earlier reflections on the extended self and autobiographical memory and identity.

The Future Time Perspective in Psychological Research

In the following, we will turn to the psychological research of the personal time perspective of the past, present, and future. In particular, the future time perspective is a traditional line of psychological research that received much attention in Western countries throughout the last century. Much empirical research was carried out in the traditional way, using designs that test hypotheses with closed questionnaires and scales in correlational and sometimes experimental studies (with the exception of Nuttin, 1984, who used incomplete sentences asking for the subjects' wishes, goals and preferences). Furthermore, I have provided some examples of future time-perspective research in elderly adults. Empirical results of my own research will be partly related to findings of future time-perspective research.

The purpose of citing some studies on future time perspective (FTP) is to give the reader an idea of this very important field of psychological research. FTP has been more often studied than the other two areas of personal time perspective, past and present. Personal time perspective is part of the larger topic of subjective time; in turn there are several variables studied when investigating FTP, such as time extension, density of FTP, content of goals and expectations, and affective time orientation.

The purpose of the sections on future time perspective is also to pave the way toward our own approach. As I will try to show with the help of empirical data from narrative self-reports, future time perspective is seen as too narrow to catch the different facets of subjective time and self-experience in later life. In contrast, it will become evident that the subjective experience of (life) time is becoming more prominent in the self-narratives of later life, compared to early adulthood. Moreover, subjective time and self experience is characterized as much by the past and present perspectives as well as a future perspective. Also, stability and change are important features of the subjective time perspective.

Empirical Research on Future Time Perspective

Lewin (1969) had introduced a life-space concept of personal and future time perspective, analogous to the regions of the life space in its spatial extension. He is cited most often in connection with his life space concept, a model of the individual locating him/herself in space and time. Dittmann-Kohli (1991) used this model to structure the categories mapping the lexical content of spontaneous self-descriptions (see the empirical section of this contribution).

Nuttin and Lens (1985) have emphasized in their theoretical and empirical work that the future time perspective (FTP) is a basic human potential associated with motivation, planning, and other behavior. In particular, FTP has been found to be positively related to achievement, career, achievement motivation, and delay of gratification. In contrast to the future time perspective, the present time perspective was found to be related to more hedonistic strivings in the here and now. In his thorough theoretical and empirical study of time perspective and motivation, Nuttin (1984) proposed that the study of a personal future perspective should have priority over the past or present because the future, rather than the past or present, has a close interrelation with the dynamics of personality.

An illustrative selection of typical research on future time perspective was assembled by Zaleski (1994). Especially in adolescence and youth, the density and extent of future perspective—the number and temporal distance of anticipated future life events, personal projects, and goals—have been related to a host of psychologically and socially important variables. In addition to planning, striving, and delay of gratification (e.g., Nurmi, 1994; Trommsdorf, 1994), self-regulation in the area of criminality and success in educational and social mobility were investigated.

A good example of the specific youthful orientation and the long tradition of the study of future time perspective is a new study by Zimbardo and Boyd (1999). Referring to earlier philosophers and to the psychological authors mentioned above, the authors describe their general conceptual model of a time perspective which is assumed to merge into a dispositional style ". . . that is characteristic and predictive of how an individual will respond across a host of daily life choices. . . . Temporal bias may include either habitual overuse or underuse of one or more of these temporal frames" (p. 1272). Judging from the item content of their instrument for measuring this temporal frame or bias in time perspective, students answering this questionnaire have to agree or disagree with statements about time perspective proper as well as with hedonistic orientations, achievement-related aspirations, lifestyle and other categories that embody specific Western cultural attitudes and values apart from time. (Example of item: I am able to resist temptation when I know that there is work to be done.)

As is to be expected, such attitudes and preferences, in connection with work behaviors and life experiences, are related to future and present time perspectives. The findings basically prove that there are indeed groups of students with a present-oriented, hedonistic alignment, and that there are future-oriented students accepting delay of gratification, striving for long-term achievement and career success, and having a more pronounced future time perspective. The association between success and future orientation, however, depends on living in cultural/economic systems that can be regulated by individual planning. Even in Western countries there are life situations in which an extended future time perspective, especially when coupled with achievement motivation and high aspirations, does not make sense in very old age. Formulated in another way: a long future time perspective will lead elderly adults to understand that their remaining years may be few, and that their opportunities for (further) social and economic success are very restricted. Even more so, their remaining years may be constrained by illness and disability. Consequently, any remaining goals (pleasures or achievements) should be reached quickly and in the present, in the here and now, or in the near future. In life situations in which future conditions cannot be controlled individually, the development of a present time perspective is not a short-sighted preference for immediate gratification but a far-sighted attitude attesting to wisdom and understanding of the *conditio humana*. In further research, the situational irrelevance of future orientation has to be taken into account.

The implicit assumption that normal studies of FTP are basically culture-free can be challenged by observations of Hagestad (1996), who makes evident that they are dependent on other broad cultural orientations. Hagestad has made revealing observations on the sociocultural embeddedness of defining individuals through their expected future. In the context of sociology of the life course, Hagestad (1996) has described the cultural emphasis on planning and a progressive future, which is the primary means of recognizing identity in American society and in Western countries. This becomes particularly evident when an individual "has no future" or has an uncertain future, as in the case of fatal illness (see also the case of AIDS, Merriam, Courtenay, & Reeves, 2001).

The value of a long-term FTP as a psychological marker of a positive personality disposition is dependent on the existence of Western sociocultural and economic structures, values, and "models of man." The usefulness of a long-term FTP can neither be generalized to all phases of life nor to different cultural and economic systems. Especially in light of the growing number of elderly people, the problems in developing countries, globalization, and Muslim/Christian collisions, the results of studies on FTP must be understood as having limited generalizability.

Future time perspective should be conceptualized in a different way, so that it is defined as an aspect of a more comprehensive construct of temporal identity. Its present restriction to certain types of people, to a certain group of personality traits, and to certain approaches to motivation and achievement should be dropped, and an adjustment in its definition should make it more suitable to research on late life and to people with other cultural backgrounds. For instance, Dittmann (1973, 1974) has studied the relation between achievement motivation and future time perspective in African and Indian secondary-school students in order to test the relation between culture and cognitive/affective structures. Though the patterns of high achievement imagery have been absorbed by the African Luo students, the culturally inherited nonmetrical social constructions of time and the life course have had a negative effect on the structure and clarity of their future time perspective, their understanding of the duration of phases of the life course, and their estimation of time span in daily life. In addition, a marked effect on the affective and cognitive meaning of the concepts of time and future could be assessed. In contrast, the Indian students (as the sons of economically motivated immigrants) had an understanding of personal and social time in line with the achievement-motivation theory that relates motivation to economic achievement: they perceived time as running faster and as being more dynamic. The future time perspective is related to economic achievement because of its closeness to planning, investment, and delay of gratification in favor of future gains. Populations stressing economic success, such as the immigrant Indians in East Africa and the Chinese in many Asian countries and in North America, provide a social structure that allows financial success if individuals plan ahead and economize time. In many African countries and tribes (as in other underdeveloped countries) this is not the case, and for many elderly adults this is not the case either.

FUTURE TIME PERSPECTIVE IN ELDERLY ADULTS

Historically, research on future time perspective started with a focus on adolescence and youth; especially on students in colleges and universities. It had been an important indicator (variable) in research on the "achievement syndrome" by McClelland and his colleagues (see Dittmann, 1973). The achievement motive is in turn a disposition that is mostly relevant for young and middle-aged adults. When empirical gerontological research expanded, FTP was also incorporated in studies on aging adults (cf. van der Meer, this volume). The study of late-life time perspective, unfortunately, has been dominated by the parameters of a certain cultural system and the value of future planning for young and middle-aged adults. The main point in the present context is the proposition that because of this transfer of the young and middle-aged paradigm to elderly adults, important differences in the cognitive, affective, and motivational aspects of the "mature" time perspective have not found the attention they deserved.

What has been found through the empirical study of the future time perspective of elderly adults? One example is the work of Bouffard, Bastin, and Lapierre (1994). They investigated the "classical time perspective" in the elderly, but they used spontaneous self-reports (incomplete sentences) to obtain narrative accounts about their wishes and preferences. Age has been observed to be one of the basic parameters in time orientation and perspective. In agreement with the above-mentioned view of the situational relevance of future orientation, the authors report that in addition to higher age, situational variables like the length of institutionalization, health, functional autonomy, and socioeconomic level (but not gender) were found to be related to future time perspective. Thus, the finding that the extension of future time perspective in late life does not just reflect chronological age, but is influenced by personality structure as well as the structure of people's life situations (i.e., social and biological constraints). Both personality and situational structure influence goal setting and motivational orientation. Psychological well-being in later life has been found to correlate positively with having goals and a more pronounced FTP; thus having goals and FTP depend on appropriate life conditions. Thus, a more extended future time perspective in old age should be the consequence of a promising life situation that invites an expectation of positive outcomes and motivates people to make plans. On this understanding, FTP can also coexist with a strong present orientation. The latter makes use of what is already given with regard to quality of life and psychological well-being (cf. Westerhof, 2001; Westerhof & Dittmann-Kohli, 2000).

Future time extension (in contrast to the content of FTP) has been the aspect of personal time perspective most heavily researched, probably because it can be operationalized in a very simple way (i.e., by the number of years goals and expectations that lie ahead). In their review, Bouffard et al. (1994, pp. 77-78) point to results and conclusions of researchers about reduced life expectations and a shortening of future time perspective in old age. Other researchers, such as Kastenbaum (1982) and Thomae (1989) have stressed individual differences. In many empirical studies on the life span, chronological age and the extension of FTP have been found to correlate negatively, whereas sometimes they appeared to be independent. A curvilinear relationship demonstrating the maximum in adulthood and a decline in old age has also been found (e.g., Lens & Gailly, 1980). More specific aspects of personal time perspective, such as the temporal extension of motivational goals and the temporal range of concerns, has been shown to be age-independent when only elderly subjects were studied, so that the life situations were similar. A wide range of variables associated with the extension of FTP was presented by Bouffard in an earlier study (see Zaleski, 1994). He found 13 variables that are related to a future time perspective in old age. One of the most influential was health, which has also been found to be related to many other variables in old age (Dittmann-Kohli et al., 2001), demonstrating that psychophysical function is a key to pursuing a desired lifestyle. Healthy and able older persons who continue to achieve and to be productive often keep their habit of setting relatively long-term goals, including postmortem reputation (e.g. in the case of artists, see Adams-Price, 1998, on creativity and aging). The relationship of such life strategies to pragmatic wisdom can be suspected (Dittmann-Kohli, 1984).

Affective time orientation is the emotional quality associated with biographical time, be it toward the future, the present, or the past. It has been included in many studies on aging and the life course. It is usually understood as one's attitude or judgment about the degree of positive or negative value of present or past life. Hence it is seen by researchers as an aspect of the subjective quality of life and as part of the study of life satisfaction and well-being (e.g., Westerhof, 2001). This type of attitude and valuation of the phases of one's life forms part of self-understanding and identity seen in a life-span perspective.

In summary, the traditional (quantitative) approach to personal time perspective has been conducted within a certain theoretical and methodological paradigm. Aging research in survey studies and in more limited questionnaire studies regularly includes variables of personal time perspective, such as time extension and affective attitudes to different periods of life (e.g., Brandtstädter & Wentura, 1994). In general, the conceptualization of these variables is behavioral and dispositional in nature and does not include changing patterns of cognitive construction and embeddedness in (narrative) self-identity. Studies on personal time perspective and affective time orientation are looking at specific measurements and their correlation to criterion variables such as well-being or resilience and use them as predictors of later behavior. Studies using open-ended instruments calling for narrative self-reports, on the other hand, represent an attempt to bridge the gap between traditional methods and narrative autobiography. In addition to the studies mentioned above, narrative data collected with the incomplete sentence method were used in studies by Timmer (2000) and Timmer, Bode, and Dittmann-Kohli (2003) in a comprehensive approach to analyze the content of the anticipations of gain, continuation of the present state, and decline. These studies put the scientific conceptualizations of gain and loss into a different perspective and particularly stress the positive and proactive content of goals and concerns in the third age or the young old.

Existential Meaning of Time

In addition to analytical research with quantitative and experimental methods, there is a certain amount of qualitative research on time and aging. In this literature, topics related to (life) time and the meaning of aging, spirituality, etc. are stressed. It is an example of work that tends to treat the topic of time and aging in a manner closer to the humanities, such as "Aging and the Meaning of Time" (McFadden & Atchley, 2001). Studies such as these tend to use little or no quantification and strict design, as is also the case with literature on discourse and narrative. At the same time, this research also contributes to our scientific understanding and qualitative findings from a more sensitive and insightful approach to existential matters, such as death, finitude, the meaning of aging, as well as aging as a time in life for contemplation, reordering of priorities, advanced self-understanding and a wise attitude toward the self in the context of many external constraints (Dittmann-Kohli, 1984). The meaning of aging as a process of maturation, individualization, integrity, and spirituality has been demonstrated by a collection of journals written over several years (Berman, 1994). Baars (1997b) and many other authors have dealt with topics of finitude and the process of dying.

Social and biological structures are the roots of existential limitations of self and life that are often the focus of this literature. It does not start with the frame of reference of a young adult but that of an elderly adult, viewing the life span as a whole. Authors explore the meaning of this fact for personhood and for its implications for mental development and identity. In this kind of research, human mortality has the quality of temporal transitoriness; existence has the quality of a fleeting, passing, or diminishing time span and limited consciousness. These qualities of experience are held to be typically human because they presuppose rich cognitive understanding.

TEMPORAL REFERENCES IN SELF-NARRATIVES AS A MARKER OF LATE-LIFE IDENTITY CONSTRUCTION

To a certain extent the use of narrative self-reports in the following part represents an effort to approach aging and subjective time in later life with sensitivity and understanding, as was promoted by authors writing about the existential meaning of time. However, it is also an effort to study these existential meanings with methodological care and empirical prudence. On the one hand it is desirable to use quantifiable data, on the other hand the data should be representations of thoughts and feelings about the self that are really held and expressed by the subjects themselves, instead of just being opinions. When identity and self-definition are studied in connection with one's own aging, they are logically connected to the theme of time, in the sense of the temporal dimension in human life. Self-understanding and self-identity are based on the way a person identifies basic properties and processes defining the self. Studying the latter must therefore be an unobtrusive approach to "temporalization" of human self-construction in later life. We should expect to find that numerous aspects and elements of the self-concept are coupled with terms (and concepts) of transitoriness as well as the expression of a preference for stability. Thus we should find references to changing patterns of life, passing events, changing characteristics of body and mind, thoughts of finitude and aging, as well as the observation and value of preservation, maintenance, and continuity. This cognitive/affective construction of the self should be marked by the frequent use of time references in narrative self-reports of elderly people, in opposition to young adults. Frequent time references are the evidence that the temporariness of existence has been assimilated into the self-concept and that identity and self-experience have been changed through the awareness of finitude.

This is not to be mistakenly identified with the abstract ("cold") knowledge that human beings are mortal and that I, in theory, am mortal too. Having an existential self-identity is equivalent to being able to activate (affectively tuned) cognitions and motivations giving rise to psychological processes (thoughts and feelings) about the nature of the self and its existence. For some time, though, young persons can also be made aware of their death by arousing vivid images and feelings. Observing a car crash or imagining being the victim of terrorism will arouse thoughts and fear responses. These mechanisms are manipulated experimentally in social psychology studies (cf. Dechesne, 2001). However, these are transitory states of mind and do not operate as a repeatedly activated cognitive framework that shapes the information processing and interpretation of almost every aspect of self-reflection and life experience. The fact that we are changing and aging, thus moving closer to old age and death everyday, may be known in theory, without being a "working self" in daily life, in self-reflection, and in appraisals of one's life situation.

In the following report on a study of temporal references in identity, a design has been used that activates a range of a person's working selves as a response to the reporting of what is most important and true about one's own person and personality.

METHODOLOGICAL CONSIDERATIONS

Concepts from narrative psychology (as cited in a previous section) may be connected with the methodology used in the study of temporal aspects of identity. In constructing narrative selves, the "I" as an author produces narratives about the self as a protagonist or "hero" of the life story or of parts thereof. This circumstance was used in my comparative study of the elements of identity in young and elderly adults. In order to compare the self-narratives of young and elderly men and women, an instrument was used that made it possible to sample and analyze a large number of subjects providing self-narratives. This is hardly possible with long texts or life stories, as is done in autobiographical research. Therefore, self-narratives and life stories were not collected in one line of temporal ordering from past to present and future, but rather in a "scrambled" fashion. The instrument was designed to activate, in a random time order, the components of a subject's identity and life story, including statements on the present, past, and future self or life situation. The self-reports were stimulated by very general, short, familiar sentence stems; and the respondents interpreted their semantic meaning and completed the sentences according to their personal choice. In a few cases, the sentence stems referred directly to a future or past time perspective, but in general no specific time reference was provided.

Methodological Foundations in Psychology and Sociology

Sarbin (1986, p. 8) presents an argument that explains the correspondence between narrative identity (as in a life story) and sentence-stem completions. The component pictures or meanings of the self-narrative are related to each other by the implicit or explicit use of a plot. When the stimulus material depicts people (such as the self as speaker in the sentence stems), the story components will reflect human sentiments, goals, purposes, valuations, and judgments. For the purpose of construction, cultural models (ideas, concepts) and metaphors on human life are being used.

In the "standard discourse" and the "ordinary" experience of everyday life (Holstein & Gubrium, 2000a, p. 183), the conventional approach of understanding the life course is to take for granted the forms of communication and interaction about the reality of experience and facts in life. Narrative schemes are used as internal models for the construction of stories and their components (Brockmeier, 2001). Holstein and Gubrium (2000a, p. 184) remarked that they wanted to investigate the construction of the life course in order to understand how ". . . the everyday work of reality construction produces a sense of personal change through time." In analyzing the self-narratives, the objective is to describe the procedures through which meaning is organized. The young and elderly adults who report in their own words about their personality and life will usually be unaware of their authorship and "neglect their own role in producing meaning, just as they overlook their own authorship of the circumstances and forces that seem to control experience" (Holstein & Gubrium, 2000a, p. 185).

Ordinary people use narrative to construct and present desired identities, whereas scientific researchers analyze claims about the course of development in the perspective of the construction process, the use of linguistic and conceptual resources, and with respect to their functions for the person who invests in the construction process in order to reach personal and social goals, such as convincing others and guiding oneself to positive affect and an optimistic, constructive future outlook. Thus, by calling oneself old, by using time frames indicating the loss of potential, or by expressing hopes to remain healthy in the next years, people confer to others and to themselves that certain things are or should be the case. And by using certain references of time, they evidence a way of activating frames that minimize or stress negative implications.

From the perspective of psycholinguistic research, additional support can be obtained on the narrative perspective. "Principles of discourse organization" (Klein, 1994, p. 14) are among the ways in which temporality is encoded in natural language. Narrative schemes are devices for encoding multiple temporal orderings and inclusions. Narrative schemes are models ordering events and durations in a complex way. A biographical story is told from the temporal point of the I, the ORIGO (Klein, 1994). This is the point from which the present, the past, and the future are seen, from which the passing of time is portrayed, and from which combinations of past and future event lines are conceived. To construct self-narratives is to use words and their combinations to form sentences that can be arranged into a story. The ways in which temporality is encoded in natural language contain, among others, the grammatical categories of tense and verb, temporal features of the verb itself, temporal adverbials of various types, or expressions indicating time and duration of an event, such as to continue smoking, etc. (Klein, 1994, p. 14).

"Temporal reference relates the time of an event, action, process, etc. to some distinguished time span, in particular the time of utterance," such that an event may temporally precede the time of utterance, follow, or overlap it (Klein, 1994, p. 16). Temporal reference may be tense, a systematic grammatical working of the verb, or adverbials of different types, such as yesterday, next week, at my age, when I retire. While an event is indicated by the lexical content of an expression or utterance, time span as such has no qualitative properties other than being before or after or contained within (Klein, 1994, p. 36). "Language has found a way to bring timeless lexical contents and time spans together. We may say that it embeds a lexical content in time, or that it hooks it up, or links, a lexical content to some time span. This is what an utterance does." If a lexical content is linked to some time interval, there are several consequences. For instance, it may be interpreted as an event, a state, or a process; it allows us to relate the situation to other situations or to other time spans (Klein, 1994, p. 37).

Most languages have temporal terms such as during, before, after, later, not any more, furthermore, until then, etc. These temporal adverbs can be used in constructing narrative schemes about the self. Such terms do not necessarily presume a metrical concept of time, but rather imply temporal structuring and ordering. In addition to temporal adverbs, there are multiple terms indicating a temporal location (of the author) on the life line, such as retirement, old age, elderly, youth, and being young, etc.

Our concepts of the life course and of getting older imply a temporal period that begins with birth and ends with death. Components of our life story and aspects of our own situated existence may depict any point or period within the life span and may also be embedded in the transpersonal past and future. Narrative schemes or forms provide the linguistic structure that is used to present the self- and life components (the multiple careers and multiple voices) to oneself and to others (Brockmeier, 2001). References to time in the sense of being in a certain life stage reflect, in their terms, the cognitive location of the self within the cultural model of human life that is predominant in a culture. This temporal framework for the self and its life is learned and observed, and will be applied to one's own life, especially when death is anticipated as a final life event.

EMPIRICAL STUDY: EXISTENTIAL TIME AS AN ASPECT OF IDENTITY

Underlying Assumptions and Hypotheses

My contention is that in later life, the quality of self- and life experience changes to include the dimension of "existential time." This is an awareness of being alive versus not being alive, with duration, decline and finitude of characteristics of human beings, and with one's own perspective on self and life at an advanced point in the life line. From that perspective, the amount of time left to live and to be used as a resource for life management becomes precious and must be used optimally.

I also assume that this awareness of being alive implies a perception of the present self as a temporal event that is running out according to a "scheme of aging." This scheme of aging is (known to be) ruled by nature, but in its special form it is individual and unique. The experience of aging spreads to more and more aspects of the person, to the physical, psychological, social, aging trajectories. According to narrative and linguistic research, these aspects of existential time should become manifest in narrative self-reports in most domains of personal meaning. The "temporal markers" in spontaneous self-descriptions reflect temporal self-identity.

The hypothesis is that time-related references in self-narratives differ qualitatively as well as quantitatively between young and elderly adults. Because motivational engagement fosters the construction of self and life in a positive way, self-reports will be phrased in favorable ways where possible, without distorting perceived reality too much.

Type of Study

The sentence completion method SELE (Dittmann-Kohli, 1991, 1995) has been used to elicit spontaneous self-narratives. Sentence stems of great generality and everyday life quality were presented, which directed attention to aspects of the self and life of the young and elderly subjects. The sentence stems represent the rudimentary form of the narrative scheme used in each sentence completion (cf. Brockmeier, 1991, 2000). In order to obtain self-reports that are considered by the subjects as being important as well as (in their own view) truthful features of the self, the instruction was phrased in a particular way. The subjects were asked to complete the sentences in a way reflecting their own authentic self. Also, the free responses to the sentence stems are a means to activate those features of personal identity that are most important to the subject. Twenty-three sentence stems were selected to form a protocol for each individual. The sentence stems were self-referring or referring to the subject's life.

The format of the "Self and Life" instrument (SELE) is subject to content analysis after each sentence stem and answers have been entered into the computer. This makes it possible to analyze the text with respect to content and frequencies. In the study reported here, type and number of existential time references have been coded either automatically (which makes it very reliable) or by using coders.

The SELE sentence completion instrument was used with 300 young and 300 elderly adults. The young adults were trainees (apprentices) and university students; they ranged from 15 to 29 years of age, with a mean age of 20 years; the elderly ranged from 60 to 90 years of age with an average of 74. The sentences were completed in settings that corresponded to everyday situations of the age groups (for greater details see Dittmann-Kohli, 1995; also Dittmann-Kohli & Westerhof, 1997).

The categories found and used to classify the temporal references were the following:

(a) Linguistic expression for stages or periods of life.
(b) References to being or becoming (not) old or feeling young, or similar statements about one's own aging process.
©) Terms of various temporal adverbs that refer to limited or further duration or to the maintenance of the present state. These temporal adverbs include states of the past that declined or ceased to exist, and future states that are anticipated to continue, to decline, or cease to exist.
(d) Expressions of the awareness of finitude and mortality.
(e) The number of past events mentioned; these are obvious when corresponding terms or grammar is used.

(f) The content of states and events occurring in the somewhat distant or very distant future or in unspecified future possibilities.
(g) In addition, linguistic statements about development and growth, as well as on becoming dependent or staying independent, were used.

The reliability of coding is high because the linguistic terms to be identified can be clearly defined.

EMPIRICAL FINDINGS

The Content of Future Time Perspective in Young and Elderly Adults

In this section, the content of the future time perspective of the young and elderly adults is presented. The sentence stems used for this purpose refer explicitly to the future, either specifying the near future or the far future, or to a nonspecified time ahead. These three future-oriented sentence stems were coded with regard to the type of expectations, goals, or intentions expressed. The categories were constructed inductively after grouping the sentence completions according to their lexical content; then categories were defined for these groups and the frequency was counted. In the process of category definition, existing scientific knowledge about goals and future orientations of young and elderly adults was also used.

The sentence stems specified that the moment of answering the questionnaire was the point in time from which an idea about events, states, and actions in the middle and distant future should be written down. The sentence stem "In the next few years . . ." covers the coming years for both groups. The sentence stem "Later, when I am older . . ." can be understood by the young adults as "Being (much or somewhat) older than now" or as referring to late old age. For the elderly adults, it refers to being still older than they already are. The third sentence stem is asking for possible selves (in the sense of Hazel Markus' concept) "Perhaps I can . . ."; it leaves open the time period as well as the reality mode of the future event or behavior.

The lexical content of these sentence stems was classified into categories and subcategories, and the frequencies for the two groups of young and elderly adults were compared (for further details, see Dittmann-Kohli, 1995). Two different profiles were found in young and elderly adults that showed marked differences in the goals and expectations of these two age groups. The type of differences found reflected a pattern that is in agreement with the expectations derived from the assumptions and hypotheses about the effect of societal and biological constraints and opportunities (or demands) specified above. The following are the main conclusions:

Young adults completed the sentence completions referring to the possibilities open to them in the middle and long-term future. These possibilities are related to roles, achievements, and other activities open for young and middle-aged adults in our society. Positive pathways and events are stated more often than negative ones. The following topics were mentioned:

- Improved living conditions with regard to independent living and one's own apartment
- Money and possessions
- Goals, wishes, and fears in the domains of education and work
- Goals, wishes, and fears in the domain of partnership and future family
- Individual improvement and expansion, such as personal growth, ideas about character, and the psychological self

The elderly adults provided answers presenting a different content of hopes, goals, and expectations. They expressed concerns and anticipations about general social issues (not the attainment of personal future goals or events); they referred to interpersonal relations of a more general kind, to the quality of family relations, and to inner states of others. The well-being of other older persons, the well-being of the partner, and the well-being and fate of children, grandchildren, and friends were particularly important to them.

Elderly adults also expressed thoughts and wishes with regard to leisure activities, about the role of past occupational work and nonpaid work activities, and they looked forward to the pleasures of well-earned rest. This type of content of future-directed thought and possible selves was not typical for young adults and could not occur because they are specific to the life situations and developmental tasks in old age.

Differences between the Distant and Not-So-Distant Future

Social and biological constraints and opportunities are different for young and elderly adults with regard to the long-term and the near future. Biological characteristics as well as social structures are quite discrepant and allow for differential goals and expectations in these age groups. Here again, the patterns and content of the future perspectives will correspond to the biological and environmental givens typical for Western countries in general and especially in Germany.

When thinking of the next few years, young adults refer most often to their vocational education or college and university years, such as expectations about passing their examinations at the end of their vocational training or study program, enabling them to find paid work. Anticipations of having to learn and work hard for school are also mentioned. The responses to the second sentence stem (Later, when I am older . . .) were more often associated with marriage and founding a family, especially in the case of young women (11:64). Trainees and students referred to the life tasks and developmental tasks of the present and immediate future, thus locating themselves on the life line as defined in our society for adolescents and young adults.

In contrast to this, the elderly associated both of the future-oriented sentence stems with themes that refer to their advanced position in the life cycle and its approaching end: they mentioned their (high) chronological age, the process of getting older or the fact of being old. All of these transmit an awareness of progressing toward the end of one's life line.

Young adults refer to their age only in rare cases, for instance when they are answering the sentence stem about getting older in the sense of their own late-life period. In those cases they often put their answer into a retrospective view of their own former life, expressing their wishes to have had a successful life.

In terms of other life events and aspects of the self, the elderly referred extensively to issues of general health and psychophysical functioning, to the question of going to an old people's home (or not), of having lived a long time, etc. Their references to the stem "Later, when I am older . . ." reflected the typical expectations for late old age or the expression of already being there.

The empirical findings on the items asking for the content of the future time perspective show indirectly but very clearly the self-localization of the young and elderly adults on the life line. Their answers refer to their age-related life situation and the normal pathways of young adults and old age, and their individual outlooks correspond with their developmental tasks and their inner situation vis-à-vis their life period.

Preservation: Future Goals and Desires that Do Not Imply Improvement

In this section, findings are presented that show age differences in the light of hopes, desires, and goals. They have been coded for all of the sentence stems asking for responses about possible selves; not only those relating explicitly to a future state. All of these imply the wish or longing for a positive state or outcome. These hopes, desires, goals, etc., may be directed to the coming years as well as to the more distant future and to possible developments or behaviors (Perhaps I can . . .). Wishes and desires may appear in response to sentence stems such as "I like to dream about . . . ," "What is most important for me . . . ," and can also be found in statements of negative goals (such as: "I fear that . . .").

More particularly, the coding of hopes, wishes, goals, and fears proceeded in such a way as to capture any expressions referring to desires of preservation, maintenance, and continuation with regard to possible selves. (It was indicated earlier that this is a type of future perspective that is absent from the traditional understanding of direction toward the future and of thinking about alternative, possible states and events for the self.)

Such future-oriented hopes for maintenance and continuation appear nine times more frequently in the elderly than in the young (480:41). The lexical content of statements coded as preservation is (in order of frequency) (1) health and general physical integrity, (2) the quality of present life, (3) functional competence and status, (4) general desires for stability and maintenance, (5) character. The appearance of preservation references in a wide range of different content categories shows that the longing for temporal attenuation is attached to many possible aging trajectories perceived by the subject.

What is basically different between young and elderly adults is that young adults have goals that mean a positive change from the present state, or an extension or addition to what they have now. Elderly adults have many future-oriented desires, hopes, and goals, which are aimed at preservation of the present state. They do not consist of growth or improvement, but of maintenance or stability. Such goals and desires do not intend change but preservation. This type of future time perspective is tied to the present and the past: what is available now should be prolonged into the future. Sentence completions coded on preservation are nearly always made in relation to positive or neutral sentence stems; the completions reflect desired possible selves that depend on the continuation of personal properties, dispositions, and quality of life.

It is evident that a preservation-oriented future time perspective does not contain goals in the way they are usually understood, where an improvement is intended. The large majority of young adults do not express hopes for a continuation of the status quo; if they use the temporal adverb "still," this occurs as an anticipation of old age and looking back retrospectively. Otherwise, young people's hopes, goals, and plans are directed toward improvement beyond present attainments. As shown previously, maintenance goals are expressed with regard to many aspects of self and life; in particular they concern contents that are expected to decline because of aging. These may endanger the positive self-regard when cognitions of negatively valued states are also present. Hopes for preservation give negative states a positive direction and thus may protect motivation.

Lexical Content Referring to Life Stage and Aging

The findings reported were coded as responses to sentence stems about the near and more distant future and to desired or feared possible selves in general. Response categories to be considered in the following section are references to life stage and state of aging. Such temporal references may occur in responses to a variety of sentence stems, whether the future and possible selves were mentioned explicitly in the stem or not. In the category of life stage and state of aging, temporal references directly indicate certain points in life, a life stage or age group, chronological or comparative age, or name the fact that the self's existence is in (or is approaching) a late or final period of the life span. The frequencies and semantic content of the responses were the following: the elderly used terms such as being very old or too old already, they mentioned their chronological age, referred to their aging process, to being or staying young, or to being or feeling older than other people thought they were. Also, expressions such as in my life stage, my time of retirement, my later years, during my old age, etc. were often used.

In the 23 sentence stems, four times as many statements were made by the elderly about how old they felt, in which life period they were, which (high) age they had reached (104 young:400 old). Within this overall category, 217 elderly as opposed to 16 young persons constructed self-reports that referred explicitly to becoming old, being very old, or being at the end of life. In these statements, the affective tone was neutral. In addition, there were positive and negative statements on this topic; the elderly provided also many more positive (48 old:3 young) and more negative (50 elderly:17 young) versions of such statements about aging, becoming old, and being old than the young adults. By choosing more emotional responses, elderly adults show that they are more involved in the issue.

Within the overall category, statements about being or feeling younger than one's actual age appeared only twice in the young sample, but were mentioned 82 times by the elderly (For instance, "I am very proud . . . that I am mostly taken for being younger than I am"). Three young adults give a retrospective comment on their former life from the viewpoint of their late life, and 49 mention their own future middle and late life in a prospective way.

A further evidence of differences in the time orientation of early and late adulthood is that the elderly stated much more often that they did not have any future goals any more or that they had already reached whatever they were striving for. Such answers were given by 114 elderly persons, whereas only 30 young persons proffered a comparable content in their responses. For instance, elderly people would state that the goal of their mental development had been reached, had been reached long ago, that they would not strive for anything anymore, or that they did not have enough time left to strive for anything. Or they would state that they would not have any more dreams for the future but would live for the present, that they had no dreams or illusions. Trainees and students, in contrast, never denied having dreams and did not say they had no goals; rather, they seemed to love to talk about their dreams and goals. In some cases, however, young persons stated that they could not say anything yet about their goals, but would see what would come along.

Overall, the various subcategories of the theme "references to life stage and state of aging" show an intensified awareness and high sensibility to features of life typical for advanced aging and for the final period of life, such as retirement, evening of life, or getting (too) old. The frequencies found in this and other categories demonstrate that the SELE protocols of elderly subjects reveal a higher awareness of one's point on the life line than young adults, which is a sign of a stronger prominence of the temporal dimension of identity.

Development and Loss of Autonomy

Another theme in subjects' narrative self-reports is also related to the different view of self and life resulting from the divergent locations of young and old persons on their life line. The theme "positive development, growth, and loss of autonomy" provides further evidence of temporal self-localization. In addition, the responses in this category suggest the presence of a "cultural model" (or social representation) of a developing and declining organism. Such social representations or cultural models are adopted by individuals as a cognitive framework that may give rise to positive and negative cognitions and concerns for the self. Self-reports in the SELE protocols often contain expressions of future hopes that go in the opposite direction for young adults. Whereas young subjects express possible selves around personal growth and self-realization, elderly adults express concerns and awareness of alternative possible behaviors when the loss of autonomy and independence is imminent.

Thoughts about personal growth are generally not formulated in relation to the environment but in relation to one's own development. These hopes are strongly related to strivings toward something in the person that is bigger, better, or an addition to what is given now. Two hundred and ten young students and trainees were found to report self-descriptions classified as responses expressing hope for or belief in personal growth. The young persons seemed to know that they are in a period of life where personal extension and growth can be expected. In principle, such hopes could be entertained by elderly adults as well. There were in fact 50 adults who expressed belief in personal growth too; but their frequencies in the subcategory of personal growth amounted to less than one-quarter compared to the young. Thus, most of the men and women in the older group did not express expectations of growth, whereas slightly more than two-thirds of the young subjects did. This result is in line with the findings on preservation, and it is in line with the findings on limited continuation that follow.

Another contrast is obtained when we compare self-descriptive statements about dependence and independence. Here too, responses reflect an identity that presupposes an ascending or descending position on the life line. Wishes for obtaining independence are expressed by the young, such as leaving the house of the parents, financial independence, self-determination, and making one's own decisions. In contrast, hopes to retain personal autonomy and worries about losing abilities for independent living are expressed by the elderly. The motivational orientations and concerns in the young and elderly adults are thus aiming in opposite directions. The frequency of answers in the category of loss of autonomy ranged from 91 in the elderly to 0 for the young adults. In addition, one of the young persons and 38 of the elderly expressed worries regarding their future home or having to give up one's house or apartment.

Limited Continuity and Finitude

The elderly think of maintenance and stability not only with respect to the future (when aging may become a serious matter and decline may occur), but also to the present. This present is a point in time that is occupied by the "author" at the moment of writing, and is at the same time the period that the author is writing about. The term used most often to express limited continuation is "still" in a temporal sense, meaning further (but limited) duration; that is, something going on for some time. The concept behind this temporal adverb connects an event or state existing at present with ones that have also existed in the past (for instance, as in the statement "I am still going strong"). It can also tie the present (together with its past) to the future, as in the statement "I hope that I will be still healthy in later life." This temporal adverb is overlapping in part with the terms used in the category "preservation"; the difference is that preservation is used for states without an explicit ending, while the temporal use of the term "still" implies the expectation of the eventual disappearance of a state, thing, or process.

Statements assigning "limited continuation" to an event, trait, circumstance, or period is a very important category found in the SELE protocols. This time category covers thoughts referring to the absence or presence of change within a certain period. Linguistically it can be combined with a diversity of other semantic content, transforming the referent into an event or a process with a certain duration. When this temporal term is used in a sentence, it functions as a simple temporal adverb assigning to the subject term a period in time as well as a certain duration that is expected to end sometime. The time category limited continuation is a concept that has not often been used in research on time and aging, nor in aging research in general. It is a phenomenon that emerges and can be easily detected in the type of self-narrative instrument used. The reason is that a limited set of terms can be specified, which can be coded through automatic searches with the computer. Raters have to check possible double meanings of temporal adverbs that can be identified close to 100% of the time.

In the group of elderly adults, the terms for limited duration were found 362 times in their protocols. By contrast, only 24 young persons used that expression, and if they did, it did not refer to typical themes of self and life that elderly people think about. Limited continuation or duration are similar in meaning to the wish for stability, preservation (see above) or maintenance; temporal adverbs for decline, however, refer to the observation that some feature of self and life has already disappeared (see section following). Examples for the time category "limited continuity" are "I am very proud . . . that I can still participate in many activities; . . . that I am still fit and independent, . . . that I can still enjoy my life for some time."

The statements on preservation—combining hopes for the future and present wishes—were coded 41 times in the group of young adults and 413 times in the group of the elderly. The category with statements expressing limited continuation of some state obtained frequencies of 24 for the young and 362 for the elderly (see above). In addition to this, the subcategory "limited life" obtained 14:178 for old and young, respectively. The statements in this subcategory contain a clear reference to the end of life (and not to a particular feature of self or life). Combining "limited continuation" in relation to some aspect of self and life with those referring to the anticipation of the passing of self and life for good, we obtain a ratio of 38:540.

Thus, the men and women in the group of the elderly produced self-descriptions that conferred an identity implying awareness of the possibility of prolongation (of an existing state or feature, or life itself) 135 times more often, while at the same time indicating that it will end. The statements referred to a very large range of circumstances, properties, processes, or states. All aspects of self and life were connected with anticipations of a final limitation after some period of stability.

An interesting characteristic is that the statements on limited continuation are usually combined with an indication of their affective or evaluative value. It became evident that positive statements are much more frequent than negative ones, in spite of the closeness between limited continuation and finitude. Elderly people cast their anticipation of advancing old age and finitude very often into forms of positive thinking. They formulate hopes and expect a maximally extended continuation, instead of regretting the future fading away and the disappearance of positive aspects of existence or personhood. This again is a sign of protecting motivation by thinking positively, even in the face of negative realities. It is a protection against depression and apathy to have positive versions of negative circumstances.

Decline

The meaning of decline is the opposite of personal growth, but also of improvement, expansion, etc. By analogy to earlier themes, decline statements indicate that an organismic model of development is used by the individual, especially if the statements refer to aging. In the case of social constraints, however, decline statements may also reflect views about societal provisions and deficiencies with respect to friends and relatives who no longer exist.

The category of decline was coded for all sentence stems and turned out to be frequently used. In opposition to growth and to educational, occupational, and interpersonal achievements mentioned by the young, a large number of statements referring to decline emerged in the elderly sample (270 times in a sample of 300). They are hardly ever mentioned in the young sample (4 out of 300).

Decline was most often indicated by the use of temporal adverbs such as "no more," "not any more", or terms like "I used to . . ." or ". . . will not last longer." Such temporal terms can be combined with all sorts of content, and indeed the variety of content provided was large. Some of the anticipations of decline were directed toward one's own properties, dispositions, psychological states, and physical functions or features. Another type of statement referred to situations, lifestyle, external conditions, or projects. Themes regarding the decline of (psychophysical) functional abilities and potentials are frequent, but also health and illness, and the reduction of desirable aspects on one's life situation.

Concerns and expectations regarding one's life potential are also the background of statements about future helplessness and fears of becoming a problem for family and neighbors. In addition, worries and considerations with respect to living conditions emerge in later life, such as about going to an old people's home, obtaining regular care, needing a smaller apartment, having to accept a loss of quality in housing, and not being able to care adequately for oneself. Statements in these categories have been expressed 70 times by older people and only once by a young person.

It is worth mentioning that the elderly had a higher percentage of nonanswers to the items, as well as "do not know" or "do not want to answer" responses. It appears that unpleasant and fear-arousing anticipations of a bad future are often suppressed by the elderly or bring them into a state of indecision or avoidance. Questionnaires used as an alternative to verbal sentence completions also indicate this possibility. There seems to be a certain resistance to visualizing existentially disastrous states in one's future life.

Decline was seen or suspected to occur in many different aspects of the self: outer appearance, not dreaming any more at night, or having to give up vocational self-employment. Also, decline was reflected in statements about having become sad or slow, feeling that work is getting harder, of no longer being able to do more than watch TV, or sitting around after a stroke. The observation that everything will be worse in the future, and the suspicion of losing abilities that one may not be aware of reflects perceived aging decline.

The contents associated with the category of decline seem to reflect public knowledge, scientific findings, negative age stereotypes, personal observations of other elderly people, as well as direct perceptions of the aging self. Decline is a concept of change that involves a temporal comparison by the individual of present and past or of future and present state(s). Another possibility to state decline used social comparisons, where decline is reported to have taken place in comparison to (most) other people or to an average standard.

Past Life

A subjective or personal time perspective includes the past, in addition to present and future. The biographical past or the past self and life history can be a very important part, or even the central piece, of self and identity. With respect to objective time, young persons have a short past life and old people a long one. It is to be expected that this is reflected in temporal identity and can be detected in the narrative self-reports. In this category, the sentence stem "My life up to now . . ." was not considered in the coding procedure. Only when past life in general was referred to spontaneously, or when autobiographical events and actions were spontaneously mentioned, was this category coded.

As expected, the past life category also reveals an important characteristic of the identity of elderly adults, and again it stands in sharp contrast to the narrative self-reports of youth. Whereas the 300 students and trainees mentioned past events spontaneously 57 times, the 300 elderly adults referred to (aspects of) their past 565 times. The elderly referred to past life events even in completions of future-oriented sentence stems. The difference in frequencies reached a probability of less than a million. This finding about spontaneous references to the past is impressive and suggests that the past self and past life indeed become a central part of identity in later life. Past events seem to be remembered automatically when thinking about one's own person. Self-understanding includes events and processes from a long past that shaped the person one is today and will be in the future.

In contrast, future roles and states loom large in the self-identity of young persons. The past self and life of young persons is usually not seen to be of great importance by them; it does not figure much in the interpretation of who they are. In fact, in the sentence completion to "My past life . . . ," many young adults referred explicitly to the shortness and insignificance of their past life.

For the elderly men and women, the precariousness of their future and their concerns over the changes accompanying the aging process can perhaps be compensated and affectively balanced by the richness of identity made up of a long past life. Even if this life is not appreciated in all its parts, personal life is valuable. The self was and is a human being that has been "impersonated" by me as a subject. The unique individual, the "I," has embodied the self and its life as a "Me" by way of the special configuration of personhood. Selfhood is an interesting and valuable feature of existence in its own right, and its dissolution at death does not eliminate the fact of its (former) existence.

The Passing of Life and the Approach of Death

The growing awareness of life's time dimension is also expressed in responses in the category about death and dying. Statements that contained a clear reference to the passing of life time and approaching death were coded in this category.

As expected, the observation that the time of life is running out emerged as another prototypical theme in late life adults and was rarely mentioned in the sample of young adults. Also, young adults never mentioned regrets about the noncontinuation of consciousness after death. The number of cases where elderly people referred to the running out of life or consciousness was 178, whereas this occurred only 14 times in trainees and university students. Examples of such statements in the elderly are "I think that I . . . cannot experience any good days any more"; "It is difficult for me . . . to think of my end, life is too pleasant"; "It is difficult . . . to know that I will not experience many things any more"; "Perhaps I can . . . live as a human being in my last ten years"; "When I think about myself . . .

I would like to live on a while in order to know how the world is developing"; "When I think about myself . . . I think I have lived my life."

When the elderly men and women referred to the end of their lives, it was mostly about the *process* and the circumstances of dying, not about the threat of being dead. On the contrary, very old persons expressed that they had nothing against death and that they sometimes thought it was time to die. Death or dying were mentioned much less often by the young, and when they did, it appeared in a less differentiated and complex manner of thinking. Young persons would simply state that they were afraid to die, or mention the possibility of dying of cancer someday. Examples of statements from the older group are "Later, when I am older . . . I want an easy death"; "I fear that I . . . might die lonely and perhaps lie dead in my apartment for weeks." Statements about one's own death were given by 34 young and 96 elderly adults. "I fear that I . . . might die young" was expressed by a young adult. The desire for a pleasant death (or the fear of a bad one) was expressed by 0 young and 23 elderly adults.

The narrative self-reports about limited continuation and finitude, the running out of life time, decline, the advanced life stage, and aging and preservation are closely related to the categories of the passing life and of death. Basically, all of the categories presented can be said to circumscribe the fact that human identity becomes heavily infused with the passing of time and the ending of life. Among the overall findings, there were a number of additional categories that pointed to the awareness of passing time and of an advanced position on the life line (Dittmann-Kohli, 1995). However, these have not been mentioned here because the age-related differences in frequencies were smaller or because their presentation would have demanded too much room. The evidence that was selected is sufficient to make the point.

CONCLUSION

Empirical data about the use of verbal references in narrative self-reports have been presented in order to substantiate the definition of a new or revised concept of subjective time. The comparative data on young and elderly adults have provided various themes (and quotations) of self-descriptions that refer to the underlying construct of existential time. This type of subjective time (perspective) is understood as a cognitive framework related to feelings and motivation; it constitutes the substance of our temporal identity. Temporal identity means a type of selfhood that includes, beyond individuality and self-awareness, the common domains of the personal meaning system (Dittmann-Kohli, 1995) and an awareness of the self as a temporary being in the process of aging. The existential time perspective is therefore meant to be more than a concept of past and future time perspective, as it is used mostly in psychology.

The results strongly indicate that later in life, basic conditions of reality like that of growth and death of organisms are accounted for in the cognitive framework and cognitive structure of identity. Also, the emotional and motivational relevance of the growing temporal awareness regarding the passing of time and the course of development and decline become evident in narrative self-reports. The assimilation of the transitory character of human life and the possibilities and constraints in the phases of human aging are the precondition to an identity that fits the *conditio humana.* This late life identity is able to balance between losses and gains in a way that intensifies sensitivity to the possibilities of "secondary control" (Heckhausen, 1999). In less technical terms, this could mean the growth of an individual's potential for a deeper understanding of life and consciousness, as well as a deeper appreciation of this understanding in light of the knowledge of what it is to be subject to the biological constraints of life.

Identifying and localizing events, states, objects, and persons within one's future period of life have important consequences for planning and action for the young as well as the elderly. Locating events, properties, states, etc., in one's past life also has an important effect: together with present awareness, a long and detailed life history is the most important part of identity. The life span construct of older persons thus becomes qualitatively quite different from that of the young members of society. In addition, we have seen that there are concerns for maintenance and decline, limited continuation, and being in an advanced position on the life line.

The narrative statements about limited continuation, aging, and finitude can be viewed against a background of cultural models of life as a process with only a certain duration, resulting in the disappearance of the self and the awareness of a world. Not only the biological life span but also the "normal life course" are concepts assimilated into the identity structure. The different contents of their future time perspectives, and the differences between the profiles of their near and far future, underscore that subjects in the two age categories localize themselves on a common life path and combine it with their knowledge of their past and present situation. Depending on the stage of late life, young and old people have different opportunities for activity and further development. Opportunities and constraints are, as I have tried to underscore, specific to sociocultural and historical structures, even if they also depend on our brain structures, on ontogenetic development, and on the long history of accumulating experiences through biological and cultural evolution. Brain structures, with their various self-functions, give us the preconditions for the acquisition of "extended selves" (Neisser, 1988), extended in a temporal dimension as well as in its symbolic content.

Narrative and other psychologists have emphasized that the self-concept is constituted as self-narrative or self-construction. This narrative structure of the self has been used by Dittmann-Kohli and her colleagues as a means to construct a data set that is quantifiable as well as "ecologically and psychologically valid" as a measure. Similar to our analysis of narratives, Pennebaker and Stone (2003) have analyzed written and spoken text with the help of automatic content analysis. They gathered material from discussion groups and literary publications in order to test hypotheses such as Carstensen's social selectivity hypothesis (Carstensen, 1993) derived from experiments on the effect of aging on people's preferences in interpersonal relations. Narrative psychologists, however, have not strongly influenced empirical research, especially not in life-span developmental psychology. The method used here, a combination of qualitative and quantitative approaches, appears to be adequate to study even very large samples (as has been done in the representative sample in East and West Germany and the Netherlands (see Dittmann-Kohli et al., 2001).

The results obtained in this study support the view that there are developmental ontogenetic changes over the adult life span. As there may be cohort effects in the reported findings, future cohorts will perhaps show somewhat altered differences between the young and the elderly. Goals and expectations for the future especially in young persons may undergo social change, but there will be goals and other expectations also that do not change. I expect that the increased late-life salience of existential time and one's point on the life line will not vanish. The recognition of this temporal dimension of human life is a universal fact, and over the second half of life this fact is internalized in the narrative identity. This universal is generally considered as a basic property of humans for self-reflection and individual personhood, in contrast to lower mammals.

Thus, the high salience of a temporal framework in nearly every aspect of self and life becomes a specific characteristic in the second half and especially of later life. In young adulthood, the future is much more important than the past; the future stands out in terms of life goals and personal growth. Only in later life does existential time (in the sense of the awareness of having passed and experienced the greater part of one's life) become a pervasive feature of self-identity and life experience. Existential time is a scientific construct that designates temporal framing in the sense of self-localization on the life line. It also provides the constant awareness of the limited existence of all aspects of self and life. Limited existence and mortality are a constant implicit knowledge and can be activated easily as a dimension of the "working self." Though the awareness of finitude is readily activated, the thoughts and feelings making up perceived personhood and existence are in their majority molded into a positive attitude toward self and life. The percentage of statements expressing a positive attitude and hope for the maintenance of a fulfilled and meaningful life is high. It can be concluded that even in the face of finitude and death, most elderly persons can maintain a positive attitude toward self and life. This corroborates numerous findings of social psychologists in studies with college students in which compensatory values and self-esteem are activated under threat (Dechesne, 2001; Steele, 1988). It is also in line with the numerous studies on life satisfaction in later life, and it may also indicate the freedom from social norms and from constant striving to be more and more successful. Aging and the existential meaning of time are very old topics indeed; however they have not been studied extensively in psychological empirical designs.

REFERENCES

Adams-Price, C. E. (Ed.). (1998). *Creativity and successful aging. Theoretical and empirical approaches.* New York: Springer.

Baars, J. (1997a). Concepts of time and narrative temporality in the study of aging. *Journal of Aging Studies, 11,* 283-295.

Baars, J. (1997b). The reinterpretation of finitude: An introduction to three articles on the philosophy of aging. *Journal of Aging Studies, 11*(4), 259-262.

Baars, J. (2000). Time, age and autonomy. *The European Journal of Social Quality, 2,* 9-27.

Bergmann, W. (1981). Zeit, Handlung und Sozialität [Time, action and being social]. *Zeitschrift für Soziologie, 10*(4), 351-363.

Berman, H. J. (1994). *Interpreting the aging self: Personal journals of later life.* New York: Springer.

Bond, L. A., Cutler, S. J., & Grams, A. (Eds.). (1995). *Promoting successful and productive aging.* Thousand Oaks: Sage Publications.

Bouffard, L. K., Bastin, E., & Lapierre, S. (1994). The personal future in old age. In Z. Zaleski (Ed.), *Psychology of future orientation* (pp. 75-94). Lublin: Towarzystwo Naukowe KUL.

Brandtstätter, J., & Wentura, D. (1994). Veränderungen der Zeit- und Zukunftperspektive im Übergang zum höheren Erwachsenenalter: Entwicklungspsychologische und differentielle Aspekte [Changes in time perspectives and attitudes toward the future during the transition to later adulthood: Developmental and differential aspects]. *Zeitschrift für Entwicklungspsychologie und Pädagogische Psychologie, 26,* 2-21.

Brockmeier, J. (1991). The construction of time, language, and self. *The Quarterly Newsletter of the Laboratory of Comparative Human Cognition, 13,* 42-52.

Brockmeier, J. (2000). Autobiographical time. *Narrative Inquiry, 10,* 1-23.

Brockmeier, J. (2001). From the end to the beginning: Retrospective teleology in autobiography. In J. Brockmeier & D. Carbough (Eds.), *Narrative and identity: Studies in autobiography, self and culture* (pp. 247-280). Amsterdam: John Benjamins.

Carstensen, L. (1993). Motivation for social contact through the life span: The positive lessons of loss. In R. A. Niemeyer (Ed.), *Meaning reconstruction & the experience of loss* (pp. 158-172). Washington: American Psychological Association.

Cohler, B. J. (1982). Personal narrative and life course. In P. B. Baltes (Ed.), *Life-span development and behavior* (Vol. IV, pp. 206-241). New York: Academic Press.

Damasio, A. R. (1999). *The feeling of what happens. Body and emotion in the making of consciousness.* New York: Harcourt Brace.

Dechesne, M. (2001) *Flexible and rigid reactions to reminders of mortality.* Nijmegen: Quickprint.

Dittmann, F. (1973). *Kultur und Leistung. Zur Frage der Leistungsdispositionen bei Luo und Indern in Kenia* [Culture and achievement: Achievement dispositions in Luo and Indians in Kenya]. Saarbrücken: Verlag der SSIP-Schriften.

Dittmann, F. (1974). *Cultural constraints on the acquisition of achievement motivation.* Menlo Park, CA: Stanford Research Institute, Educational Policy Research Center, Research Note 18.

Dittmann-Kohli, F. (1984). Weisheit als mögliches Ergebnis der Erwachsenenentwicklung [Wisdom as possible result of adult development]. *Sprache und Kognition, 2,* 112-132.

Dittmann-Kohli, F. (1991). *Code-Manual zur Erfassung des persönlichen Sinnsystems—Einführung und Beispiele aus dem Projekt "Lebenssinn und Selbstverständnis im Erwachsenenalter."* Berlin: Max-Planck-Institut für Bildungsforschung.

Dittmann-Kohli, F. (1995). *Das persönliche Sinnsystem. Ein Vergleich zwischen frühem und spätem Erwachsenenalter.* Göttingen: Hogrefe.

Dittmann-Kohli, F., & Westerhof, G. (1997). The SELE sentence completion questionnaire: A new instrument for the assessment of personal meaning in research on aging. *Anuaria de Psicologia, 73,* 7-18.

Dittmann-Kohli, F., & Westerhof, G. (2000). The personal meaning system in a life span perspective. In G. T. Reker & K. Chamberlain (Eds.), *Exploring existential meaning: Optimizing human development across the life span* (pp. 107-123). Thousand Oaks, CA: Sage.

Dittmann-Kohli, F., Bode, C., & Westerhof, G. (Eds.). (2001). *Die zweite Lebenshälfte: Psychologische Perspecktiven. Ergebnisse des Alters-Survey* [The second half of life—Psychological perspectives. Findings of the German Aging Survey].

Donadoni, S. (1990). *Der Mensch des alten Ägypten.* Frankfurt a. M.: Campus.

Epstein, S. (1973). Entwurf einer integrativen Persönlichkeitstheorie. In S. H. Philipp (Ed.), *Selbstkonzept-Forschung* (pp. 15-45). Stuttgart: Klett-Cotta.

Gell, A. (1992). *The anthropology of time. Cultural constructions of temporal maps and images.* Oxford, PR: Berg Publishers.

Greenwald, A. G. (1980). The totalitarian ego: Fabrication and revision of personal history. *American Psychologist, 35,* 603-618.

Hagestad, G. (1996). On-time, off-time, out of time? Reflections on continuity and discontinuity from an illness process. In V. Bengtson (Ed.), *Adulthood and aging: Research on continuities and discontinuities* (pp. 204-223). New York: Springer.

Heckhausen, J. (1999). *Developmental regulation in adulthood. Age-normative and socio-structural constraints as adaptive challenges.* New York: Cambridge University Press.

Hendricks, J. (2001). It's about time. In S. H. McFadden & R. C. Atchley (Eds.), *Aging and the meaning of time* (pp. 21-50). New York: Springer.

Hermans, H. J. M. (1996). Voicing the self: From information processing to dialogical interchange. *Psychological Bulletin, 119*(1), 31-50.

Holstein, J. A., & Gubrium, J. F. (2000a). *Constructing the life course* (2nd ed.). Dix Hills, NY: General Hall.

Kastenbaum, R. (1982). Time course and time perspective in later life. In C. Eisdorfer (Ed.), *Annual review of gerontology and geriatrics* (pp. 80-101). New York: Springer.

Klein, S. B. (2001). A self to remember. A cognitive neuropsychological perspective on how self creates memory and memory creates self. In C. Sedikides & M. B. Brewer (Eds.), *Individual self, relational self, collective self* (pp. 25-46). Philadelphia: Psychology Press.

Klein, W. (1994). *Time in language.* London and New York: Routledge.

Lens, W., & Gailly, A. (1980). Extension of future time perspective in motivational goals of different age groups. *International Journal of Behavioral development, 3,* 1-17.

Lewin, K. (1969). *Grundzüge einer topologischen Psychologie* [Foundations of topological psychology]. Bern: Huber.

McFadden, S. H., & Atchley, R. C. (Eds.). (2001). *Aging and the meaning of time.* New York: Springer.

Merriam, S. B., Courtenay, B. C., & Reeves, P. M. (2001). Time and its relationship to development in the life course: Some reflections from a study of HIV-positive adults. *Journal of Adult Development, 8,* 173-182.

Neisser, U. (1988). Five kinds of self-knowledge. *Philosophical Psychology, 1*(1), 35-59.

Neisser, U., & Fivush, R. (Eds.). (1994). *The remembering self. Construction and accuracy in the self-narrative.* Cambridge: Cambridge University Press.

Neimeyer, G. J., & Metzler, A. E. (1994). Personal identity and autobiographical recall. In U. Neisser & R. Fivush (Eds.), *The remembering self. Construction and accuracy in the self-narrative* (pp. 105-135). Cambridge: Cambridge University Press.

Nurmi, J.-E. (1994). The development of future orientation in life-span context. In Z. Zaleski (Ed.), *Psychology of future orientation* (pp. 63-74). Lublin: Towarzystwo Naukowe KUL.

Nuttin, J. (1984). *Motivation, planning, and action: A relational theory of behavior dynamics.* Leuven: Leuven University Press/Hillsdale, NJ: Erlbaum.

Nuttin, J., & Lens, W. (1985). *Future time perspective and motivation.* Leuven and Hillsdale, NY: Leuven University Press and Erlbaum.

Pennebaker, J. W., & Stone, L. D. (2003). Words of wisdom: Language use over the life span. *Journal of Personality and Social Psychology, 85,* 291-301.

Piaget, J. (1970). *The child's conception of time.* London: Routledge.

Polkinghorne, D. E. (1991). Narrative and self-concept. *Journal of Narrative and Life History, 1,* 135-154.

Roth, G. (2001). *Fühlen, Denken, Handeln.* Frankfurt a. M.: Suhrkamp.

Sarbin, T. R. (1986). The narrative as a root metaphor for psychology. In Sarbin, T. R. (Ed.), *Narrative psychology: The storied nature of human conduct* (pp. 3-21). New York: Praeger.

Sedikides, C., & Skowronski, J. J. (1997). The symbolic self in evolutionary context. *Personality and Social Psychology Review, 1,* 80-102.

Smith, M. B. (2002). Self and identity in historical/sociocultural context: "Perspectives on selfhood" revisited. In Y. Kashima, M. Foddy, & M. J. Platow (Eds.), *Self and identity: Personal, social, and symbolic* (pp. 229-243). London: Lawrence Erlbaum Associates.

Staudinger, U. M., & Dittmann-Kohli, F. (1992). Lebenserfahrung und Lebenssinn [Life experience and meaning of life]. In P. B. Baltes & J. Mittelstraß (Eds.), *Zukunft des Alterns und gesellschaftliche Entwicklung* [The future of aging and societal development] (pp. 408-436). Berlin: De Gruyter.

Steele. C. M. (1988). The psychology of self-affirmation: Sustaining the integrity of the self. *Advances in Experimental Social Psychology, 21,* 261-302.

Stuss, D. T., Gallup, Jr., G. G., & Alexander, M. P. (2001). The frontal lobes are necessary for "theory of mind." *Brain, 124,* 279-286.

Thomae, H. (1989). Veränderungen der Zeitperspektive in höheren Alter [Changes of temporal perspectives in advanced old age]. *Zeitschrift für Gerontologie, 22,* 58-66.

Timmer, E. (2000). *Antizipation von Gewinn, Fortsetzung des Status Quo und Verlust. Eine Untersuchung über persönliche Zukunftsbezüge in der zweiten Lebenshälfte* [Anticipation of gains, continuation of status quo, and loss. A study on personal future in the second half of life]. Nijmegen: Nijmegen University Press.

Timmer, E., Bode, C., & Dittmann-Kohli, F. (2003). Expectations of gains in the second half of life: A study of personal conceptions of enrichment in a life span perspective. *Ageing & Society, 23,* 3-24.

Trommsdorf, G. (1994). Future time perspective and control orientation: Social conditions and consequences. In Z. Zaleski (Ed.), *Psychology of future orientation* (pp. 39-62). Lublin: Towarzystwo Naukowe KUL.

van der Meer, E. (this volume). *Psychological time. Empirical evidence—Theories—Aging effects.* Berlin: Department of Psychology, Berlin Humboldt University.

Vroon, P. (1978). *Stemmen van vroeger. Ontstaan en ontwikkeling van het zelfbewustzijn* [Voices of the past: Emergence and development of self-awareness]. Baarn: Amboboeken.

Wallace, M. (1956). Future time perspective in schizophrenia. *Journal of Abnormal Social Psychology, 52,* 240-252.

Welzer, H., & Markowitsch, H. J. (2001). Umrisse einer interdisziplinären Gedächtnisforschung [Framework for interdisciplinary memory research]. *Psychologische Rundschau, 52,* 205-214. Göttingen: Hogrefe Verlag.

Westerhof, G. J. (2001). Lebensevaluierung: Bewertungsdimensionen und Vergleichsprozesse [Evaluation of life: Value dimensions and comparisons]. In F. Dittmann-Kohli, C. Bode, & G. Westerhof (Eds.), *Die zweite Lebenshälfte: Psychologische Perspektiven. Ergebnisse des Alters-Survey* [The second half of life—Psychological perspectives. Findings of the German Aging Survey].

Westerhof, G. J., & Dittmann-Kohli, F. (2000). Work status and the construction of work-related selves. In K. W. Schaie & J. Hendricks (Eds.), *The evolution of the aging self: Societal impact on the aging process* (pp. 1123-1157). New York: Springer.

Whitbourne, S. K. (1985). The psychological construction of the life span. In J. E. Birren & K. W. Schaie (Eds.), *Handbook of the psychology of aging* (pp. 594-618). New York: Van Nostrand Reinhold.

Zaleski, Z. (1994). *Psychology of future orientation.* Lublin: Towarzystwo Naukowe KUL.

Zimbardo, P. G., & Boyd, J. N. (1999). Putting time in perspective: A valid, reliable individual-differences metric. *Journal of Personality and Social Psychology, 77*(6), 1271-1288.

CHAPTER 5

The Concept of Event Time in the Study of Adult Development

K. Warner Schaie

When I was invited to share my thoughts on the subject of time and age sponsored by a group of philosophers, I was at loss at first to determine how a methods-oriented developmental psychologist ought to proceed. Much has been said about the nature of time as a relative phenomenon whose meaning may be no more than the subjective experience of the rate at which time passes. The simplest form of measuring such an experience would, of course, be merely the ratio of a unit of time experienced over the total time previously experienced. We could then argue over whether this ratio should be expressed as a logarithmic or exponential function; but all we would really say is that the subjective passage of time accelerates rapidly as people age (cf. Ornstein, 1969; Richardson & Rosen, 1979; Schroots, 1996).

DIFFERENT CONCEPTS OF TIME

There have been a number of thoughtful discussions of the meaning of time as related to the dynamics of development and aging (cf. Schroots & Birren, 1988, 1990; Schroots & Yates, 1999). Some of these discussions have focused on the role of entropy in aging processes (Strehler, 1977; Yates, 1996) or have implicated chaos theory as explanatory processes for asynchronous relationships between time and aging (cf. Prigogine, 1979).

In his overview encyclopedia article, Schroots (1996) distinguishes between physical time, biological time, psychological time, social time, and intrinsic time. Physical time is thought to be linear and irreversible, with the characteristics of a ratio scale. This would imply that equal time intervals have equal meaning at any life stage, a proposition that is hardly tenable within the human experience. *Biological time* is thought to be irreversible but also related in a nonlinear fashion to calendar time. Since such relationships must be defined for specific biological processes, it is difficult to conceive of a single biological time, except for the probability of dying in any particular species. Again, biological time does not easily conform to the equal intervals specified by a calendar time model.

Schroots suggests that four attributes are required for a plausible definition of *psychological time:* it may follow a nonlinear path; it's metric may be perturbed by both internal and external influences; it's present experience may be detached from past experience; and it's metric may be unrelated to causality. He also suggests that the units of a psychological time scale consist of psychological events each of which has "its own unique place on the absolute time scale of personal history and future . . ." (Schroots, 1996, p. 587). This is the major issue that I will expand upon later in this chapter.

Social time is based on the notion that every society has social expectations for behaviors that are thought to be appropriate at different life stages (a concept often called age grading). One can therefore argue that a person's position in social time depends upon whether they are on-time or off-time with respect to their age-graded roles and role behaviors (cf. Neugarten, Moore, & Lowe, 1968).

Intrinsic time, finally, is assumed to be the time scale that is generated by the nonlinear dynamics or energy transformation that are emergent properties of any system (Richardson & Rosen, 1979). The metric for this scale would involve the entropic (and negative entropic) properties of psychological processes and events. The metric of intrinsic time must therefore be studied as the dependent variable.

CONCEPTUALIZING TIME IN TERMS OF EVENTS

As a developmental psychologists, I am obviously interested in finding ways of describing the timing of psychological processes and events. But measuring the empty passage of time does not attract me greatly, especially since I have argued again and again that the mere passage of time has no explanatory power whatsoever. Hence the primary interest in assessing calendar time in the study of development and aging is in the prediction of the occurrence, duration, and timing of significant behavioral events. Therefore, calendar time is best measured as a dependent rather than independent variable (Willett & Sayer, 1994). This position is, of course, equally valid for the measurement of chronological age as was suggested over 30 years ago by Wohlwill (1973).

Instead, I want to consider here the possibility of alternate conceptions of the passage of time that might offer greater psychological meaning. The question then is how could we best assess the psychologically meaningful content of events occurring in time? The astute reader will notice immediately that this discussion must include the possibility of transforming raw calendar time into something that is more meaningful than calendar time. Such an effort also represents a special case of an attempt to remove the dependencies for one of the components of the age-cohort-period model, such that the proportion of variance due to this component alone can be independently estimated.

It is the purpose of this chapter to show how the explicit dependency between chronological age, birth-cohort membership, and measurement period so troubling in developmental studies of adulthood can be broken by redefining the scaling of one or more of these basic components in terms other than calendar time. I will begin my discussion by summarizing the properties of the age-cohort-period model (Ryder, 1965; Schaie, 1965) and by reviewing previous attempts to substitute alternatives for calendar time. I will then expand my previous discussion (Schaie, 1986) on how one might redefine calendar time as *event time* and propose some new models that would allow the study of event time in adult cognitive psychology. After which I will identify possible relevant empirical data sets that might be appropriate for testing these models and try to chart the direction of promising future research.

THE AGE-COHORT-PERIOD MODEL

The need to understand the relationship between cross-sectional and longitudinal data studied by those interested in development in the social and behavioral sciences led to the specification of what sociologists call the "Age-Cohort-Period Model" (Mason, Mason, Winsborough, & Poole, 1973; Ryder, 1965), which I independently introduced to the psychological sciences as the "General Developmental Model" (Schaie, 1965, 1967). The two approaches are virtually identical, although different approaches to the estimation of these models have been variously advocated.

The general developmental model characterizes the developmental status of a given behavior B to be the function of three components, such that $B = f(A, C, T)$. In this context, *age (A)* refers to the number of units of calendar time from birth to the chronological point at which the organism is observed or measured. *Cohort ©)* denotes a group of individuals who enter the environment at the same point in calendar time or the same range of calendar time (usually but not necessarily at birth), and the *time of measurement (T),* referred to as *period* by sociologists, indicates the temporal occasion on which a given individual or group of individuals is observed or measured. The three components of this model are confounded in the sense that once any two of them are specified, then the third is known—similar to the confounding of temperature, pressure, and volume in the physical sciences. Nevertheless, each of the three components may, of course, be of primary interest for different questions in the developmental sciences. Efforts are therefore made frequently to obtain estimates of the specific contribution attributable to each of the three component of the model, even though only two of the three can be independently measured, given the above specifications.

The general developmental model further permits specification of how the three components are confounded in research designs traditionally used by developmentalists. For example, a single cross-sectional study will confound age and cohort, while a single-cohort longitudinal study will confound age and time of measurement. In addition, novel designs can be derived from the model that allow us to estimate the components confounded in different ways. For example, it is possible to unconfound age and cohort when multiple cohorts are studied over the same age range (cohort-sequential strategy). Likewise, age and time of measurement can be unconfounded when cross-sectional studies are replicated over the same age range at different times of measurement (time-sequential strategy; cf. Schaie, 1977; Schaie & Willis, 2002, ch. 5). Nevertheless, time of measurement remains confounded in the cohort-sequential strategy, while cohort remains confounded in the time-sequential strategy.

The unconfounded estimation of all components of the general developmental model still eludes us except under special circumstances and with certain collateral assumptions (Schaie, 1986, 1994, 2005). Nevertheless, the expanded designs have lead to new departures in theory building (Schaie, 1988, 1992, 2000). In particular, it has been recognized that breaking the dependencies in the model are likely to be achieved by redefining one of the components in ways such that it is no longer directly dependent upon calendar time. For the purposes of this chapter, the logical candidate for such redefinition is, of course, time of measurement or period, the component that is concerned explicitly with the timing of events of interest to the researcher.

THE CONCEPT OF EVENT TIME

As we begin our search for a possible alternative to scaling human experience within a calendar time framework, we should note once again that calendar time may not have any other significance than its role in marking the "white space" within which those events occur that are perceived by the individual and society to possess significant meaning and which therefore enter into our individual or collective consciousness. Consciously perceived events, indeed, represent the "matter" of our experience.

I have suggested earlier that there are historical periods that may either show a paucity or a richness of such events (Schaie, 1986). Here, I would add that over the human life span there are also maturational periods that are likely to be characterized by a sparse occurrence of significant events or that may contain an unusual fullness of experiences. In this context, a maturational period could be defined as a particular chronological age span, but it could also be characterized as a *functional* age span (i.e., one characterized by the individual's relative status with respect to his or her chronological age peers on dimensions such as the level of physical maturation or decline (cf. Schaie & Parr, 1981).

Other examples of noncalendar-defined age spans would be the concept of mental age to denote the relative level of cognitive development (cf. Terman, 1916) or a person's social age referencing his or her relative life-course role status (as being on-time or off-time (Neugarten, Moore, & Lowe, 1968) In the context of understanding individual lives, of course, it is the interaction between the individuals maturational stage and the event density provided by the environment during that stage that becomes of primary interest.

It will immediately be noticed then that event time can be characterized as a macrosocietal phenomenon that requires sociohistorical analyses of the timing of events that have broad impact on most (but not necessarily all) individuals exposed to these events (cf. Schaie, Willis, & Pennak, 2005). Interestingly, it is probably the duration of the event in terms of exposure time that ought to be measured. That is, the duration of the event from the point in chronological time when the first impact occurred to that point in time when all or most individuals exposed were affected. Alternatively, an event duration could be characterized by an occurrence from that point in time when universal acceptance of a societal practice or technology first started to erode to the point where the event has virtually dissipated.

But before we can seriously go about measuring events impacting society or individual lives, we must heed Sorokin and Merton's (1937) admonition that it is the nature of a particular event that lends meaning to its occurrence rather than its particular calendar date. This statement must be qualified, however, by the recognition that in the measurement of individual event time, the maturational stage of organisms may show critical interactions with the characteristics of the event. That is, the same event may have different impact on an individual depending upon that individual's life stage when the event occurred. Thus for Americans, the Vietnam war affected primarily males who were of the right age to be inducted into the armed forces, and their parents who feared for the lives of their young adult children. For others, this war was largely a political problem that had little impact on their lives.

In order to measure events that could be used as a suitable marker, we need to identify classes of event attributes that deserve our attention. I have previously identified five classes of such events: substantive type of event, impact of event, direction of event, event density, and perceptions of the event (Schaie, 1986). In Figure 1, I provide nonexclusive examples of these event attributes.

Taxonomic studies are needed to provide the substantive domains of types of events. Since many different types of events can obviously co-occur, event time should be thought of as a multidimensional phenomenon. Thus it may be profitable to chart event density in different experiential domains, such as the introduction of a new technology, changes in societal attitudes and values, the effect of wars and changes in political systems, changes in societal acceptance of personal habits, or the diffusion of knowledge (cf. Schaie & Elder, 2005).

A second attribute is concerned with the manner in which the *impact* of an event is to be defined. Impact can be defined, using the criteria in Figure 1, to refer to a specific population and time frame. But impact might differ across successive population cohorts and might be unique to a historical time period. For

Type of Event
- Technological Innovation
- Attitudinal Change
- Lifestyle Change
- Diffusion of Knowledge
- Historical Event

Impact of Event
- Initial Occurrence
- Universal Recognition
- Dissipation

Direction of Impact
- Linear
- Accelerating
- Decelerating
- Recursive

Event Density
- In Population
- In Individuals

Perception of Event
- Defined by Professional Judges
- Defined by Population Survey
- Subjectively Perceived by Individuals Studied

Figure 1. Examples of attributes of noncalendar event time.

example, the historical impact of apartheid in South Africa might have had differential consequences depending upon cohort membership (cf. Bluen & Odesnik, 1988).

There have been many admonitions in the literature on adult development regarding the multidimensional nature of events for populations as well as individuals (cf. Baltes, 1987). Hence, we would argue that linear models of event time would at best offer first approximations.

The third attribute of event time is concerned with its direction. Most likely it will be necessary to specify a variety of nonlinear models that need to be fitted to the direction of impact. Figure 2 charts event time against calendar time for the adoption of several common technologies and practices. Note in particular that event duration thus defined often has linear form, but it can also be recursive, as in the example of the length of women's skirts.

The fourth attribute of event time is the density of events experienced during given periods of historical time or over specific maturational stages in the lives of individuals. Later on I shall have more to say about the distinct analytic paradigms that are required for the study of event time in individuals as contrasted to those required for the study of populations.

The fifth and final attribute concerns the distinctions of how one is to characterize the perception of significance and impact of events. For populations, it would obviously be necessary to rely either on population surveys or on objective

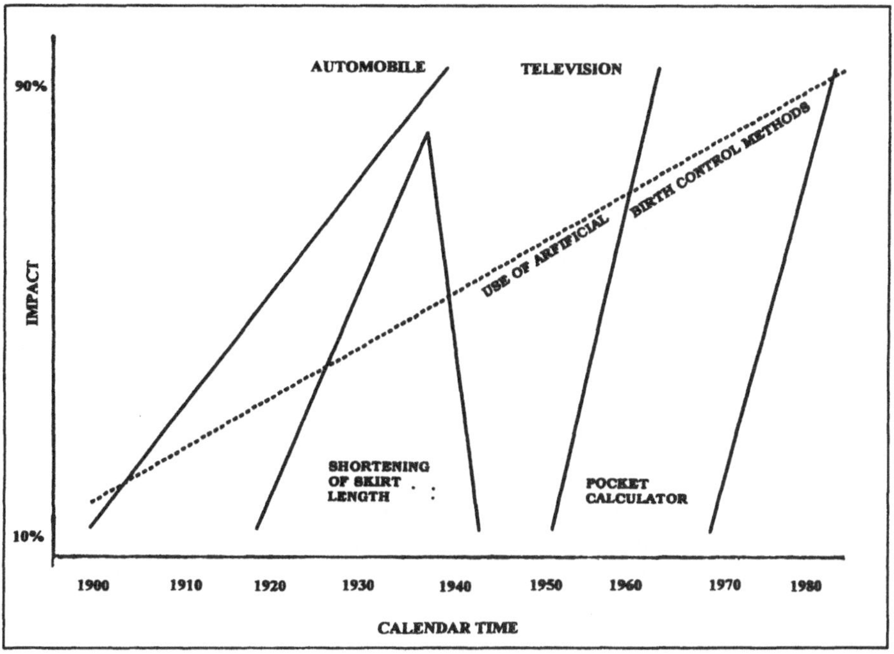

Figure 2. Examples of markers of event time scaled against calendar time.

definitions provided by professional judges. On the other hand, chronicling the life events affecting an individual may require assessing subjective perceptions as experienced by the affected individual.

If we are to employ event-time analyses to individual lives, we must begin by identifying the types of event that are likely to have an impact on individual development. There is a substantive literature on the contextual aspects of life events that can provide guidance on the choices that may be appropriate (e.g., Brim & Ryff, 1980; Cui & Vaillant, 1996; Lerner, 1995; Schaie, Willis, & Pennak, 2005; Von Eye, Kreppner, Spiel, & Wessels, 1995). What remains to be done is to investigate the multiple domains that provide salient markers over a person's life course. Some relevant scales may be found to be widely dispersed across a number of literatures. Many of these scales were constructed to discover possible environmental influences that act as precursors of chronic disease and psychological problems (e.g., Cui & Vaillant, 1996; Rahe & Arthur, 1978; Segrin, 1999). They may nevertheless provide good models for our purposes as well those efforts that were explicitly directed toward normal life-course events such as success in marriage, in careers, or in retirement. (e.g., Suedfeld & Bluck, 1993; Szinovacz & Washo, 1992).

MODELS FOR THE STUDY OF EVENT TIME

The notion of studying the timing of the occurrence of specific events began in the actuarial sciences in order to be able to compute the appropriate cost premiums required to cover the cost of insurance for common hazards (risks or end points) the probability of which could be computed for classes of individuals or events. It's use has also been common in fields such as epidemiology, industrial engineering, criminology, and other social sciences. However, until recently it has been only rarely applied in the behavioral sciences. In most of its applications, the emphasis is upon the occurrence of some end point, whether the time required for a disease, to cause disability or death, the time to criminal recidivism, or the failure of light bulbs. However, in each case the goal is usually a dual one: identification of the predictors of the event and estimation of a time point (including a confidence interval about that time point) at which the event will occur.

The independent variables in event time analyses represent the conditional probabilities attributable to mediating influences; they can be both fixed in time or can be time-varying. The dependent variable in such analyses is typically defined as a dichotomous variable (the occurrence of the event and the log time, cf. Allison, 1984; Singer & Willett, 1991). Both continuous and discrete algorithms are available for the estimation of event time. For our purposes, we would prefer the discrete methods because in the behavioral sciences, we would be most likely to be able to sample events at specific times or ranges of times rather than in a continuous manner (Allison, 1982).

I have pointed out previously that the events to be studied by means of event history analyses do not necessarily have to be of a naturalistically defined dichotomous nature (Schaie, 1989a). That is, events could also be defined as the attainment of a threshold value. Events thus defined are quite common. The definition of legal blindness, for example, does not imply that a person must have no sight whatsoever to be classified as being blind. Likewise, sociologists often treat divorce as a discrete event, timing it when the divorce decree has been awarded. Realistically, that date can only be interpreted as a threshold attainment, since marital disruption started much earlier, and residues of the marriage will continue far beyond the divorce date, especially when there are minor children involved.

In the study of human aging, I have further argued that it might be useful to substitute log age (calendar age) for log time (Schaie, 1989a). I would like to make the distinction here that the age at which an event occurs would seem to be the proper dependent variable when we are interested in studying the timing of events with respect to maturational age-related variables. However, time must be the appropriate dependent variable when we are speaking of the timing of events within a historical framework or of the duration of time-dependent events that occur regardless of the maturational stage of the organism at which they occur. Given the likely interaction between life stage and event duration, both approaches may be indicated in many instances.

The Study of Multiple Events

I began my discussion of event time by advocating the concept of event density. This concept, of course, entails the notion that we should not be attending primarily or exclusively to singular events as is commonly done in the event-history literature cited above. Instead we are concerned with the co-occurrence of multiple events. Most discussions of methods for event history analysis include prescriptions for the assessment of competing or cumulative risks, such as in the study of co-morbidity or multiple drug use (cf. Allison, 1982). However, if we wish to create an alternative scale to calendar time, we must instead attend to the issue of the temporal structuring of multiple events. In order to consider designs that might be appropriate for time-ordered events it may be useful to refer to Cattell's (1957) data cube (see Figure 3).

As Figure 3a suggests, there are three facets to the data cube. The front facet designates a matrix of conventional data collected at a single point in time. The rows of this matrix normally indicate persons (study participants) or in more general the entities across which observations are to be generalized. The columns of this matrix represent the variables or attributes of the entities that have been measured. Analysis of such a data matrix is generally designed to discover the concurrently observed relationships among the variables (denoted by Cattell as R methodology). This matrix, however, could also be utilized to determine

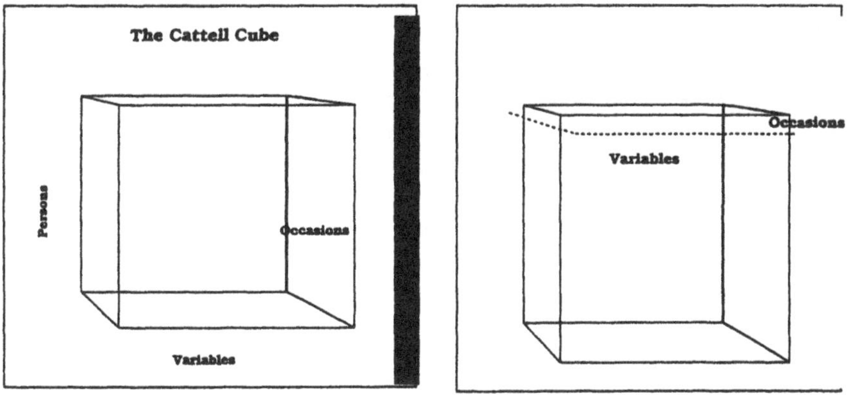

a. The Cattell Data Cube

b. Single Subject Facet

Figure 3. The three facets of the Cattell data cube (a) and an example of a single subject longitudinal data matrix derived therefrom (b).

the typology of individuals who have been measured, by analyzing the relationships among the entities as generalized across the variables (denoted as Q methodology).

The side facet of the cube represents a longitudinal data matrix. It's rows also represent the entities over which observations are to be generalized, while the columns represent the multiple points in time at which a single variable has been measured. This matrix can be analyzed to study the temporal relationship of the variable of interest across the entities under study (T methodology), generating what is sometime known as a simplex model of temporal relationships for a particular variable. This is the analytic approach taken in a typical longitudinal inquiry, albeit usually more than a single facet is examined in complex multivariate designs (cf. Schaie, 1996, 2004). This facet can also be analyzed to structure a typology of individuals who experience similar temporal life courses on a given variable or variables (S methodology; e.g., Schaie, 1989b).

Of particular interest for our purposes is the top facet of the cube shown in Figure 3b. This matrix represents measures or observations taken on a single individual, with the rows representing successive (longitudinal) occasions of measurement, and the rows representing the multiple variables or attributes under observation. This matrix can be analyzed by studying the relationships among the attributes across time (similarity or dissimilarity in the temporal structuring of attributes; P methodology; cf. Jones & Nesselroade, 1990; Nesselroade, 1994). Studying facets for several persons allows contrasting timing of events among members of family dyads or other social systems. P methodology has been utilized in the study of aging and development to model individual patterns of change primarily over relative short time intervals (e. g., Nesselroade & Jones, 1991; Schulenberg, Vondracek, & Nesselroade, 1988). This facet can also be analyzed to study relationships among temporal patterns across the attributes (consistency or inconsistency of temporal patterning of attributes; O methodology; e.g., Shifren, Hooker, Wood, & Nesselroade, 1997).

In order to discover the density of multiple events over time utilizing a macrosocial approach, we would need to identify the major societal events of interest. We could then study the temporal pattern of each event across a given population (culture) with the T methodology approach and then use Tucker's (1966) three-mode factor analysis approach for the multidimensional factor analysis of this system for multiple classes of events (also see Bentler & Lee, 1979; Snyder & Law, 1979). Alternatively, it might be useful to employ methods of latent class analysis, to develop the latest constructs needed to describe event type, or to combine latent class analysis with three-mode factor analysis (Tucker, 1972). Utilizing any of these statistical approaches, I believe that, whether at the direct observable or latent construct level, we would discover a temporal structuring of events that would reveal a nonlinear relationship of event density with respect to calendar time.

POSSIBLE RELEVANT EMPIRICAL DATA SETS

Clearly, cross-sectional data can not be relevant to the issues at hand, since whether one uses the calendar or a scale of event time, it is necessary for time to pass in order to study time-related processes. Our targets of inquiry must therefore be existing longitudinal studies; preferably those that have been conducted over large segments of the human life span. However, there are additional criteria that must be met. First, there has to be reasonably complete information as to the historical point in time and the maturational stage (whether defined chronologically or otherwise) when data on the dependent variables of interest were collected. Second, the data sets ought to include sufficient time-varying sociodemographic indicators. And third, in the study of individuals, time- and age-indexed life-event indicators should be available.

Archival data of this type may be found for many currently conducted longitudinal studies as well as for some that have now been concluded and are available to the public (cf. Schaie & Hofer, 2001). What is needed, however, is the identification of variables in such studies that can be used to quantify the event time attributes discussed in this chapter. Once this is done, it is then possible to create an appropriate event time scale or scales, and substitute such scales in order to study time-dependent processes in a more meaningful manner. Development of these scales would also permit full estimation of the three components of development change by breaking the dependencies in the age-period-cohort model.

From the point of view of researchers in the field of human aging, examination of event time over large portions of the adult life span would allow testing hypotheses regarding the differentiation and dedifferentiation of the event space (i.e., changes in the multidimensionality of the event space) at various adult life stages (cf. Schaie, 2005). Such hypotheses could be tested both in terms of maturational hypotheses related to the demands of given life stages (cf. Erikson, 1964; Schaie & Willis, 2000) and with respect to the impact of different historical periods or their interaction with life stage. We would hypothesize that event density would be greatest in young adulthood and middle age (cf. Willis & Reid, 1999), but would decline as old age is reached. This follows from what we know about the restriction of role functions and the selection of more restricted interaction with the environment (cf. Carstensen, Gross, & Fung, 1997). Historically, we could test hypotheses about periods full of conflict contrasted with those of relative calm (Schaie, Willis, & Pennak, 2005), Finally, we may want to take advantage of experiments of nature where cross-cultural propositions could be tested in those data sets that provide comparable data for different social systems over the same historical period (e.g., Rudinger & Minnemann, 1997).

SUMMARY AND CONCLUSIONS

In this chapter, I have argued that calendar time is a rather unsatisfactory scale in the behavioral and social sciences. Just as chronological age simply indexes position in the life span, so does calendar time index the point of occurrence or duration of an event. Neither have explanatory meaning in their own right. I have therefore suggested that it may be desirable to substitute the concept of event time; the attributes of this construct were described in some detail. In particular, I showed that many definitions of event time would be independent of chronological age; hence, the indeterminacy posed by the age-period-cohort model can be successfully resolved by substituting event time for the traditional concept of calendar time. I then showed how appropriate designs for the study of event time could be derived from the Cattell cube and suggested that O and P techniques might be particularly suitable study designs. Given full data sets (such as in the Seattle Longitudinal Study (Schaie, 1996, 2004), it is also possible to apply three-mode latent factor analyses. Once the appropriate metric for defining event density is developed, it is then possible to apply event history methods to determine the structural and time-varying predictors of this concept. Finally, characteristics of data sets that would be suitable for the identification of events and their dimensionality were suggested. Much work lies ahead, but also the opportunity to put psychological and social meaning into the concept of time.

ACKNOWLEDGMENT

Work on this chapter was supported in part by grant R37 AG08055 from the National Institute on Aging.

REFERENCES

Allison, P. D. (1982). *Discrete-time methods for the analysis of event histories.* In S. Leinhardt (Ed.), *Sociological methodology* (pp. 61-98). San Francisco: Jossey-Bass.

Allison, P. D. (1984). *Event history analysis: Regression for longitudinal event data.* Beverly Hills, CA: Sage.

Baltes, P. B. (1987). Theoretical propositions of life-span developmental psychology: On the dynamics between growth and decline. *Developmental Psychology, 23,* 611-626.

Bentler, P. M., & Lee, S. Y. (1979). A statistical development of three-mode factor analysis. *British Journal of Mathematical and Statistical Psychology, 32,* 87-104.

Bluen. S. D., & Odesnik, J. (1988). Township unrest: Development of the Township Life Events Scale. *South African Journal of Psychology, 18,* 50-57.

Brim, O. G. Jr., & Ryff, C. D. (1980). On the properties of life events. In P.B. Baltes & O. G. Brim Jr. (Eds.), *Life-span development and behavior* (Vol. 3, pp. 368-388). New York: Academic Press.

Carstensen, L. L., Gross, J., & Fung, H. (1997). The social context of emotion. In K. W. Schaie & M. P. Lawton (Eds.), *Annual review of gerontology and geriatrics* (Vol. 17, pp. 325-352). New York: Springer.

Cattell, R. B. (1957). *Personality and motivation: Structure and measurement.* Yonkers-on-Hudson, NY: World.

Cui, X. J., & Vaillant, G. E. (1996). Antecedents and consequences of negative life events in adulthood: A longitudinal study. *American Journal of Psychiatry, 153,* 21-26.

Erikson, E. H. (1964). *Insight and responsibility.* New York: Norton.

Jones, C. J., & Nesselroade, J. R. (1990). Multivariate, replicated, single-subject, repeated measures designs and P-technique factor analysis: A review of intra-individual change studies. *Experimental Aging Research, 16,* 171-183.

Lerner, R. M. (1995). Developing individuals within changing contexts: Implications of developmental contextualism for human development, research, policy and programs. In T. A. Kindermann & J. Valsiner (Eds.), *Development of person-context relations.* Hillsdale, NJ: Erlbaum.

Mason, K. G., Mason, W. H., Winsborough, H. H., & Poole, W. K. (1973). Some methodological problems in cohort analyses of archival data. *American Sociological Review, 38,* 242-258.

Nesselroade, J. R. (1994). Exploratory factor analysis with latent variables and the study of processes of development and change. In A. Von Eye & C. Cliff (Eds.), *Latent variables analysis: Applications for developmental research* (pp.131-154). Thousand Oaks, CA: Sage.

Nesselroade, J. R., & Jones, C. J. (1991). Multi-modal selection effects in the study of adult development: A perspective on multivariate, replicated, single-subject, repeated measures designs. *Experimental Aging Research, 17,* 21-27.

Neugarten, B. L., Moore, J. W., & Lowe, J. C. (1968). Age norms, age constraints, and adult socialization. In B. L. Neugarten (Ed.), *Middle age and aging.* Chicago: University of Chicago Press.

Ornstein, R. E. (1969). *On the experience of time.* New York: Penguin.

Prigogine, I. (1979). *From being to becoming.* San Francisco, CA: W. H. Freeman.

Rahe, R. H., & Arthur, R. T. (1978). Life changes and illness studies. *Journal of Human Stress, 4,* 3-15.

Richardson, I. W., & Rosen, R. (1979). Aging and the metrics of time. *Journal of Theoretical Biology, 79,* 415-423.

Rudinger, G., & Minnemann, E. (1997). Conditions of life of elderly women and men in East- and West-Germany: First results from the Interdisciplinary Long-Term Study of Adulthood and Aging (ILSE). *Zeitschrift für Gerontopsychologie und Psychiatrie, 10,* 205-212.

Ryder, N. B. (1965). The cohort as a concept in the study of social changes. *American Sociological Review, 30,* 843-861.

Schaie, K. W. (1965). A general model for the study of developmental problems. *Psychological Bulletin, 64,* 92-107.

Schaie, K. W. (1967). Age changes and age differences. *Gerontologist, 7,* 128-132.

Schaie, K. W. (1977). Quasi-experimental designs in the psychology of aging. In J. E. Birren & K. W. Schaie (Eds.), *Handbook of the psychology of aging* (pp. 39-58). New York: Van Nostrand Reinhold.

Schaie, K. W. (1986). Beyond calendar definitions of age, time and cohort: The general developmental model revisited. *Developmental Review, 6,* 252-277.

Schaie, K. W. (1988). The impact of research methodology on theory-building in the developmental sciences. In J. E. Birren & V. L. Bengtson (Eds.), *Emergent theories of aging: Psychological and social perspectives on time, self and society* (pp. 41-58). New York: Springer.

Schaie, K. W. (1989a). The hazards of cognitive aging. *The Gerontologist, 29,* 484-493.

Schaie, K. W. (1989b). Individual differences in rate of cognitive change in adulthood. In V. L. Bengtson & K. W. Schaie (Eds.), *The course of later life: Research and reflections* (pp. 68-83). New York: Springer.

Schaie, K. W. (1992). The impact of methodological changes in gerontology. *International Journal of Aging and Human Development, 35,* 19-29.

Schaie, K. W. (1994). Developmental designs revisited. In S. H. Cohen & H. W. Reese (Eds.), *Life-span developmental psychology: Theoretical issues revisited* (pp. 45-64). Hillsdale, NJ: Erlbaum.

Schaie, K. W. (1996). *Intellectual development in adulthood: The Seattle Longitudinal Study.* New York: Cambridge University Press.

Schaie, K. W. (2000). The impact of longitudinal studies on understanding development from young adulthood to old age. *International Journal of Behavioral Development, 24,* 267-275.

Schaie, K. W. (2005). *Developmental influences on adult intelligence: The Seattle Longitudinal Study.* New York: Oxford University Press.

Schaie, K. W., & Elder, G. H., Jr. (Eds.). (2005). *Historical influences on lives and aging.* New York: Springer Publishing Co.

Schaie, K. W., & Hofer S. M. (2001). Longitudinal studies in research on aging. In J. E. Birren & K. W. Schaie (Eds.), *Handbook of the psychology of aging* (5th ed., pp. 55-77). San Diego, CA: Academic Press.

Schaie, K. W., & Parr, J. (1981). Concepts and criteria for functional age. In J. E. Birren (Ed.), *Aging: A challenge to science and social policy* (Vol. III, pp. 249-264). Oxford, UK: Oxford University Press.

Schaie, K. W., Willis, S. L., & Pennak, S. (2005). A historical framework for cohort difference in intelligence. *Research in Human Development, 2,* 43-67.

Schaie, K. W., & Willis, S. L. (2000). A stage theory model of adult cognitive development revisited. In R. Rubinstein, M. Moss, & M. Kleban (Eds.), *The many dimensions of aging: Essays in honor of M. Powell Lawton* (pp. 175-193). New York: Springer.

Schaie, K. W., & Willis, S. L. (2002). *Adult development and aging* (5th ed.). Upper Saddle River, NJ: Prentice-Hall.

Schroots, J. J. F. (1996). Time: Concepts and perceptions. In J. E. Birren (Ed.), *Encyclopedia of gerontology* (Vol. 2; pp. 585-590). San Diego, CA: Academic Press.

Schroots, J. J. F., & Birren, J. E. (1988) The nature of time: Implications for research on aging. *Comprehensive Gerontology, C2,* 44-66.

Schroots, J. J. F., & Birren, J. E. (1990). Concepts of time and aging in science. In J. E. Birren & K. W. Schaie (Eds.), *Handbook of the psychology of aging* (3rd ed., pp. 45-64). San Diego, CA: Academic Press.

Schroots, J. J. F., & Yates, F. E. (1999). On the dynamics of development and aging. In V. L. Bengtson & K. W. Schaie (Eds.), *Handbook of theories of aging* (pp. 417-433). New York: Springer.

Schulenberg, J. E., Vondracek, F. W., & Nesselroade, J. R. (1988). Patterns of short-term changes in individuals' work values: P-technique factor analyses of intra-individual variability. *Multivariate Behavioral Research, 23,* 377-395.

Segrin, C. (1999). Social skills, stressful life events, and the development of psychosocial problems. *Journal of Social and Clinical Psychology, 18,* 14-34.

Shifren, K., Hooker, K., Wood, P., & Nesselroade, J. R. (1997). Structure and variation of mood in individuals with Parkinson's disease: A dynamic factor analysis. *Psychology and Aging, 12,* 328-339.

Singer, J. D., & Willett, J. B. (1991). Modeling the days of our lives: Using survival analysis when designing and analyzing longitudinal studies of duration and the time of events. *Psychological Bulletin, 110,* 268-290.

Snyder, C. W., & Law, H. G. (1979). Three-mode common factor analysis: Procedure and computer programs. *Multivariate Behavioral Research, 14,* 435-441.

Sorokin, P. A., & Merton, R. K. (1937). Social time: A methodological and functional analysis. *American Journal of Sociology, 42,* 615-629.

Strehler, B. L. (1977). *Time, cells, and aging.* New York: Academic Press.

Suedfeld, P., & Bluck, S. (1993). Changes in integrative complexity accompanying significant life events: Historical evidence. *Journal of Personality and Social Psychology, 64,* 124-130.

Szinovacz, M. E., & Washo, C. (1992). Gender differences in exposure to life events and adaptation to retirement. *Journal of Gerontology: Social Sciences, 47,* S191-S196.

Terman, L. M. (1916). *The measurement of intelligence.* Boston: Houghton.

Tucker, L. R. (1966). Some mathematical notes on three-mode factor analysis. *Psychometrika, 31,* 279-311.

Tucker, L. R. (1972). Relations between multidimensional scaling and three-mode factor analysis. *Psychometrika, 37,* 3-27.

Von Eye, A., Kreppner, K., Spiel, C., & Wessels, H. (1995). Life events' spacing and order in individual development. In T. A. Kindermann & J. Valsiner. Hillsdale, NJ: Erlbaum.

Willett, J. B., & Sayer, A. G. (1994). Using covariance structure analysis to detect correlates and predictors of individual change over time. *Psychological Bulletin, 116,* 363-381.

Willis, S. L., & Reid, J. E. (Eds.). (1999). *Life in the middle: Psychological and social development in middle age.* San Diego, CA: Academic Press.

Wohlwill, J. B. (1973). *The study of behavioral development.* New York: Academic Press.

Yates, F. E. (1996). Theories of aging: Biological. In J. E. Birren (Ed.), *Encyclopedia of gerontology* (Vol. 2; pp. 545-555). San Diego, CA: Academic Press.

CHAPTER 6

Time and Aging: A Physicist's Look at Gerontology

Jos Uffink

To enter as a physicist into the field of gerontology brings along certain dangers. I will presumably fall into pitfalls of misunderstanding or step on some other booby traps, which those who are familiar with the terrain have learned to avoid. This danger is probably even greater since the so-called science wars and the Sokal affair have sensitized the relation between the physics community and those working in the humanities and social sciences in general.

To be sure, unlike Sokal's (1996) contribution, my chapter is not a hoax. But like him, my intention will be more or less skeptical and aimed at toning down overrated and uncritical expectations of the benefit of importing physical concepts into other fields of research. I will argue that, although modern physics has lots of interesting things to say about time, it has very little to say about aging. Moreover, the little it has to say about aging has no practical relevance for gerontology.

I will avoid trying to define aging. I take it that aging is a phenomenon that is familiar to every one who has looked into a mirror more than once. The field of gerontology aims to study the physiological, social, and psychological aspects of human aging. There are, *prima facie*, two good reasons to expect that this field might have some interesting relationships with physics.

The first reason is that both fields share a common interest: the concept of time. I will try to describe in this chapter some aspects of time in modern theoretical physics and address the question whether they shed light on the topic of aging. The second reason is that aging and its ultimate consequence, death, is a universal phenomenon. One of the few certainties that humans have is that they cannot remain young forever and will eventually die. The inevitability of this fate strikes us with such force that one might suspect this to be due to a general law of nature. Since physics is traditionally regarded as the discipline most intimately conversant with laws of nature, it is natural to turn to physics in order to see whether there is such a law. Some authors claim it is the Second Law of Thermodynamics. They argue that all living beings evolve toward death because of the universal tendency toward ever-increasing entropy implied by this law.

The chapter is organized as follows. First, I will review some aspects of the notion of time that usually arise in discussions of this topic in physics and the foundations of physics literature. After that I shall give a description of the well-known Twin Paradox of relativity theory, which is arguably the result most relevant to aging in modern physics, followed by a discussion of some themes connected with the "arrow" of time and the Second Law of Thermodynamics. Finally, I shall debate some recent claims in the gerontology literature about the relevance of physical theory for the understanding of time and aging.

TIME IN CLASSICAL (PRERELATIVISTIC) PHYSICS

Time is a central notion in physics. And although theoretical physics has developed exact ways to deal with this notion and experimental physics has devised accurate instruments to measure times, it is not easy to say what it is. If you ask a "physicist on the street" what is meant by time, the most likely answer will be "time is simply that quantity which is measured by a clock." This answer is not very helpful for two reasons. First, the obvious objection is that one can define a clock, in turn, as an instrument designed to measure time. Thus, the answer is in danger of circularity. Second, it only addresses the quantitative aspect of how time is measured and not the meaning of the term.

In fact, I think it is fair to admit that physics simply does not have the wherewithal to specify the meaning of time or to define time in terms of more fundamental, nontemporal notions. The meaning of time is a problem belonging to metaphysics or, more generally, to the philosophy of physics. If we resist the temptation to dive into metaphysics, at least for the moment, one can only say that even in theoretical physics the meaning of time still has to be grasped on the basis of our common everyday language. In some sense this is embarrassing, because in our everyday speech time can mean many things. For example, on some occasions we speak of it as if it were a commodity: it is something we can spend, or save, waste or share. Here, it seems to be almost synonymous with effort or attention or, as the saying goes: money. This is clearly not the meaning intended in physics.

The intended meaning of time is more closely approached by the idea that all events can be ordered in an organized whole, by means of the primitive temporal relations "earlier than," "later than," or "simultaneous with." To be more precise, let us denote the relation that event E is earlier than, later than, or simultaneous with event F as

$$E \prec F,\ E \succ F, \text{ and } E \sim F.$$

It is customary in classical physics to assume that these relations interlock in such a way to provide a complete, continuous, and linear ordering. This means that we postulate several properties of this ordering (which I won't spell out here). The upshot from these postulates is that one can derive the result that the ordering can be represented by means of a continuous parameter t. That is to say, we can attribute a real number $t(E)$ to every instantaneous event E, such that

$$t(E) < t(F) \text{ if and only if } E \prec F,$$
$$t(E) > t(F) \text{ if and only if } E \succ F, \text{ and}$$
$$t(E) = t(F) \text{ if and only if } E \sim F.$$

An equivalent view is to represent the events geometrically as ordered along a straight line.

But even if we focus on this intended meaning, it is remarkable how underdeveloped our vocabulary for temporal concepts really is. Consider the analogy with space. In this case too, we can start with primitive spatial relations like "E is to the left of F" etc., and build up spatial geometry from them. Once we have the geometry, we will readily distinguish various further spatial notions, for example, location, region, and distance. These terms are so familiar that no one would confuse them. Now, it is not hard to find temporal analogs for these fine-tuned distinctions. For example, we could use the terms instant, duration, and lapse to refer to temporal location, temporal region, and temporal distance. However, such specialized terminology has never become popular. Instead, one usually speaks of the "time of birth" when we refer to an instant, "the time of the Crusades" when we mean a temporal region, or an athlete's "time" for the 100-meter race, when we consider the lapse between start and finish. Apparently, common language favors equivocation between distinct temporal notions. Below we will encounter further examples of this lack of precision in our temporal vocabulary.

The quantitative representation of time by a parameter t immediately raises a further problem. Once we have found one such parameter, we have many of them because every transformation, say from t to $t' = f(t)$, with f a monotonic continuous function, provides us with another parameter that represents the temporal ordering just as well. The choice of a unique parameter is obtained by introducing a standard time scale; it is fixed by the choice of a standard clock.

It is not easy to give criteria for the choice of such a clock; that is, to specify in what sense one particular clock is "better" than any other. The most compelling criterion one can come up with is the idea that this choice should make the physical laws of motion look simple. That is to say, one identifies certain physical systems, which we have good reason to believe are relatively free from external disturbances, and for which physical theory predicts that, if undisturbed, their evolution should be regular (e.g., periodic). Then, the best standard clock is one that makes their motion indeed come out perfectly regular. Thus, in the final analysis it is the theory that dictates the choice of an appropriate time scale and not the other way around.

This procedure might look a bit like cheating: the validity of our laws of motion seems to be guaranteed from the outset. Doesn't this mean that the validity of the laws of motion becomes a pure, empty convention? No. After all, in principle, it could very well be that there are no such clocks. It is an empirical fact, and not a conventional choice, that one can actually find clocks that make the laws of motion true (at least to excellent approximation) for all physical systems.

An obvious standard clock, which has served very well for centuries, is given by the various rotations in the solar system, from which we derive the units of the day, the month, and the year. But it is well known that these rotations are not completely regular, neither with respect to each other, nor with respect to clocks constructed by other means. Hence, by the seventeenth century, astronomers had replaced a solar-based year by the sidereal year, which is measured with respect to the "fixed stars." But then the fixed stars are also not really fixed. So, keeping up with the progress in observation and instrumentation, new and different standards have been devised. The most accurate standard currently accepted is the International Atomic Time (TAI), obtained from a statistical average over a large number of atomic clocks (see e.g., http://tycho.usno.navy.mil/systime.html).

Even after a standard clock system has been fixed, we are still left with the choice of a unit and a zero (origin) of the scale. Here we have nothing but convention and pragmatic reasons to guide us. The customary choice is to define the unit (the second) in such a way as to most closely correspond to existing practice. The choice of a zero is fixed by reference to some arbitrary event such as high noon in Greenwich England.

Note that the choice of a particular time scale is often called "Time." Thus, one refers to the various scales in common use as atomic time, sidereal time, Greenwich Mean Time, Central European time, summer time (or Daylight Saving), etc. This might easily suggest that by changing time scale, we are in fact adopting a completely new concept of time. It should be clear that this is not the case. The underlying concept is still given by the same qualitative temporal ordering, which is unaffected by the choice of scale. The choice of a scale is a pragmatic one. In fact, the habit of referring to different scales as different times again points to the paucity of common language regarding temporal notions. The analogous questions concerning space (e.g., the choice between miles and kilometers etc.) would never be considered to involve different notions of length, let alone different concepts of "space."

Perhaps the above remarks are already so obvious that some readers wonder why I mention them at all. The reason is that some authors in gerontology claim that the notion of time in classical physics is characterized by "reification," that is, by an identification of the notion of time with its measurement by a clock. And indeed, one must grant that the "physicist on the street" tends to confirm this view. It is therefore not entirely trivial to point out that classical physics does not support such a naïve identification. The choice of a clock is a subtle issue, settled by the current state of the art in instrumentation and by considerations about simplicity and convention. But it does not bear on the underlying nature of physical time.

In order to prepare for later discussions, I will briefly discuss the question how one could attribute an age to physical systems in classical physics. Of course classical mechanics envisions systems as being composed of classical particles: immutable, nondestructible grains of matter, that cannot be subject to any aging. But another meaningful question is whether there is some quantity we can ascribe to the system that keeps track of the passage of time. Hilgevoord (1996) calls them *clock variables*.

For many simple systems there are such quantities. For a free moving particle, it is just the distance covered; for a harmonic oscillator, it is the phase; for a free-falling body in a uniform gravitational field, it is its velocity. Not surprisingly, the question is closely related to that of finding a good clock. Indeed, the systems just mentioned are all reasonable candidates to act as a standard clock.

However, there are good reasons why the study of such clock variables, which can be seen as measuring the age of the system, is not a prominent feature in theoretical physics. Usually, their analytical treatment is notoriously obstreperous. This is due, among other things, to the fact that in general a system may pass through the same state at different stages of its evolution. A clock variable, which is a function of state, will then become ambiguous.

It is often convenient to join the time parameter t of an event with its spatial coordinates. In that case, we end up with a four-dimensional space-time picture, in which every instantaneous and extensionless event in our universe is represented by four coordinates, specifying when and where it occurs. In doing so, however, an important implicit assumption of the classical time concept in classical physics becomes explicit. This is the idea that the temporal ordering applies universally, without regard for spatial locations. For example, it is assumed that one can always specify exactly whether or not two events are simultaneous, regardless of how distant they are from each other in space. This four-dimensional space-time picture provides a method to represent or order events and physical processes, which, in most cases, suffices for the purpose of physics. But it leaves many interesting issues untouched.

The first of these is the metaphysical problem of what time *is*. One of the best-documented issues in this problem is the debate between the so-called absolute and relational views on time (and space). The question here is whether time (or space) exists as an entity independent of events and processes, or whether it is no more than an abstraction derived from the spatiotemporal relations between such events. The debate between these two views has a long history, starting with Aristotle and culminating in the seventeenth century in a clash between Newton (leading the absolutist camp) and Huygens and Leibniz in the relationist camp.

The contrast between these two views can be illustrated by imagining a world in which there are no changes; a world which is completely dead and still. The two views give very different answers to the question whether there would be time in such a world. According to the relationist, the notion of time is dependent on change, and therefore, in such an imaginary universe the notion of time ceases to exist. But from the point of view of the absolutist, time and space are conceived of as an arena or stage on which events are enacted. So even if there are no such events, the empty stage still continues to exist, and it remains meaningful to distinguish different instants and durations, even though there would be no instrument to measure them.

This debate on metaphysical issues is often coupled with issues from epistemology. Thus, relationism is often, but not necessarily, accompanied by the epistemological point of view (empiricism) that the meaning of scientific concepts has to be specified in terms of empirical observations. Since a universe without change clearly does not contain clocks to measure time, it is natural from this perspective to conclude that the very notion of time becomes meaningless. By contrast, the absolutist viewpoint seems more congenial to the epistemological view (realism) that science aims to describe an independently existing reality. Of course, we gain information about such entities by means of observation. But in this view, observation does not exhaust the meaning of our concepts. Their meaning is to be judged in terms of how they represent reality. So even if there are no means for measuring time, the notion itself can still be meaningful.

Apart from the above metaphysical problem, another question is how adequate the classical picture of time is. One can easily imagine other structures that differ more or less from the linear continuum. For example, one might assume that on a very small scale, time is not continuous but discrete. That is, one might drop the assumption that for any two distinct instants t_1 and t_2, there exists a third instant t_3 ,which lies between them. Indeed, many modern physicists expect that at a scale of 10^{-43} seconds (the so-called Planck time), the present theories of physics will collapse and have to be replaced by some theory as yet unknown.

Another issue is the question whether time extends linearly to plus and minus infinity. It is possible to imagine the ordering of time to be cyclic rather than linear: in other words, one might assume that events are recurrent after a long period. This would mean that instead of considering the space-time manifold as a flat infinite sheet, it would be curled up as a cylinder. Of course this entails that the relation of "earlier than" and "later than" do not define a global ordering. However, if the radius of that cylinder is large, it will be locally indistinguishable from the flat plane, just as the surface of the earth appears on a small scale as a horizontal plane. However, our evidence suggests that the history of the universe is not recurrent for at least 10^{10} years.

Above, we have mentioned some issues that come up, time and again, in the physical and philosophical literature on time. Are any of such issues relevant to gerontology; that is, to an understanding of human aging? I do not believe so. The choice between, say, a Solar Year and the Sidereal Year might have occupied astronomers in the seventeenth century, but on a human scale the difference is so minute that it is not noticeable at all. Similarly, the debate on the relational and absolute nature of space and time only becomes relevant in a universe that is devoid of change or contains only three or fewer objects. The universe in which we live is not of that kind. Finally, doubts about the continuity or linearity of the time ordering appear only at scales so small or so large that again they are irrelevant to any gerontology that is concerned with human affairs. We can conclude that the relevance of these problems for gerontology is therefore negligible.

TIME IN RELATIVITY THEORY

The advent of the theory of relativity has brought radical changes to our conception of time and space. In particular, it brought about a whole new episode in the debate between the absolutist and the relationist views of time and space. Einstein struggled with the question how to unite certain aspects from the theory of mechanics with the theory of electromagnetism, developed in the nineteenth century by Maxwell and Lorentz. The details of his work are not important here, and so I merely mention that a crucial point in Einstein's reasoning was the recognition that we have no *a priori* way of assessing whether or not two distant events are simultaneous. This can only be accomplished by means of a synchronization procedure. Einstein proposed a natural procedure (synchronization by means of the exchange of light signals). This weaves the properties of light into the fabric of space and time. Given his further postulates about the behavior of light (its speed being independent of the source, and the relativity principle), he was able to show that the Newtonian notions of absolute space and absolute time had to be abandoned. In particular, the notion of simultaneity between distant events became dependent on the state of motion of the observer.

It is commonly believed that Einstein's theory of relativity favors the relationist viewpoint above the absolutist one. There are several reasons for this belief. The first is of course Einstein's rejection of absolute space and absolute time as such. The second reason is that his argument adopted an empiricist strategy, by analyzing how different observers, equipped with standard clocks and rods, would go about measuring space and time intervals. As mentioned before, this point of view is traditionally associated with relationism. The third and worst reason is that sometimes the close etymological resemblance between relativity and relationism leads to a conflation of the two.

However, it later became clear that this belief is not tenable. The special theory of relativity replaces the notions of absolute Newtonian space and time by a more elaborate structure, usually called Minkowski space-time. However this new structure is just as absolute as its two separate predecessors. The most striking distinction is that Minkowski space-time does not possess a notion of absolute simultaneity. More precisely, it is not meaningful in this structure to ask whether two distant events are simultaneous or not. However, Minkowski space-time does acknowledge a notion of "space-time interval," or a "metric" as it is often called, which is every bit as absolute as the structures of Newtonian space and time. In particular, the metrical properties of Minkowski space-time are independent of, and not reducible to, events or processes.

The issue becomes more complicated when we pass from the special to the general theory of relativity. In this theory, the metrical properties are influenced by the presence of matter. I will not go into this topic. Suffice it to say that even in this case, there is no prospect for the claim that these metrical properties can be reduced to the spatiotemporal relations of matter (Hoefer, 1998). The project of designing a fully relationist theory of space-time thus remains an elusive one, although work on this topic is still being pursued; for example, in Julian Barbour's recent book, entitled (somewhat misleadingly) *The End of Time*.

The Twin Paradox

Perhaps the most straightforward case in which modern physics has relevance for aging is the particular consequence of the relativity theory known as the Twin Paradox. In special relativity, the rate of a clock depends on its state of motion. Consider two clocks, which are constructed in an identical fashion; and assume they are moving uniformly with respect to each other. That is, their relative motion is at constant speed and in a constant direction. For simplicity, let's adopt a frame of reference in which one of them, say A, is at rest. The theory of relativity predicts that, judged from this frame of reference, the moving clock B will run *slower* when compared with the rate of the resting clock A. This is the famous time dilation effect.

But now consider the case where one of the clocks makes a round trip and returns to the one that remains at home. From the point of view of clock A, the moving clock runs slow during both legs of the journey. So when it returns, it is lagging behind the resting clock. This is not a relative effect: it is a definite fact that, at the point where both clocks can be compared locally, the one that has travelled indicates an earlier time than the one that remained at rest. In general, the time indicated by a standard clock is now called its *proper time* τ. The rate depends on the velocity of the clock through

$$d\tau = \sqrt{}\,(1 - (v/c)^{\wedge 2})\, dt$$

where c denotes the speed of light.

One can add some human interest to the story by replacing the clocks by a twin. Imagine that one of two twin sisters departs on a trip in a fast spaceship. After a long journey, in which she roamed the depths of the galaxies, she returns to earth. On her arrival, her sister is there to greet her. But when they meet, the space voyager is still in the prime of life; for her, the expedition has lasted only a year. Her stay-at-home sister, however, is already old and grey, because by earthly reckoning 50 years have passed. So, these twin sisters experience differential aging, even though both were born at the very same time.

This conclusion has been regarded as so paradoxical that it has been called the Twin Paradox. Many authors hasten to declare that it is not a real paradox at all, since it does not involve a contradiction. But it has been appropriately named, in the original sense of the term paradox, meaning contrary to common sense. Needless to say, the above story is, of course, only a thought experiment. In actual fact, the velocities needed to achieve even the smallest difference in aging are enormous, and it seems unlikely that a spaceship with the required specifications will ever be built. However, there is no doubt about the validity of the Twin Paradox, since the effect has been observed for elementary particles, which are easier than humans to accelerate to speeds near that of light.

One question that has often been raised about the Twin Paradox is whether it is reasonable to assume that the relativistic time-dilation effect should affect humans in the same way as it affects physical clocks. Of course, generally speaking, physics has little to say about how humans perceive time durations. This issue falls under the province of "Psychological Time." It is an acknowledged fact of human experience that an hour spent in boredom, waiting for a delayed airplane, for example, is perceived as longer than an hour spent in pleasant company and entertaining conversation. There is no reason to doubt that this distinction between psychological and physical time will apply in space travel as it does in a terrestrial environment. Thus, whether the journey will be perceived as long or short will depend on whether the traveller is bored and lonely or not (whether NASA will provide entertaining company, on board movies, etc.) and not on the theory of relativity.

But apart from our mental perception of time, there are also physiological processes involved in aging: our metabolism, our hair and nails growing, the formation of wrinkles, etc. Again, it is well known that the rate at which some of these processes take place varies from individual to individual and is influenced by nonphysical factors. A well-known series of portraits of Jimmy Carter, taken at different stages during his four-year presidency of the United States, provides a telling example of how stress can speed up physiological aging. Again, there is every reason to expect that such factors will influence the aging of a space traveller in the same fashion as it does on earth.

But even if we acknowledge such effects, it seems reasonable to say that they represent relatively small variations on an underlying trend: roughly, humans do age proportionally to chronological time. Moreover, the relativistic time-dilation effect can be made as large as one pleases by increasing the speed to be arbitrarily close to that of light. In principle, it is possible to make the space traveller return to earth thousands of years after her sister died, while by her own clock the journey took less than an hour. No amount of boredom or psychological stress can compensate for such drastic differences. Hence, human beings are not essentially different from other physical systems or clocks, albeit very irregular ones, and the predictions of relativity will apply to them. So, regardless of whether the journey is boring, exciting, or stressful, the traveller will experience less aging than the earthbound twin sister.

So the theory of relativity has some impact on gerontology. If high-speed space travel someday becomes available to the common household, our perspective on aging will change dramatically, and the theoretical concepts to describe it will have to be modified. For example, one would no longer be entitled to assume that persons born at the same time belong to a single cohort. Still, I would argue that, until that day, one may safely conclude that the impact of this aspect of relativity theory on the problems of gerontology is negligible. The only lesson is this: if it is your dream to travel to the future and see what life on earth looks like in the twenty-fourth century, and if you happen to be a multimillionaire who can afford to build the required spacecraft, then, according to the theory of relativity, it is possible to realize your dream. (Although I would recommend cryogenics as a cheaper and more promising alternative.)

THE ARROW OF TIME

The geometric representation of time, employed in both Newtonian and relativistic space-time, however, leaves out some aspects that are very deep-rooted in our experience of time, as well as in certain macroscopic physical phenomena. I am referring to what is often called "Time's Arrow." Eddington coined this phrase in a popular but very influential book of 1929. It was Eddington's aim to point out that physics systematically turns a blind eye to a certain "one-way property of time" that has no analogy in space. Exactly what that property is, is not so clear from Eddington's writing. It could stand for the idea that time goes on, the asymmetry between past and future, the distinction between being and becoming, and the irrevocable nature of certain physical processes. Again, there are quite a number of separate issues at stake here, conveniently but confusingly packed into a single phrase. Let's try to disentangle them.

One important aspect of time that is involved here is the idea of a *flow* or passage of time. Human experience includes the sensation that time moves on and that the present is forever shifting toward the future and away from the past. This idea is often illustrated by means of the famous two scales of McTaggart. Scale B is a one-dimensional continuum in which all events are ordered by means of a date. Scale A is a similar one-dimensional continuous ordering for the same events, employing terms like "now," "yesterday," "next week," etc. This scale shifts along scale B as on a slide rule.

Another common way of picturing this aspect is by attributing a different ontological status to the events in the past, present, and future. Present events are the only ones which are "real" or "actual." The past is not actual: it is gone and forever fixed. The future is no more actual than the past but still "open," etc. The flow of time is then regarded as a special ontological transition: the creation or actualization of events. This process is often called *becoming*. In short, this viewpoint holds that grammatical temporal tenses have counterparts in reality.

Is this idea of a flow of time related to physics? Many authors (e.g., Eddington, 1929; Prigogine, 1980; Reichenbach, 1971) have indeed claimed that the Second Law of Thermodynamics provides a physical foundation for this aspect of our experience. But according to contemporary understanding, this view is untenable (Grünbaum, 1967; Kroes, 1985). In fact the concept of time flow hardly ever enters in any physical theory. Newton's conception of absolute time that "flows equably and of itself" seems the only exception. But there is no evidence, as far as I know, that Newton's flow was the above idea of becoming. In a physical description of a process, it never makes any difference whether it occurs in the past, present, or future. Thus, scale B is always sufficient for the formulation of physical theory, and the above-mentioned ontological distinctions play only a metaphysical role.

It seems clear that tenses cannot be defined in physical terms, and that if they are to be used at all in a physical description, they have to be imposed or motivated from some external source. This is not to say, however, that these distinctions are illusions or only subjective. In fact I think there are two plausible viewpoints on the relation between tenses and physics. The first, a physicalistic viewpoint, is that we should take the physical conception of reality as (a provisional proposal for) a literally true description of reality. This point of view, and the fact that no physical theory yet has ever provided clues on how to ground tenses in physical reality, provides an argument in favor of the nonreality of tenses.

On the other hand, one might also argue that physics is an enterprise that, by its very nature and purpose, is limited and abstract. It considers only those aspects of reality that can be connected to or expressed in terms of general laws and repeatable events. This aim of physics naturally leads it to discard all aspects of reality that are accidental, nonrepeatable, and specifically tied to a unique "here-now." According to this point of view, the fact that physics finds no evidence for the concept of tense is not an argument that it is unreal, but just indicates that physics persistently ignores this aspect of reality.

A second theme, which is more relevant to physics, is that of *symmetry* under time reversal (Horwich, 1987). Suppose we record some process on film and play it backwards. Does the inverted sequence look the same? If it does, for example, a full period of a harmonic oscillator, we call the process time symmetric. But such processes are not in themselves very remarkable. A more interesting question concerns physical laws or theories. We call a theory or law time symmetric if the class of processes that it allows is time-symmetric. This does not mean that all allowed processes have a palindromic form like the harmonic oscillator, but rather that a censor, charged with the task of banning all films containing scenes that violate the theory or law, issues a verdict that is the same for either direction of playing the film.

Note that the term "time reversal" here is not meant literally. That is to say, we are considering a reversal of processes that is or is not allowed by some physical theory, not the underlying time ordering. Note also that in this conception, time (a)symmetry is a property of the theory and not of the processes. That is to say, it is very well conceivable that one and the same process is characterized by some theory as time symmetric, while another theory judges it to be time asymmetric.

In many cases, the reversal of physical processes looks rather strange. Maxwell writes in 1868:

> . . . if every motion great & small were accurately reversed, and the world left to itself again, everything would happen backwards. The fresh water would collect out of the sea and run up the rivers and finally up to the clouds in drops which would extract heat from the air and evaporate, and afterwards, in condensing, would shoot out rays of light to the sun and so on. Of course all living things would regrede [sic] from the grave to the cradle and we should have memory of the future but not of the past (Maxwell, 1995, pp. 187-188).

This image of a time-reversed world has been used by many novelists to exploit its weird and amusing consequences.

But it is hard to say whether a hypothetical censor would ban such a world as being in conflict with physical laws. It is a remarkable fact that on the microscopic scale, all fundamental physical theories are time symmetric. Thus, judged from those theories' point of view, the world described by Maxwell is just as physically possible as our own. However, many macroscopic physical laws are not time symmetric. Examples are the diffusion equation, Fourier's heat equation, etc. The most famous example is the Second Law of Thermodynamics. The question how this can be so, especially if one wishes to see the macroscopic equations as reducible to the microscopic ones, is a vexed question.

Another main theme in discussions on the arrow of time is irreversibility. A process is called irreversible if it cannot be fully undone. Once it has taken place, the original state cannot be completely restored, even with the help of the most sophisticated auxiliary apparatus imaginable. Examples of such processes are erosion, corruption, decay, and of course, aging. Planck famously argued that all processes in the real world are irreversible. He also claimed that this was a consequence of the Second Law of Thermodynamics.

It is not a trivial matter to state what the Second Law of Thermodynamics actually says (cf. Uffink, 2001). There are, as Bridgman (1961) conservatively estimated, as many formulations as there have been discussions of it! A relatively safe formulation is the statement that according to thermodynamics, all systems in an equilibrium state are characterized by a quantity called entropy, and that in all transitions that a system can go through during adiabatic isolation, ending in another equilibrium state, this quantity can never decrease.

However, the confusion surrounding the Second Law of Thermodynamics is not confined to classical thermodynamics, the theory developed by Clausius, Kelvin, Gibbs, and Planck. During the twentieth century, many modifications of the theory have been proposed, in order to make it applicable to more general types of systems and situations. This has resulted in a plethora of theories, calling themselves "generalized" thermodynamics, "extended" or "rational" thermodynamics, thermodynamics of irreversible processes, nonequilibrium thermodynamics, continuum thermodynamics, etc. On some occasions, the same name is even claimed by rather different theories.

One of the best known of these approaches is probably the theory of Prigogine (1955) and De Groot (1951) which deals with open dissipative systems, generally assumed to be in nonequilibrium. Here it is assumed that such systems can still be characterized by an entropy function S. Changes in the entropy are supposed to be governed by two factors: an internal entropy production, $d_i S$, and an exchange of entropy, $d_e S$, with the environment. In other words:

$$(1)\ dS = d_i S + d_e S.$$

It is postulated that the internal entropy production is never negative

$$(2)\ d_i S \geq 0.$$

While this theory has scored a number of successes, in particular after the incorporation of the so-called Onsager relations, and in special cases where the adoption of a minimum entropy production principle was helpful, its status in physics has remained controversial and contested.

For example, it is always possible to resolve a change of entropy as a sum of two terms. In fact, this can be done in an infinite number of ways, even under the condition that the first term be positive. In order to obtain a unique identification of the entropy production and the entropy exchange, a more stringent definition of these terms is needed. Secondly, the justification usually offered for the assumption that the internal entropy production should be positive is the old second law of (orthodox) thermodynamics. But since orthodox thermodynamics is not applicable to nonequilibrium systems, one would expect some independent and more general arguments to be given in support of this extension to general systems.

Finally, Truesdell (1980) has severely criticized this and other theories for their rather liberal use of the differential calculus. He points out, among other objections, that in ordinary differential calculus there can be no meaningful differential inequalities.

In this section I have sketched various aspects involved in the notion of the arrow of time. The question how, if at all, these themes relate to gerontology is much more difficult than it was for the themes of the previous sections. Notions like the passage of time or becoming do have a strong connotation with our human experience of time and arise also in studies of psychological time. They are clearly relevant in gerontology. The main difficulty is rather that their relationship with physics, if any, remains unclear and controversial. Time asymmetry remains a major and unresolved issue in the debate on the foundations of physics. Irreversibility is perceived to be essential to the Second Law of

Thermodynamics, but again the issue is controversial. The question whether this second law, properly construed, has an impact on gerontology is the subject of the next section.

IS AGING DUE TO A FUNDAMENTAL LAW OF PHYSICS?

Up until now, my effort has been devoted to a discussion of those aspects of time that capture the attention of physicists and philosophers of physics. In the present section I will reverse my approach. Instead of taking the physics literature as my point of departure, I will now start from the work by some gerontologists who argue that theoretical physics provides an important clue to the understanding of aging. This view is advocated particularly by Yates (1988) and also by Schroots and Birren (1988). The work by Schroots and Birren provides a convenient starting point, since it reviews much earlier work on the nature of time and aging in gerontology.

Of course the first question to be asked is what is meant by the distinction between time and age. The basic definition of age, mentioned by Schroots and Birren (1988), is that age is the time elapsed since birth. This is called chronological age. However, this concept is not all there is to age. We are all familiar with the expression that someone is young (old) for his or her age. A central quest of theoretical gerontology seems to be to give a scientific meaning to such locutions. Obviously, the intended notion of age here is not the chronological age; rather, one has to think of it as a quantity that characterizes a certain stage of development of an individual. The problem is whether one can find some objective markers from which an alternative to chronological age can be constructed. Depending on where the ingredients are drawn from, such constructs are called biological, psychological, or social age. The process of aging itself; that is, the increase of age, taken in these three distinct senses is called senescing, geronting, and eldering.

From the biological perspective, much research has been devoted to the various physiological phenomena that exhibit oscillatory behavior; for example, the heart beat, breathing, the sleep/wake cycle, etc. Indeed, in this research, the human organism has been likened to a clock shop, with complicated mutual hierarchical relations between them (master and slave clocks). Several such biological functions have been studied as indicators of biological age: maximum heart rate, lung capacity, hearing sensitivity to high frequencies, etc. Still, Schroots and Birren (1988) are not impressed by the results of such investigations. They conclude that "measures of functional or biological age were considered useless" and "Until now, there is no evidence of a better predictor of length of life, residual life-span, time until death, residual longevity or nearness to death than plain chronological age" (p. 7).

Schroots and Birren provide a similar overview for the topic of psychological time and its components, such as the notions of time experience, time perspective, and temporal awareness. Again, they reach rather pessimistic conclusions about the prospects for this research. In particular, the problem seems to be that the variability of psychological time notions is observed to increase with age. They summarize the implications of this investigation drily as "every older man is in certain respects (a) like all older man (b) like some older man and ©) like no other older man, with strong emphasis on ©)" (p. 15). Their conclusion is that "the idea of a new psychological age variable can be dismissed immediately."

Their discussion on social time mentions, among other things, the concept of eldering or social aging, which is defined as the process of social role change and behavior in mature adults in a direction expected and displayed by others in a society. An important difference from the previous notions is of course that an analysis of social aging involves a strong reliance on normative concepts. But again, Schroots and Birren are not happy with what they find in this literature. They observe that "the fundamental criticism of the concepts of biological age and psychological age also applies to social age, which is scaled on a physical time-scale, and is consequently measured in units of calendar or chronological time" (p. 16). In conclusion, "the quest for social time has merely resulted in *tautologies*, implicitly or explicitly" (p. 19).

Clearly, previous work in gerontology has failed to provide a proper analysis of aging, according to Schroots and Birren. Yates (1988) expresses similar complaints about the lack of coherent theory building in gerontology. Together, they advocate a new approach, which Schroots and Birren term "gerodynamics." Generally speaking, there are three main characteristics of this approach. First, it regards humans as instantiations of a general species of "living" or "biological" systems, to be described by thermodynamics of irreversible processes. A second characteristic is the claim that aging is to be seen as an accumulation of entropy in the system, due to the Second Law of Thermodynamics. Third, it involves the introduction of another concept of time, called "intrinsic time." I will expound and comment on these three points below.

HUMANS AS LIVING SYSTEMS

Schroots and Birren provide a clear description of the conception of human beings in gerodynamics. According to this viewpoint,

> . . . humans are regarded primarily as living systems, hierarchically organized from many subsystems, such as cells, cell tissues, organs, and so on, according to levels of complexity. As a system, humans can be conceived of as part of an even more complex larger system—for example, the physical and social environment. From a thermodynamic or energetic point of view, a living system of any sort is *open*.
>
> That is to say, a current of energy passes through the hierarchically organized (sub)systems in a chain of reactions. This flow of energy starts with the sun as solar energy and gets transformed into chemical energy via plants and animals, which are our food. Metabolism introduces further

> *transformations*, in which food with a relatively high energy level is converted into waste products such as carbon dioxide and water, with low energy levels of biological systems (p. 22).

While this quotation greatly emphasizes the role of physical concepts, the fact that Schroots and Birren include the social environment in their scheme shows that their approach is not exclusively physical and allows for nonphysical factors.

By contrast, Yates is more outspoken in his physicalist outlook. His stated aim is to provide "the physical foundation for a general gerontological theory" (Yates, 1988, p. 91) and indeed a full "epistemological reduction of biology to physics" (p. 94). Succinctly, his goal is

> . . . to close the gap between biology and physics so that we can make some progress toward a comprehensive scientific theory of the aging of biological systems. In that physical theory aging will be seen as a progressive loss of dynamical stability dependent on changing constraints. That alteration of constraints is the touch of the Second Law [of thermodynamics] in biochemical networks. The theory will also require that there are two kinds of time for biological organisms" (p. 97).

Strangely, Yates (p. 91) accompanies this stated goal by an admission that his point of view is anthropocentric; that is, concerned with humans only. This seems to me incoherent with the quest for a comprehensive and general theory.

THE SECOND LAW OF THERMODYNAMICS

As is apparent from the last quotation, a second main theme in the approach advocated by Yates as well as Schroots and Birren is the role of the Second Law in the explanation of aging. The main idea is that living organisms are to be regarded as open thermodynamical systems in a steady state. As mentioned above, this means that we associate an entropy S to such a system, whose change is governed by an internal entropy production and exchange with the environment. In order to maintain a steady state, in which the entropy of the system remains constant, these two terms should compensate each other.

$$(3)\ \mathrm{d}S = \mathrm{d_i}\, S + \mathrm{d_e}\, S = 0.$$

In other words, in a steady state, the internal entropy production is compensated by an equal amount of entropy exportation to the environment.

But Yates claims that the Second Law also has another interpretation; namely "Constraints shall not last!" (p. 99). He argues that an organism cannot maintain a steady state indefinitely, because "the internal thermodynamical engine cycles are not perfect, being themselves subject to the Second Law" (p. 102). The result is that

$$(4)\ \mathrm{d_i}\, S > \mathrm{d_e}\, S,$$

which implies dS > 0. Hence, by the continual loosening of internal constraints, there will be an entropy accumulation in the system. It is this accumulation that "drives senescence," according to both Yates and Schroots and Birren. Indeed, as the latter argue

> Generally speaking, one might then say that each living system moves toward maximum disorder or entropy, in short toward death. In terms of general systems theory from a thermodynamic perspective aging can now be defined as the process of increasing entropy with age (p. 22).

There are several remarks and objections to be made. First, Yates' interpretation of the Second Law is rather unorthodox. The version of the Second Law of Thermodynamics proposed by Prigogine implies nothing more than $d_i S > 0$. The inequality (4) does not follow from this and cannot be said to be an expression of this law. Of course, this is not to say that this relation is generally false. In many systems, whether living or not, we do see a loosening of constraints as time goes on (by wear and tear, etc.), and they are often accompanied by an increase of entropy. But in many other cases, the passage of time will not loosen constraints but merely change them, or indeed even impose additional new constraints. All this is entirely compatible with thermodynamics as commonly understood. Therefore, Yates' reinterpretation of its Second Law has no lawlike validity within thermodynamics.

Further, even if one admits that living systems are in many circumstances truly characterized by an accumulation of entropy, it is not thereby established that one can *define* aging as the accumulation of entropy. An obvious counterexample is obtained by considering an experiment in which one avoids internal entropy accumulation by increasing its exchange with the environment. If you lock me in a freezer cell for several hours without protective clothing, the entropy production of my body will not keep up with the heat that it loses to the environment. So here we have

$$(5)\ d_i S < d_e S,$$

and my total entropy S will decrease. Note that in spite of the violation of (4), this is not at all in conflict with the Second Law. But still, my losing entropy does not mean that I will become younger. Instead, I will die from cold. Incidentally, the example also shows that death cannot be equated with a state of maximum entropy. Indeed, it seems likely that in many cases, dying is not accompanied by any change of entropy in the organism at all and hence is a thermodynamically rather insignificant event. A development toward maximal entropy occurs only during the subsequent process of decay or cremation. Clearly then, it is too naïve to expect that a complex phenomenon such as human aging can sensibly be reduced to the increase or decrease of a one-dimensional physical quantity.

As noted before, Schroots and Birren allow for a role of the social environment in their conception of living systems. They envisage that this role can be included in the general scheme by means of a concept of "social entropy." But this seems hardly a viable option. Social entropy is at best a dubious metaphor, which has lost all relationship to thermodynamics. It does not and cannot appear as a term in the entropy balance of an open thermodynamical system simply because this relation applies equally to cars and stars and microwave ovens as it does to living organisms. If one wishes to pursue this idea seriously, then the whole evocation of the thermodynamical formalism becomes nothing but a speculative metaphor rather than a physical foundation for a theory of aging. As an aside, I note that the introduction of social entropy (interpreted by Schroots and Birren as a form of information) is not favored by Yates. He regards information as a "toxic juice," which ought to be wrung out from gerontological theory (Yates, 1988, p. 97).

INTRINSIC TIME

Another main ingredient of gerodynamics is the proposal of a new notion of time, called "intrinsic time." This notion is supposed to stand in contrast to the ordinary (chronological) concept of time, which is henceforth also called "external time." It is claimed that intrinsic time is relevant for the explication of aging. Thus Yates writes

> External . . . time gives us the clock time by which we measure chronological age, *but it does not necessarily give us intrinsic human age*, which is determined by internal process time as described below. . . . Intrinsic time is created by biological processes as an emergent property of their non-linear dissipative dynamics, leading to the result . . . that the intrinsic biological significance of a unit of external time cannot be itself constant but must change with chronological age (p. 98).[1]

Schroots and Birren argue similarly, but are more explicit about what to understand by intrinsic time:

> Paraphrasing Richardson and Rosen, it may be stated that any given dynamics of any given system will generate its own *intrinsic time* scale. That is, intrinsic time is created by physical, biological, psychological and social processes as an emergent property of their dynamics. As already known, any dynamical process can serve as a clock, time being measured by monitoring one of the variables undergoing change. The dimensional unit of this intrinsic time is simply the unit of the state variable chosen for observation" (p. 24).

They illustrate this concept by the example of a burning candle. Here, one can consider the length of the candle as the state variable undergoing change and indicating the intrinsic time of this process.

A number of questions may be raised about this notion of intrinsic time. The most important one, in my opinion, is that this discussion of intrinsic time seems to

[1] Amusingly, he presents this as "the simplest view consistent with Einsteinian locality."

suffer from a pervasive confusion. What is really meant by this concept? From the texts available to me, I think there are two ways in which one can understand it. The straightforward, literal, way would be to read these authors as proposing a different time *scale* or unit for measurement of time. But this proposal immediately runs into difficulties. As we have seen before, the question of the choice of scale is one that is settled largely by considerations of convenience. Nothing substantial is at stake in this issue, as long as we do not upset the underlying temporal ordering relation. It is hard to see how one particular scaling convention would possess more explanatory power than any other, or would in some other way provide an essential element in the analysis of aging. Indeed, it seems that once more, the poverty of our language concerning temporal concepts lures one into the misconception that by choosing another scaling convention, we have actually created a different concept of time altogether. This confusion also appears in Schroots and Birren's "fundamental criticism," mentioned above, against previous notions of time; namely, that they rely on a scale measured in chronological time.

However, there is a second way of reading the proposal. One can understand the vague claim that intrinsic time "is created as an emergent property of the dynamics" as intending to say that it is a variable of the dynamical state of a system. In this sense, the notion of intrinsic time would be analogous to the proper time of special relativity theory, which depends on the velocity of a system. Indeed, if the purpose is to provide a basis for the idea that different individuals age at different rates, this should be the type of concept we are after. One only has to assume that some other dynamics than that of relativity could produce a similar differential effect on at least some variables of the system.

It is to be noted that in this second reading, intrinsic time is an attribute of a system, and hence, there can be as many different intrinsic times as there are systems. But it has nothing to do with a choice of a scale. (Although one can, of course, choose some intrinsic time as a standard scale.) Indeed, in the Twin Paradox we only arrive at the definite result that the two sisters age differently because we apply the same scale (i.e., the same standard clock) to both of them. If one could say that one sister has aged 50 units in one scale and the other only one unit of a different scale, then we have no basis to compare them: it might be that the former units are weeks and the latter years.

Now in spite of these misgivings, it should be clear that the desire for a time scale that fits the study of aging is a perfectly natural and legitimate enterprise. We have seen before that in physics, the choice of a time scale is largely a conventional issue. It is picked out by the desire to make the laws of motion look simple. And just like physicists, gerontologists may also wish to design a scale in which gerodynamical laws (if there are such things) take their simplest form. Ideally, one would like to obtain a scale that reflects the fact that the human life at certain stages goes through rapid transformation and more or less tranquil periods at other stages. In other words, such a scale should be proportional to the transformational rate rather than chronological time.

In fact it is not hard to find such scales. The main problem for the prospect of using an intrinsic time scale is that there appear to be so many choices for such a scale. For example, Yates considers an intrinsic time determined by mortality rate. That is to say if t represents the ordinary chronological time scale and $f(t)\,dt$ represents the probability that an organism dies between t and $t+dt$, then

$$d\sigma = f(t)\,dt$$

defines a time scale σ in which the mortality rate is constant.

An advantage of this scale is that it is readily obtainable from demographic data. Moreover it has the appealing feature that it depicts humans as aging faster at those stages in which mortality is higher (i.e., during infancy and old age) and relatively slower in between. (It would, however, give less prominence to early adolescence, a stage that, although arguably the scene of important transformations, does not appear to be accompanied by high mortality.)

However, this choice of time scale also has disadvantages. Obviously, the mortality rate is, strictly speaking, a property of the population as a whole rather than of an individual. It is well known that the mortality rate is highly dependent on the social environment. A person living in an industrialized and peaceful society has a higher life expectancy than one who is born into a poor or combative society. Moreover, a society can itself witness transition from poverty to affluence, from peace to war or back again, in just a couple of years or decades. This means that, as a measure of intrinsic age, the mortality rate suffers from the same problem as measuring money by its nominal value: it may show considerable inflation or deflation within an average life span.

Another proposal for the definition of intrinsic time scale, discussed by Schroots and Birren, is the rate of metabolism. They refer to Hershey and Wang (1980), who report work on the metabolic rate, as calculated from respirational data on mammals, and were subsequently able to obtain a metabolic age for human subjects. This is a time scale whose increments are proportional to the metabolic rate. An advantage of this scale is that it is more explicitly internal and tied to the individual organism itself.

Both Yates and Schroots and Birren express the hope that a general connection between intrinsic time and thermodynamics can be obtained. This hope seems to be based on a paper by Richardson and Rosen (1979), which claims to derive an entropic metric for intrinsic time in a certain class of dissipative processes.

Their paper makes it clear that it is not concerned with the choice of a particular time scale, but with the second alternative mentioned above; namely, the introduction of a quantity determined by the state of the system, which can be used to calibrate its age. Unfortunately, I doubt very much whether this hope will come to fruition. When dealing with open systems, one has to give up the idea of intrinsic dynamics. The fate and evolution of an open system depends, not only on its own initial state and constitution, but also on its environment and its modes of interaction with its environment. The notion of intrinsic time is therefore anything but intrinsic to the system.

Although Richardson and Rosen claim that they have obtained an intrinsic time in a certain class of dissipative processes in terms of an entropy metric, their actual results are much more modest. The intrinsic times they consider can only be compared to systems of the same dynamical class (e.g., one may compare two candles with each other, and two harmonic oscillators to each other, but one cannot compare the intrinsic time of a candle with that of an oscillator). Given the fact that every human will in some sense undergo its own unique dynamics ("every old man is like no other old man"), this means one has no basis for comparing intrinsic ages of different individuals. This is enough to shatter any prospect of a general gerodynamical science. Secondly, their claim to have derived an entropic metric for the intrinsic time in certain dissipative processes is not substantiated. Indeed, the concept of entropy never occurs in their treatment of intrinsic time, and its metric; that is, its relation to ordinary time is always determined completely by the constitutive parameters of the system. Thirdly, their approach only works straightforwardly for a single variable. The generalization they offer (and characterize as "immediate") to treat more than one variable, which is in fact mathematically flawed.[2]

Yates (1988) goes even further in his claims about a physical underpinning of intrinsic time. He claims that "the origin of intrinsic time is quantized action" (p. 99). This last term is meant to refer to Bohr's postulate that certain action integrals of atomic orbits are only allowed to assume integer multiples of Planck's constant. This postulate forms part of a precursor of quantum mechanics, nowadays called "old quantum theory" or Bohr-Sommerfeld theory. He claims that the quantization of action assumed by Bohr's theory also applies to macroscopic processes such as metabolism, and leads to a natural time scale. He also claims that the discretization of action arises out of the general dynamics of complex systems.

This is an astonishing set of claims, and frankly, I believe not a single one of them is true. First, in physics Bohr's quantization of action has long been discarded in favor of the "new" quantum mechanics, created in 1925–1926 by Heisenberg, Born, Jordan, Dirac, and Schrödinger. Second, it is certainly not a consequence of general dynamics, nor does it involve complex systems.

[2] Technically speaking, they argue that in this case, several intrinsic times can be defined, one for each variable separately. They show that in the case of coupled linear transport equations, the substitution of these into the differential equations results in a sum that formally resembles the expression of a distance in terms of a metrical tensor. But the metric is given here by the coupling coefficients in the transport equations, not by entropy. Moreover, Richardson and Rosen do not address the question whether the various intrinsic times are mutually independent. Without an answer to this issue, the partial derivatives in terms of those that they use are not well defined.

Finally, quantization of action does not lead to a natural time scale; in the Bohr-Sommerfeld theory, it is used to obtain stationary states in which no change occurs.

CONCLUSIONS

Does theoretical physics have anything to contribute to gerontology? In the first part of this chapter, I have taken a short tour around some topics in the study of time that capture the interest of physicists and philosophers of physics. Generally speaking, one can say that there is little here that should arouse the attention of gerontology.

In the second part, I have looked at the work of some gerontologists who turn to physics for the development of a general theory of aging. Again, the main findings here are disappointing. The view of a human as a physical system is a valuable point of departure. Of course, this is not to deny that humans also have complex psychological and social relationships. In fact, many will argue that it is these relationships that define who we are as human beings. But notwithstanding that fact, a scientific account of humans as physical systems, rather than disembodied rational agents, is certainly needed to get a comprehensive account of aging.

There is also no doubt that the human organism is subject to the laws of thermodynamics and, in this respect, is not essentially different from other, less complex, open thermodynamic systems, such as microbes or combustion engines. However, we do not age in the same way as microbes or combustion engines or even other mammals. It seems unlikely to me that the vocabulary of nonequilibrium thermodynamics, or any other general physical theory, is rich enough to account for this distinction. Hence, a proper explanatory account of aging cannot be conducted in terms of general physical concepts; it must relate to some very special aspects of our physical and biological make-up, and presumably our psychology and social make-up as well.

So does physics have anything useful to teach gerontology? When I started writing this chapter, I was convinced the answer would be no. But now, looking back, I think there is maybe one lesson. In physics one can draw a sharp distinction between the choice of a time scale and the conception of age as a dynamical variable of the system. Perhaps this example may help gerontologists to draw a similar distinction in their study of human aging.

REFERENCES

Barbour, J. (1999), *The end of time.* London: Weidenfeld & Nicolson.

de Groot, S. R. (1951). *Thermodynamics of irreversible processes.* Amsterdam: North-Holland.

Earman, J. (1989). *World enough and space-time: Absolute versus relational theories of space and time.* Cambridge, MA: The MIT Press.

Eddington, A. (1929). *The nature of the physical world.* Cambridge: Cambridge University Press.

Grünbaum, A. (1967). The anisotropy of time. In T. Gold (Ed.), *The nature of time.* Ithaca: Cornell University Press.

Hilgevoord, J. (1996). The uncertainty principle for energy and time. *American Journal of Physics, 64,* 1451-1457.

Hershey, D., & Wang, H. H. (1980). *A new age scale for humans.* Toronto: Lexington Books.

Hoefer, C. (1998). Absolute vs. relational spacetime: For better or worse, the debate goes on. *British Journal for the Philosophy of Science, 49.*

Horwich , P. (1987). *Asymmetries in time.* Cambridge, MA: The MIT Press.

Kroes, P. A. (1985). *Time: Its structure and role in physical theories.* Dordrecht: Reidel.

Marder, L. (1971). *Time and the space-traveller.* London: Allen and Unwin.

Maxwell, J. C. (1995). Letter to the editor of the *Saturday Review,* April 7, 1868. In E. Garber, S. G. Brush, & C. W. F. Everitt (Eds.), *Maxwell on heat and statistical mechanics.* Bethlehem: Lehigh University Press.

Prigogine, I. (1955). *Introduction to thermodynamics of irreversible processes.* Springfield: C. C. Thomas.

Reichenbach, H. (1971). *The direction of time.* Berkeley: University of California Press.

Richardson, I. W., & Rosen, R. (1979). Aging and the metrics of time. *Journal of Theoretical Biology, 79,* 415-423.

Schroots, J. F., & Birren, J. E. (1988). The nature of time: Implications for research on aging. *Comprehensive Gerontology, C*(2), 1-29.

Sokal, A. (1996). Transgressing the boundaries: Toward a transformative hermeneutics of quantum gravity. *Social Text* 46/47, 217-252, 1996. See also http://physics.nyu.edu/faculty/sokal/.

Truesdell, C. A. (1980). *The tragicomical history of thermodynamics 1822-1854.* New York: Springer.

Uffink, J. (2001). Bluff your way in the second law of thermodynamics. *Studies in Philosophy and History of Modern Physics, 32,* 305-394.

Yates, F. E. (1988). The dynamics of aging and time: How physical action implies social action. In F. J. Birren & V. L. Bengtson (Eds.), *Emergent theories of aging* (pp. 90-117). New York: Springer.

CHAPTER 7

Biological Time as an Emergent Property

F. Eugene Yates

Terrestrial *biological time* flows from a past through a present toward a future and is irreversible. It is anisotropic and has a direction. Time anisotropy is a major, hoary problem for physics (Halliwell, Perez-Mercader, & Zurek, 1994), but living systems, through their development, adaptations, aging, and evolution, provide one of the strongest "arrows of time" of which we are aware. We biologists assume that we must model biological time by starting with Newton's absolute time, adding the familiar concepts of past, present, and future—a "flowing"—that the great theories of physics absolutely reject. But how would one measure the rate at which time flows? Relative to what?

Since 1905, physics has abandoned the Newtonian concept of absolute time. Modern physics is doing away with time entirely. As David Mermin (1990) has written:

> Clocks do not measure some preexisting thing called "time," but our concept of time is simply a convenient way to abstract the common behavior of all those objects we call "clocks." While such a distinction may sound like splitting hairs, it is remarkably liberating to realize that time itself does not exist except as an abstraction to free us from having always to talk about this clock or that. The discovery that there is no time—only clocks—has deep and surprising consequences . . . (p. 111).

However, we biologists smile knowingly while watching physicists inevitably grow old and die, killed by nonrelativistic time, cherishing the thought that they might actually be growing younger!

Having a preferred direction, biological time is definitely not that of general relativity, of relativistic quantum field theory, of quantum mechanics, or of supersymmetric quantum string theory, even though strictly, these theories are not time invariant. The problem is that, in practice, they all perform as if they actually are time invariant with respect to positions of particles on forward or backward paths. One might say they are "partially" time reversible (Albert, 2000). The emerging (so far unconventional) physics of multiple string theories extend the dimensionality of space-time beyond the four expressed in an Einsteinian manifold, to as many as 10 + 1 (the ten being "space" and the extra being "time," but only vaguely). If some version of string theory ever emerges as dominant, it may eliminate space and time entirely, at which point it will be either the long sought for "theory of everything," or an empty, useless physical theory of nothing. Here I adopt an ultraconservative position that accepts the well-known, classical, and clarifying views of Karl Popper and Patrick Suppes; namely, a useful physical theory is a text that after formalization can be specified by ancillary statements so that a predictive or descriptive *model on theory* results. This model is then compared to a *model of data* generated from empirical observations and measurements. The comparison is accomplished by a set-theoretic entity. If the models are concordant (e.g., technically isomorphic), the theory survives for further testing; if not, the observations must be improved, and the theory modified or abandoned. It is not yet clear that any version of string theory will meet those tests.

Even by looking at a small sample of the voluminous literature on the nature of time, it becomes clear that physical time has not been a neglected subject by either the technical or the lay press. We can agree with Uffink (this volume, p. 138) that: "Time is a central notion in physics . . . (but) in fact, I think it is fair to admit that physics simply does not have the wherewithal to specify the meaning of time, or to define time in terms of more fundamental, non-temporal notions." He might have added that, as many of the above references show, physics is now busily doing away with time entirely.

In contrast, irreversible biological time correlates and sequences macroscopic events and processes. It is that time dimension in which we irreversibly grow old and die. Those events and processes are chemical, electrochemical, and chemomechanical. (So-called psychological time, as a variant of consciousness, though subjectively different from biological time, nevertheless has an electrochemical basis.) Of course some biological processes, being chemical, may involve reversible, microscopic, quantum-mechanical resonant bond-energy exchanges. The anisotropy of biological time arises at a higher, macroscopic level.

Fundamental physical theories deal effectively only with simple systems; they can't do glasses (spin glasses are about as far as they can go, and even that is not a strong accomplishment), nor the commonplace flow of particles through funnels, as in a grain silo. Nor does physics know what to do about complexity, diversity, or reproducing systems that store their deep historical past as a highly conserved code—all features of living systems. (Witness the struggles reported by the Santa Fe Institute for the Study of Complex, Adaptive Systems.) All electrons in the universe are alike (though their behaviors may vary in different settings), whereas no two living organisms are exactly alike. The diversity of the physical universe is of some interest (there are classes of galaxies), but it is not comparable to the diversity of living systems, which is truly astonishing.

Now, if physics, or at least the physicist, has no competence to illuminate biological time, we biologists have to do the job ourselves. Uffink seems to not approve of one of my earlier attempts to do the job. Unfortunately, he mistakenly claims that "when dealing with an open system one has to give up the notion of intrinsic dynamics!" This is an astonishing remark, suggesting that he is not sufficiently acquainted with the extensive literature on biological "clocks" establishing beyond any doubt that, for example, the circadian (about 24h) rhythm, ubiquitous if not universal among all living systems, persists in spite of complete *experimental isolation of the living system from all environmental time cues* that it could potentially sense. Of course, in these studies, organisms are not actually isolated from their environments; as thermodynamic open systems, they depend on interactions with an environment. The point is that in these demonstrations, the environment itself provides no time cues, so all dynamics (motion and change) within the organisms so constrained by a time-clamped environment reflect the intrinsic dynamics of the organisms themselves. They express a strong internal dynamic that is intrinsic to the living state of matter. The rhythms sometimes damp out in time-isolated organisms, but often do not. Many of the endogenous rhythms are easily entrained to geophysical time cues (especially light/dark cycles), but that fact does not diminish their inherent intrinsic genesis. But the situation is more profound than that: all self-organizing systems that persist, animate or inanimate, are self-scaling in both time and space.

Consider your own size and metabolism—the sum total of all your internal transfers and transformations of matter and energy. Human beings are scaled at an energy expenditure rate of about 2000 to 3500 kcal/day. For short periods you can increase the throughput (Tour de France cyclists hit about 6000 kcal/day for a limited time—three weeks) and decrease it by fasting. Like all other living systems, you are temporally organized by a set of near-periodic processes with periods ranging, for example, from milliseconds (electroencephalogram), seconds (heartbeat, breathing), minutes (pulsatile endocrine signals), hours (basic rest-activity cycle of 90–120 minutes), one day (the circadian rhythm mentioned above), months (the menstrual cycle), and, for seasonal breeders, to the year. The spectrum is only sparsely filled with broad peaks. Most of these cycles continue in constant environments. They are all endogenous signs of our intrinsic dynamics arising out of nonlinear modes. They are the dynamic signs of life.

Because it is abundantly clear that conventional physicists cannot do the job of illuminating biological time, we biologists need a fresh approach. We must find a "fix" for the physics if we are to hold to our conviction that biological entities are ultimately physical through and through. The alternative is recidivism—a retreat to some naïve version of vitalism, entelechy, *élan vital,* or what have you. I believe that the physics can be fixed by modest extensions, and the path toward doing so uses fluid mechanics (e.g., Navier-Stokes) and the thermodynamics of irreversible processes and open systems as guides. Physicists A. S. Iberall and H. Soodak, founders of the physical science *homeokinetics,* have been showing the way for over twenty-five years (see References), and I have brought together many of the salient concepts, and added some of my own, as *homeodynamics* (Yates, 1994). Below I shall just give some of the elements, showing where standard physics fails, and suggest remedies.

SOME LIMITATIONS OF CONVENTIONAL PHYSICS: COMPARISONS TO BIOLOGY

As preamble, I list some of the issues that have to be acknowledged before any progress can be made. They include the following points:

1. Physical theory addresses simple systems; life is complex.

2. Particles in physics have very little internal structure or dynamics with any significance at mesoscopic or macroscopic scales. Some particles have both static and dynamic properties (e.g., rest mass and spin), and some particles are not fundamental, but have internal structures (e.g., quarks). Some have no mass or associated time (e.g., photons), while others are unstable and reveal themselves to an observer through a characteristic time—a "half-life" of existence. However, usually in our modeling of terrestrial-scale events, physical particles behave as billiard balls having dead interiors, making all their mechanical exchanges with their environments in a Newtonian fashion, via external momentum exchanges.

3. In contrast, living systems all have very active interiors, with delayed internal equipartitioning of energy or matter when either crosses their boundary with the environment. That property is captured in the concept of internal bulk (associational) viscosity (λ) as seen in the Navier-Stokes equations of motion. The external momentum exchanges are captured in the shear (or kinematic) viscosity term (υ). Both viscosity terms are creative of dissipative processes that produce entropy in a nonconservative field in which the Second Law of Thermodynamics is operating. Instead, the fundamental physical theories favor conservative fields, with only the First Law of Thermodynamics operating.

4. Living systems carry their histories with them, even across generations, as a highly conserved genetic code, and in most multicellular, individual animals, also as a neural-based memory, established dynamically and then stored structurally. In contrast, the simpler, semireversible "memories" of hysteretic loops, elastomeres, and some other inanimate objects, including computers, are not complex.

5. Living systems are very obviously goal directed. (This feature is not merely an anthropomorphic projection on our part.) In contrast, physical systems are predominantly ahistorical—just responding to the fields in which they are embedded (though they can affect the fields locally). Strictly, in the fundamental theories of nonchaotic dynamical systems, a complete history of the world's dynamical conditions would imply one complete and unique history of its states, and even, in the vision of Laplace, a unique future. But that history isn't

recoverable from any present state; initial conditions of chaotic systems cannot be retrodicted, and any physical process that passes through an equilibrium loses all its history. In contrast, we biologists routinely retrodict biological origins from studies of DNA and RNA, even looking back 3.9 billion years.

HOMEODYNAMICS: A PHYSICS FOR COMPLEXITY

To get beyond these limitations of standard physics, I believe that the following views should be considered as a preliminary:

1. The concept of a particle must be extended to allow for very active interiors.
2. Dynamics (motion and change) in open, dissipative systems are best characterized through physical action (energy × time).
3. Self-organizing systems that persist are all thermodynamically open.
4. At terrestrial scales, internal actions in open systems that are stable enough to persist for times that are long compared to the relaxation times of their interior interactions must be cyclic, so that initial conditions are recovered periodically.
5. Each near-periodic cycle is nonlinear, dissipative, limit-cycle-like, with a characteristic period.
6. The limit cycles have the effect of quantizing actions at mesoscopic and macroscopic scales. (Planck's constant quantizes action at the microscopic level.)
7. The dimensionless ratio λ/υ (bulk/shear viscosities) expresses and scales the ratio of internal action/external action ($E_i\tau_i/E_e\tau_e$), where E is energy (per cycle), τ is a cycle period, and the subscripts i and e refer to internal and external regions, respectively.
8. Reynolds number (R_e) must be expanded to reflect not just the traditional ratio of inertial to viscous "forces," but also the ratio of convection/diffusion as velocities that distribute matter and energy. At conditions of low R_e values, a perturbation will be handled mainly by diffusions, and system integrity will be maintained. At high values, diffusive processes (which are too slow) will fail to equipartition the energy or materials before the system is severely altered by convective processes that then sop up the energy. The system will then have to adopt a new form or break up.
9. A complex system has an intermediate value of λ/υ between that of an ideal gas (very low value) and a rigid solid (high value). In fluid systems, such intermediate values support highly nonlinear behaviors.
10. Homeodynamics relaxes the traditional view that thermodynamics is a statistical science applying only to macroscopic systems consisting of an enormous number of particles. It recognizes that all three transport modes of fluid mechanics (diffusion, convection, and wave propagation) are realizable in a fluid system of only about 100 particles. (Although all living systems are treated as being physically macroscopic, some of them are so small that they contain only a few of each species of the macromolecules essential for their metabolism.)

In brief, the proposal is that some of the familiar pieces of standard physics can be slightly modified to achieve approximations suitable for a physical biology, out of which biological time emerges. (For a general discussion of phenomena of emergence, see Morowitz, 2002.) The emergence follows from the fact that at all levels of dynamics, action is nature's most basic, quantized variable. In complex adaptive systems, action is (approximately) a conserved variable as well—a summational invariant. *Homeodynamic processes do not occur in time—they make their time.*

At this point it should be clear that I reject Barbour's timeless, static models of the universe (Barbour, 2000) and embrace instead his youthful starting point, as expressed in the Preface (p. 2) to his engaging book ". . . time is nothing but change. . . . Physics must be recast on a new foundation in which change is the measure of time, not time the measure of change." (However, I would add that the change must be cyclic.) His struggle to accommodate the Wheeler-DeWitt equation as the fundamental equation of a static universe need not concern us biologists. Contrary to Einstein, we biologists believe that our lives progress in time to a certain concrete, timeless, nonillusive, and irreversible death state (except for our bodily decay completing the "ashes-to-ashes, dust-to-dust" trajectory, which is still dynamic). Indeed, we biologists seek and find chemical agents (i.e., some genes and proteins) that profoundly affect how long fruit flies, or the nematodes *Caenorhabditis elegans,* mice, and probably we, actually live (see Baker et al., 2004 for a recent, dramatic example). These genes and their products, acting as controlling influences or chemical constraints, partially determine life span—a fundamental biological, dynamic unit of time for all multicellular organisms that stop growing in adulthood. However, even genetically identical living systems exposed to similar environments do not all die on the same day. In fact, the dispersion of the data on their life spans almost equals that of the wild types (Finch & Kirkwood, 2000).

As physics abandons time to our illusions, it disqualifies itself as a basis for a hoped-for strategic physical biology, and so guarantees its continuing incompleteness, revealing that even at its best, physics is nongeneric. If it stays its current course, it will never achieve the "theory of everything!" *The only truly generic science is—biology* (Rosen, 1991, 2000).

REFERENCES

Albert, D. Z. (2000). *Time and chance.* Cambridge, MA: Harvard University Press.

Baker, D. J. et al. (2004). BubR1 insufficiency causes early onset of aging-associated phenotypes and infertility in mice. *Nature Genetics, 36,* 744-749.

Barbour, J. (2000). *The end of time.* New York: Oxford University Press.

Finch, C. E., & Kirkwood, T. B. L. (2000). *Chance, development, and aging.* New York: Oxford University Press.

Halliwell, J. J., Perez-Mercader, J., & Zurek,W. H. (1994). *Physical origins of TIME asymmetry*. Cambridge: Cambridge University Press.

Mermin, N. D. (1990). *Boojums all the way through: Communicating science in a prosaic age*. New York: Cambridge University Press.

Morowitz, H. J. (2002). *The emergence of everything: How the world became complex*. New York: Oxford University Press.

Rosen, R. (1991). *Life itself: A comprehensive inquiry into the nature, origin, and fabrication of life*. New York: Columbia University Press.

Rosen, R. (2000, posthumous). *Essays on life itself*. New York: Columbia University Press.

Yates, F. E. (1994). Order and complexity in dynamical systems: Homeodynamics as a generalized mechanics for biology. *Math and Computer Modelling 19*, 49-74.

Additional References of Literature on the Nature of Time Not Cited in Text

Cole, K. C. (2001). *The hole in the universe*. New York: Harcourt.

Colonna, S. (Ed.). (1997). *What is time*? Proc. VI International Conference Milano: Fondazione Carlo Erba.

Covenet, P., & Highfield, R. (1990). *The arrow of time*. New York: Fawcett Columbine.

Davies, P. (1995). *About time*. New York: Simon & Schuster.

Flood, R., & Lockwood, M. (1986). *The nature of time*. New York: Basil Blackwell.

Gibbon, J., & Allan, L. (Eds.). (1984). *Timing and time perception* (Vol. 423). New York: New York Academy of Sciences.

Gould, S. J. (1987). *Time's arrow time's cycle*. Cambridge MA: Harvard University Press.

Hawking, S. (1988). *A brief history of time*. New York: Bantam.

Landes, D. S. (1983). *Revolution in time*. Cambridge, MA: Harvard University Press.

Macey, S. L. (Ed.). (1994). *Encyclopedia of time*. New York: Garland.

Morris, R. (1984). *Time's arrows*. New York: Simon & Schuster.

Prigogine, I. (1996). *The end of certainty*. New York: The Free Press.

Reichenbach, H. (1927, in German; English trans. 1957). *The philosophy of space and time*. New York: Dover. *Scientific American Special Issue: A Matter of TIME*. Sept. 2002.

Veneziano, G. (2004, May). The myth of the beginning of TIME. *Scientific American*, pp. 54-65.

Additional References on Homeodynamics Not Cited in Text

Yates, F. E. (1979). Physical biology: A basis for modeling living systems. *Journal of Cybernetic Information Science, 2*, 57-70.

Yates, F. E. (1982). Outline of a physical theory of physiological systems. *Canadian Journal of Physiology and Pharmacology, 60*, 217-248.

Yates, F. E. (1992). Fractal applications in biology: Scaling time in biochemical networks. In L. Brand & M. Johnson (Eds.), *Numerical Computer Methods (Methods in Enzymology*, Vol. 210, pp. 636-675). New York: Academic Press.

Yates, F. E. (1993). Self-organizing systems. In C. A. R. Boyd & D. Noble (Eds.), *The logic of life* (pp. 189-218). London: Oxford University Press.

Yates, F. E. (1996). Homeostasis. In J. Birren (Ed.), *Encyclopedia of gerontology* (Vol. 1, pp. 679-686). New York: Academic Press.

Yates, F. E., & Benton, L. A. (1995). Biological senescence: Loss of integration and resilience. *Canadian Journal of Aging, 14,* 106-130.

Yates, F. E., & Iberall, A. S. (1973). Temporal and hierarchical organization in biosystems. In J. Urquhart & F. E. Yates (Eds.), *Temporal aspects of therapeutics* (pp. 17-34). New York: Plenum.

Yates, F. E., Marsh, D. J., & Iberall, A. S. (1972). Integration of the whole organism: A foundation for a theoretical biology. In J. A. Behnke (Ed.), *Challenging biological problems: Directions towards their solution* (AIBS 25-Year Celebration Vol., pp. 110-132). New York: Oxford University Press.

Additional References on Homeokinetics Not Cited in Text

Iberall, A. S., & Soodak, H. (1987). A physics for complex systems. In F. E. Yates (Ed.), *Self-organizing. systems: The emergence of order* (pp. 499-519). New York: Plenum Press.

Iberall, A., & Soodak, H. (1978). Physical basis for complex systems—Some propositions relating levels of organization. *Collective Phenomenon, 3*, 9-24.

Iberall, A. S., Soodak, H., & Hassler, F. (1978). A field and circuit thermodynamics for integrative physiology. II. Power and communicational spectroscopy in biology. *American Journal of Physiology, 234,* R3-R19.

Soodak, H., & Iberall, A. (1978). Homeokinetics: A physical science for complex systems. *Science, 201,* 579-582.

Iberall, A. S. (1977). A field and circuit thermodynamics for integrative physiology. I. Introduction to the general notions. *American Journal of Physiology, 233,* R171-R180.

CHAPTER 8

Whence an Emergence of Biological Time?

Jos Uffink

In Chapter 6 I have discussed the role that modern theoretical physics might play in our understanding of those aspects of time and aging that are prominent in gerontology. My main purpose was, frankly, didactical. I pointed out that many discussions of these issues suffer from confusion by using the same words to denote different concepts. My overall conclusion was that the help of theoretical physics in the problems of gerontology can only be very limited. I also took the opportunity to criticize some authors who argue that the theoretical framework of gerontology should be grounded in the laws of physics. In particular, I have criticized Yates (1988) for his fanciful interpretation of the Second Law of Thermodynamics, his claim that a notion of "intrinsic time" would follow from Bohr's quantum postulate, and the curious inconsistency between his self-professed aim to develop a general, physics-based biology and the admission that his approach is anthropocentric and thus applicable to human beings only.

Now Yates has responded to my essay in the foregoing chapter. His response does not touch upon any of my critical comments mentioned above, so my present rejoinder will mostly consist of some general observations about his response. I will postpone a discussion of the single point on which Yates does criticize my previous chapter to Section 5.

FROM PHYSICS TO BIOLOGY?

The theme of Yates' reply is the "emergence of biological time." It is clear that the main topics characteristic of Yates' conception of biological time are its flow, its direction, and its alleged irreversibility. Note that the concept of aging (or the more specialized concept of senescence) is not mentioned here, nor are they addressed elsewhere in his chapter. Neither is the distinction between intrinsic and extrinsic time, which appeared to be such a crucial ingredient in his previous work. Accordingly, I will not return to my criticism on these issues either. The central topic of Yates' reply is the question whether and how biological time might emerge from physics. This question, of course, is intimately connected with the wider problem of the relationship between biology and physics in general. In fact, it is this general problem that occupies the main part of his chapter.

The most striking point in the chapter is that it involves a complete withdrawal of the view Yates espoused previously on this relation. His earlier chapter advocated a thoroughly reductionist view of the relation between physics and biology, as can be seen from the following quotations:

> Life obeys all the known laws of physics. No new fundamental postulates are needed to explain the dynamics of life (Yates, 1988, p. 106).

and

> To me the issue is: Can we strengthen biology through epistemological reductions to physics? I see no chance for expunging intellectually pernicious or vapid vitalism, entelechy, *élan vital,* and "Just So" stories from biology unless we strive for that reduction, at least in principle (Yates, 1988, p. 94).

Yates' present manuscript, however, advocates a diametrically opposed view. It argues that physics is just incompetent to deal with complex systems, such as living beings, and claims

> Because it is abundantly clear that conventional physicists cannot do the job of illuminating biological time, we biologists need a fresh approach (Yates, this volume, p. 163).

Moreover,

> as physics abandons time to our illusions, it disqualifies itself as a basis for a hoped-for strategic physical biology . . . revealing that even at its best, physics is nongeneric. . . . *The only truly generic science is biology*! (Yates, this volume, p. 166).

Clearly, Yates has given up all of his previous hope for a reduction of biology to (conventional) physics. Instead, he now argues that physics should be extended by various new postulates in order to explain the dynamics of life. One naturally wonders what may have caused such a radical change of mind. Could my previous chapter have convinced Yates to revise his previous views? If so, I would of course welcome this as a silent compliment. But, in fact, I doubt that my chapter deserves such credit. The reason is that I never criticized Yates for his previous reductionist outlook. Indeed, I am more sympathetic to his previous views on the relation between physics and biology than to those adopted in his present chapter.

Let me explain this in more detail by stating my own view of this relation (for which I obviously do not claim any originality). I fully agree with Yates' previous view that living beings are physical systems, and that physics needs no extension, in the form of new fundamental postulates or otherwise, to describe life. That is to say, I adhere to reductionism on the ontological level.

However I am skeptical about reductionism on the epistemological level. I do not expect that biological concepts and theories will be derived from the laws of physics by means of mere correlative definitions or bridge principles and the application of certain special conditions. In short I do not believe that a "theory reduction" is feasible. My skepticism on this point is based on two considerations. First of all, the ideal of a successful theory reduction has proved to be very hard to come by. Even those cases that were previously thought to be paradigmatic successes of theory reduction (such as the relation between thermodynamics and statistical mechanics) turn out to be much more obstreperous upon closer analysis. In fact, there seems to be hardly any example of successful theory reduction within physical science. But then, since epistemological reduction is already so difficult to attain, even for theories such as thermodynamics and statistical mechanics, which are relatively close to each other in their conceptual apparatus, it seems implausible that it will be obtained between more distant sciences like physics and chemistry, let alone physics and biology. A second point is that theory reduction presupposes that both theories involved are formulated in terms of a formal calculus or in terms of set-theoretical predicates. It is, however, obvious that biology as yet does not adhere to this format.

Now, it may seem that the above point of view on the relation between physics and biology (ontological reduction yes; epistemological reduction no) is somewhat disappointing. Surely, one might argue, if one admits that living organisms are physical systems, one ought to expect some kind of intertheoretical relationship between their descriptions in physics and in biology. A flat rejection of epistemological reduction might easily seem like a denial of such a relationship. My response would be that the requirement of some intertheoretical relationship is indeed natural, but that it need not take the special form of theory reduction, or, for that matter, the form of "emergence." My own expectation is that some form of the notion of "supervenience," which is currently receiving much attention in the philosophy of science literature, is most likely to account for this relationship (cf. Kim, 1984). But it would take us too far afield here to argue for this in detail.

To end this section, allow me to make one final comment on Yates' claim that, in contrast to physics, biology is the only truly generic theory. I think this remark is inconsiderate. With all due respect for the immense progress that biology has achieved in the last century and a half, it seems fair to say that we have no clue whether even the most celebrated results of biology (e.g., the theory of evolution or the determination of the genetic code) have any validity outside of planet Earth. For all we know, biology depends essentially on highly contingent and very special conditions of our local cosmic environment. To claim that biology is generic and physics is not is to mock the meaning of the word.

THE "FAILURES" OF CONVENTIONAL PHYSICS

Having explained my own views on the relation between physics and biology, I now return to a discussion of Yates' chapter. He claims that conventional physics suffers from limitations, which ought to be acknowledged before any progress can be made. He lists a total of five such flaws, but for brevity, I will comment on only two of them.

His first point is that physics is unable to deal with complex systems. It is somewhat hard to discuss the merits of such a claim without a definition of the term "complex systems." What does one mean by a complex system? Is it one with a huge number of degrees of freedom? Is it a system whose dynamics are complicated and unstable? Must it be an open system? Is it far from equilibrium in the thermodynamic sense? Is it necessary that it should have an active interior, displaying periodic or almost periodic cyclic processes or processes that are nearly cyclic? There are passages in Yates' chapter that suggest he regards each of these criteria as essential, but no clear-cut definition is provided that would help to sharpen the discussion on this issue.

Nevertheless, it is not too difficult to rebut the claim. Whatever criterion used to define a complex system, it seems to me that the sun qualifies on all counts. It consists of a huge number of particles; it is far from in thermodynamic equilibrium with its environment; it is open (emitting radiation into empty space) and possesses a very active interior, producing solar protuberances on a scale of hundreds of thousands of kilometers, and a stable internal cycle of sunspot activity of about 11 years. But is physics incompetent to describe the sun? Visit the section of any university library devoted to solar physics and one will be convinced of the absurdity of such a claim.

A second claim laid down by Yates is that

> Living systems carry their histories with them. . . . In contrast, physical systems are predominantly ahistorical—just responding to the fields in which they are embedded . . . (Yates, this volume p. 164).

This view of physical systems is plainly false. Obvious counterexamples are the phenomena of magnetic hysteresis, and the "form memory" displayed by certain metals, or the hard disc of any personal computer. My impression is that Yates confuses the general idea of a physical system with that of an elementary particle, and mistakenly assumes that physics is only interested in the latter.

Now it is true, of course, that our physical understanding of complex systems in general, and of living organisms in particular, still leaves much to be desired. Most of our theories concerning macroscopic systems are still semiphenomenological and do not depart from "first principles." But that is no surprise. In general, the study of complex systems is also complicated, and it is quite natural that progress on this topic is slow and involves a lot of hard work. The fact that our understanding of macroscopic and complex systems within conventional physics is still incomplete is, in my opinion, no indication that physics is flawed or in need of repair.

A FIX FOR THE "FAILURES" OF PHYSICS

However, Yates' conclusion is a different one. He argues that the flaws mentioned in the previous section need to be "fixed" in order to obtain a new, extended physics, for which he has coined the name of "homeodynamics." This new theory is allegedly capable of dealing with complexity and the emergence of biological time. Of course I welcome every effort to improve or extend physics and wish this new theory every bit of success. But the stakes in this game are high: every proposal of a new theory will be judged by comparing its success with that of its predecessors and competitors, in particular the conventional physics that Yates wishes to leave behind.

Thus, we have the right to ask how homeodynamics competes with conventional physics. In particular, one might ask whether homeodynamics meets the standards of Yates' own "ultraconservative position" (Yates, this volume p. 162), which requires any useful physical theory to be formalizable in set-theoretical terms and to specify predictive theoretical models that can be tested against empirical data. Unfortunately, no such formalization of homeodynamics is offered. Indeed, from the list of 10 assumptions provided by Yates, I cannot make out much of the content of his new theory. His description is no more than a set of slogans.

Be that as it may, it is apparent that Yates has high expectations of the role of fluid mechanics in his new theory, and of the Navier-Stokes equation in particular. This strikes me as odd, because fluid mechanics and the Navier-Stokes equation have been part and parcel of conventional physics for more than a century and a half. Yates' proposal to "extend" physics by incorporating this equation is thus, at best, a little late.

What is more, the conception of time employed in fluid mechanics is really the same as in Newtonian theory. Since Yates considers the latter to be incompatible with biological time, one wonders how biological time is going to emerge in homeodynamics. What Yates offers in support of this claim is surprisingly little. It consists merely of the exclamation that "Homeodynamical processes do not occur in time—they *make* their time" (Yates, this volume, p. 166). There is, however, no argument whatsoever about how this metaphysical claim would follow from the listed elements of homeodynamics. Nor does Yates explain how the kind of "time," allegedly generated by homeodynamical processes would lead to "biological time"; that is, how it obtains direction, flow, and irreversibility. Finally, if one really believes that such processes do not occur in time, one faces the onus of explaining what the variable t, figuring so prominently in the Navier-Stokes equation, refers to.

INTRINSIC DYNAMICS VERSUS INTERNAL GENES

Let me finally also comment on the one occasion where Yates addresses a point I raised in my previous chapter, and that is my claim that the dynamics of an open system are anything but intrinsic to that system. To me this is just a point of simple logic: an open system is one that can interact with its environment. Dynamics is the common name for the equations that determine the evolution of a system. For an open system, these equations will have to refer to parameters of the particular state of its environment. Consequently, these equations are not intrinsic to the system. However, Yates thinks that my remark is astonishing and reveals "that he [i.e., me] is not sufficiently acquainted with the extensive literature on biological clocks" (this volume, p. 163).

He quotes the example that in many organisms the circadian rhythm persists even when the system is isolated from all environmental time clues. This example is beside the point. To say that a system is isolated from time cues does not mean that it is isolated in a physical sense. It would be more relevant if the circadian rhythm could be shown to persist in organisms deprived of food and oxygen. And although genes are internal to the organism, they remain material bodies, whereas dynamics are a set of equations. They belong to different categories. Even if internal genes explain the behavior of biological clocks, the dynamical equations describing this behavior will still depend on the characteristics of the environment of the organism. To state that dynamics itself are internal, as Yates does, is as strange to me as it would be to say that the law of gravity is internal to a falling stone.

FINAL REMARKS

I agree with Professor Yates that differences between our perspectives remain, and that it would overstretch the patience of readers to continue discussion.

So let me just sum up. Yates' present position is that standard physics fails because it does not provide adequate models for human life. He believes that physics needs radical revision and extension, and he offers the theory of homeodynamics to fulfil this need. I have argued that in order to be considered as an alternative candidate to standard physics, homeodynamics would have to be judged by the same criteria of exactness and empirical content. There is no way in which Yates' theory passes such a test. As it stands, homeodynamics is little more than an incoherent collection of slogans.

Yates complains that I have nothing to offer in comparison. But I actually did present my own views on the subject. In my opinion, the standard body of physical theories is working just fine. Of course, there are relatively unexplored fields, even in classical physics, and new insights are still being developed every day. That just shows how rich the conceptual structure of physical theory is, and that the enterprise is in healthy shape. There is no need for a radical departure from ordinary physics in order to achieve compatibility with biology.

Instead, we need a more sophisticated view of intertheoretical relations. If one hopes to find a complete and strict reduction of biology or social science to physics or, as Yates calls it, an "analytical derivation" of models of human life from the fundamental principles of physics, one is bound to be disappointed. The idea of theory reduction is not going to work; there is no way a useful or interesting description of human life can be derived analytically from physics. Attempts at analytical derivation have already failed in other cases where the intertheoretical relationships are much simpler, such as between the theories of thermodynamics and statistical mechanics or between chemistry and physics. It would be naïve to expect that such attempts will succeed in the case of biology and physics.

But we need not go in this direction. It seems to be more fruitful to analyze the relationship between biology and physics in the form of "supervenience" relations. Quite roughly, one says that X is supervenient on Y, just in case there can be no change in X without a change in Y. Thus, taking X to be any biological or social condition of a human being and Y a complete physical description of the state of his or her body and its environment, supervenience of biology from physics implies that any change of biological conditions corresponds to a change in the physical state. This view thus allows for the underlying idea that, ontologically, a human being (or any living organism), is really just a particular kind of physical system. At the same time, it allows for autonomy in theoretical description. Supervenience of biology or social science from physics does not pretend that the most meaningful notions in human life, notions like happiness, pain, love, senescence, aging, etc., can even be defined in the vocabulary of fundamental physics.

To be sure, much more work would be necessary to analyze the supervenience relation in detail. Nevertheless, it seems to me that this approach holds more promise than Yates' desperate attempt to discard physics for the flimsy framework of homeodynamics.

REFERENCES

Kim, J. (1984). Concepts of supervenience. *Philosophical and Phenomenological Research, 65,* 153-176.

Yates, F. E. (1988). The dynamics of aging and time: How physical action implies social action. In F. J. Birren & V. L. Bengtson (Eds.), *Emergent theories of aging* (pp. 90-117). New York: Springer.

CHAPTER 9

Further Conjectures on the Nature of Time in Living Systems: Causes of Senescence

F. Eugene Yates

BIOLOGICAL DYNAMICS

Life is a fourth major state of matter (after gases, liquids, and solids, and their intermediates of plasmas, glasses, and viruses). In 1944 Schrödinger asked, Does an understanding of its dynamics require any new physical laws? None have been found. However, the laws of standard, terrestrial-scaled mechanics are deterministic, time symmetric, and conservative (i.e., still Newton-dominated); whereas life, conspicuously and universally, is not state determined, not time symmetric, and not thermodynamically conservative. (Informationally, there are evolutionary, so-called conservations of some genes and their products, but that is a different meaning of the term.)

I believe that a mature dynamic description of living systems will ultimately require recognition of a nonlinear, non-Lipschitz, terminal dynamics (Zak, Zbilut, & Meyers, 1997); an emphasis on physical action rather than momentum; an emphasis on bulk (associational) viscosity as well as shear; an emphasis on broken symmetries rather than symmetries; an emphasis on nonholonomic constraints rather than holonomic; and continuing recognition of the creative, in addition to the more familiar destructive, contributions of the Second Law of Thermodynamics, appreciating what Prigogine has tried to do (1980, 1996), without necessarily accepting his Dissipative Structure Theory as a foundation of life (see Anderson & Stein, 1987).

Distinguished physicists are making pleas for a physics of intermediate scales (Anderson, 1972; Laughlin, Pines, Schmalian, Stojkovic, & Wolynes, 2000). Laughlin et al. calls for "a middle way." As I proposed in Chapter 7 of this volume, a modest extension of standard physics, ***homeodynamics***, may suffice as a useful heuristic for the new descriptions. Chaotic dynamics as illustrated, for example, by Glass and Mackey (1988), Bak (1996), and Lorenz (1993) are not predominantly involved, but fractals (Mandelbrot, 1983) definitely are (Yates, 1992).

Living organisms are nonlinear, complex adaptive systems, autonomous in the sense that their dynamics are self-organized, while they show goal-directed behavior with respect to external conditions. They are full of broken symmetries and operate internally in anisotropic, irreversible time that they self-generate and self-scale. Their dynamic signatures appear largely as near-periodic fluctuations, arising in part out of competing influences (e.g., symmetry vs. broken symmetry, diffusion vs. convection, energy vs. entropy, anabolism vs. catabolism).

The essence of homeodynamics is a scheme of functional organization for physical action, consisting of a marginally stable hierarchy (vertical organization) and heterarchy (side-to-side organization). This functional organization consists of many loosely coupled oscillators. Each oscillator expresses a thermodynamic-process cycle obeying both the First and Second laws, each having its own (average) period (τ). There is variability (wobble) in the periods, so successive cycles are not precisely of the same duration, and each cycle is independently generated, unlike the case for idealized, harmonic oscillators that "ring" indefinitely after starting once from their initial conditions. Homeodynamic action cycles are nonlinear, limit-cycle-like, and dissipative. Such a constellation of highly entailed and constrained cyclic processes generates near-periodicity and the $1/f^m$ background noise seen in spectral analysis of the behavior of many physiological and behavioral variables. Chaos may be seen occasionally, but more commonly, trajectories that start from close-by initial conditions stay close, contrary to the requirements of the chaotic regime. The limit cycles have asymptotic orbital stability and resist perturbations (except for phase). Stochastic fluctuations, both internal and external, further shape behaviors.

Of course a complete dynamical description of living systems must acknowledge environmental contributions; after all, that's why we have the science of ecology. *The important point is to make the essential distinction between an immediate stimulus/response of a simple system and the time-generating potential latent in delayed equipartitioning of energy within complex systems having active interiors and intermediate values of the dimensionless ratio λ/υ*. This ratio of bulk/shear viscosities is also the ratio of internal/external actions (see Chapter 7).

COMPLEXITY

One kind of complexity of a dynamic system, and its resilience, are convex-upward, parabolic functions of the λ/υ ratio mentioned above. Any entropic accumulation in the factors determining the λ associational parameter (that represents, among many other things, bonds and communications across hierarchical levels) will powerfully affect stability in their neighborhoods. At the extremes, if most system transactions are external (λ very small), the system is Newtonian and simple, and dominated by momentum exchanges (the game of billiards is an example). There is no possibility for the emergence of complexity of form or function, though the Newtonian trajectories can be complicated. Alternatively, if most of the energetic activity is internal (υ very small compared to λ), there is little or no possibility for different parts or regions to interact, and again complexity is lost. The optimal and maximum richness of form and function lies in between.

BIOLOGICAL TIME

What do I mean by "biological" time? It is the *coordination* by a living system of its internal actions (in which biological membranes play a dominant role). That coordination is both side-to-side in the heterarchical network organization of organisms and also up-down through their hierarchies; it is both serial and parallel. The coordination leads to a conspicuous appearance of temporal organization when observations of the system are referred to an external, macroscopic physical clock (see Careri, 1984). That external clock neither creates nor influences the internal temporal organization that results from intrinsic dynamics.

BIOLOGICAL TIME AS A HELIX: A METAPHOR FOR AGING

I offer here a new picture of internal biological time, conceptualizing it as a helix with a tapered ellipsoid boundary enveloping lifetime action (energy x time). Time as an arrow and time as a cycle are familiar metaphors, but incomplete. The helix of homeodynamic common time (Figure 1) is generated by an orthogonal intersection between action temporal cycles, especially the intrinsic (approximately 24h, circadian) daily metabolic and behavioral rhythms ubiquitous among living things and the physically imposed thermodynamic Second-Law-process arrow that is forcing the daily circadian cycles into the future via its "flowing," anisotropic time (see Chapter 7 for mention of contrary views of nonflowing physical time). But the Second Law has another internal effect that surreptitiously degrades the amount of Gibbs free energy that can be extracted from metabolic networks as time goes by. The result is a lifetime energy budget, even for those of us in the best of health, having the form of a truncated ellipsoid, as conceptualized in Figure 1, whose volume is the lifetime action.

Biological time (for a human being) is sketched as a daily cycle of metabolic action. The cross-sectional area seen as a circle at the left end of the object is the daily amount of processed energy. That daily, cyclic energy budget is being pressed into the future by the orthogonal flow of anisotropic, absolute physical time so that each daily cycle can't recover its initial condition and close exactly, thus creating a helix from the succession of cycles. A separate senescence process diminishes the action obtainable metabolically each successive day, so the circular areas get smaller, until too little obtainable daily action is left: the organism becomes fragile, and a previously tolerable fluctuation can now kill it.

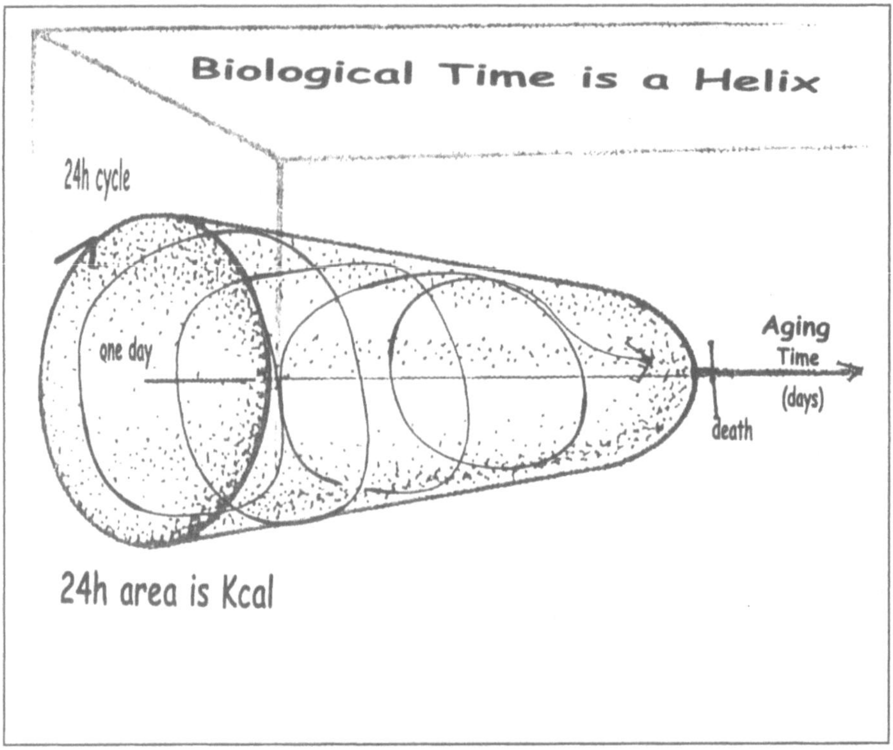

Figure 1. Homeodynamic time.

SENESCENCE: WHY DO WE GROW OLD AND DIE?

As far as we know, all multicellular living systems that reach a fixed size after a period of growth eventually grow old and die, even in the absence of accidents or adverse circumstances. At their beginnings, self-organizing homeodynamic systems create new forms and functions out of transformations of energy internally, as long as there are degrees of freedom available for major constructions. Construction requires that degrees of freedom be available for creation of new parts. While that condition is met, the net effect of energetic transactions can be internally negentropic. At maturity, those degrees of freedom will have been frozen out by the very structures made, and all further (scaled) energy transformations must then follow a scenario in which an accumulation of internal entropy is inevitable, even in open systems. Energy throughput can now erode constraints and weaken couplings and connections (represented by the λ parameter discussed above and in Chapter 7).

It will be readily appreciated that energetic/entropic attacks on λ/υ will profoundly affect the fate of a complex system: some regions or elements may appear to simplify or become more regular, while others become more randomized. At that point, the entropic accumulation begins to displace a living system from its normal optimal operating point of "orderly disorder" (neither structurally crystalline nor amorphous; neither functionally regular nor random) toward some increases in local order as insoluble aggregates precipitate out, and toward some increased regularity of function as processes become isolated from active inputs. But the main effect is breakdown of controls, so behaviors lose coherence. Overall, the system moves away from its optimal operating point in its high-dimensional-phase space, becomes fragile, and the risk of failure increases. This is the central, most general, homeodynamic cause of senescence and it is a generic property of self-organizing systems.

HOW FAST DO WE AGE?

We human beings, of course, would like to know how fast our senescence progresses, even among the healthiest. In answer, Sehl and Yates reported two relevant findings: (1) the calculation of quasi-linear loss rates for human structural and functional variables, based on a substantially larger data set than has been previously studied (2001), and, with S. Pincus, (2) the establishment of an argument from first principles demonstrating how the nonlinearity of death rate curves can arise from the apparent linearity seen in mean decay rates for a wide variety of systems (2004, manuscript in review).

Data were collected for healthy, nonsmoking human subjects of both sexes from a literature search of cross-sectional, longitudinal, and cross-sequential studies. The number of studies analyzed was 445, and the total number of subjects 54,274. Linear loss rates as a percentage decline from reference value at age 30 were calculated for variables from 13 organ systems and for integrative variables such as maximum oxygen consumption and exercise performance. The frequency distribution of linear loss rates (as percentage loss per year) for a very healthy *population* is approximately a partial or skewed Gaussian, with mean 0.65, median 0.5, and variance 0.32. The loss rates were clustered between 0 and 2% per year for variables from most organ systems, with exceptions being the endocrine, thermoregulatory, and gastrointestinal systems, for which wider ranges (up to ~3% per year) of loss rates were found.

The *ab initio* calculation of the probability of death showed a nonlinear increase in the probability of death with age for an *individual*. That increase was steeper for those with a large standard deviation among their set of linear loss rates (Sehl, Pincus, & Yates, 2004).

In summary, taken together these observational and theoretical studies showed formally (as might have been guessed informally) *that healthy, successful aging is dynamically both slow and uniform.*

REFERENCES

Anderson, P. W. (1972). More is different. *Science, 177,* 393-396.

Anderson, P. W., & Stein, D. L. (1987). Broken symmetry, emergent properties, dissipative structures, life: Are they related? In F. E. Yates (Ed.), *Self-organizing systems: The emergence of order* (pp. 445-457). New York: Plenum.

Bak, P. (1996). *How nature works.* New York: Springer-Verlag.

Careri, G. (1984). *Order and disorder in matter.* Menlo Park, CA.: Benjamin.

Glass, L., & Mackey, M. C. (1988). *From clocks to chaos: The rhythms of life.* Princeton: Princeton University Press.

Laughlin, R. B., Pines, D., Schmalian, J., Stojkovic, B. P., & Wolynes, P. (2000). The middle way. *PNAS (USA), 97,* 32-37.

Lorenz, E. (1993). *The essence of chaos.* Seattle: University of Washington Press.

Mandelbrot, B. (1983). *The fractal geometry of nature.* New York: Freeman.

Prigogine, I. (1980). *From being to becoming.* San Francisco: W. H. Freeman & Co.

Prigogine, I. (1996). *The end of certainty.* New York: The Free Press.

Schrödinger, E. (1944). *What is life?* Cambridge: Cambridge University Press.

Sehl, M. E., & Yates, F. E. (2001). Kinetics of human aging: I. Rates of senescence between ages thirty and seventy years in healthy people. *Journal of Gerontology and Biological Science, 56B,* 191-197.

Sehl, M. E., Pincus, S. M., & Yates, F. E. (2004). Kinetics of human aging II. A model of linear losses predicting a nonlinear, increasing risk of mortality. (Under review).

Yates, F. E. (1992). Fractal applications in biology: Scaling time in biochemical networks. In L. Brand & M. Johnson (Eds.), *Methods in enzymology* (pp. 636-675). New York: Academic Press.

Zak, M., Zbilut, J. P., & Meyers, R. E. (1997). *From instability to intelligence. Complexity and predictability in nonlinear dynamics.* New York: Springer.

ADDENDUM

In his essays in this volume, Jos Uffink challenges some of my ideas, and I shall respond briefly to a few of these. A more extensive reply would demand a level of attention from the readers of this book much greater than I think they may wish to invest. The differences between Uffink's perpectives and mine are irreconcilable, and I do not intend to try to resolve them. Uffink did not offer any new ideas on the subject of a physical approach to biology and aging, whereas I have put forth a novel and fresh heuristic to help us understand the striking peculiarities of the dynamics of living organisms, compared with those of any inanimate physical systems. In so doing, I fully expect readers to have one of three responses to my efforts: (1) to ignore them, (2) to let them stretch your mind, or (3) to feel abused because they have scrambled your brains.

In the text of my two chapters, I have already very explicitly expressed my views on the nature of biological time, emergent properties, and intrinsic dynamics, so I'll not repeat them here. I have chosen three themes from Uffink's complaints for consideration here; my comments will touch on Newton, Navier-Stokes, and hysteresis as memory.

NEWTON AS STARTING POINT

Newton is still an essential starting point for dynamical analysis of macroscopic systems at terrestrial scales. He invented his scheme by imagining, first, a featureless three-dimensional, absolute space into which he placed a particle with no property other than inertial mass and invoked a flowing time. He recognized that the particle's state required independent specification of two values: position and momentum. Next, he permitted the environment of the particle to interact with it, and if the momentum changed via velocity change (i.e., an acceleration occurred), he defined the influence of the environment as a force, in his second law equation of motion. (His inertial mass is passive, just responding to forces. In contrast, his gravitational masses are in a sense active—in multiples they generate force. Even after Einstein's Principle of Equivalence and geometric description of gravity, there is a residual mystery.) Later, of course, mechanics was generalized by Hamiltonians and Lagrangians, but these still require a fully reversible time, even when frictional terms are involved; that is, only the First Law of Thermodynamics is operating. Furthermore, models of the physical world in which differentials are exact, or at least meet the Lipschitz condition that guarantees the uniqueness of solutions subject to prescribed sets of initial conditions, is very nongeneric (Rosen, 1991; Zak, Zbilut, & Meyers, 1997), and fails to help us biologists in the face of nonholonomic constraints and inexactness typically encountered in our simulations. So, dynamical analysis of living systems must start with Newton and stay on the road with him until a branch point is reached at which he becomes a poor guide; but much can be learned about biological complexity from that fact.

Modern science and engineering are still in the thrall of the state-determined causality of motion and change at the heart of the Newtonian dynamics. Its initial successes with regard to planetary motions were stunning. But, are living systems really so state-determined in their causalities? They are not. States do not imply their rates, and at every level of organization states and rates have to be newly and separately specified, partly because of emergent properties. Furthermore, in biology, *information* is causal in a very special manner (Pattee, 1968, 1977, 1987, 2001; Rosen, 1991).

HYSTERESIS

How about hysteresis as a model of memory, as Uffink offers? I think "memory" is a rather poor (though conventional) metaphor for hysteresis, which, in the case of circuits with inductances, arises because of lags. I think a more modern view of hysteresis loops would involve topological manifolds, velocity vectorfields, and cusp catastrophes, such as described for physiologists by Abraham (1983) and by Garfinkel (1983). The concept of memory need not enter in. As for computer memory chips, we have an object with physical expressions interpretable (by us) as 0 or 1, at numerous locations. Again, to call that "memory" is metaphorical. Except for the real switching dynamics (that designers do everything possible to keep hidden), computers running programs can express absolutely arbitrary dynamics. If you want a negative mass or frequency, you can have it (abstractly). Living systems do not enjoy that freedom from physical reality. Their memories go back perhaps 3.9 billion years or more and support (nearly) invariant reproduction, autonomous morphogenesis, and teleonomic behaviors (Monod, 1971; Monod & Jacob, 1961), a triad utterly absent from standard physics.

NAVIER-STOKES (NS) EQUATIONS

Just as spin glasses seem to appeal to some physicists looking at complex self-organizing systems and critical phenomena, so I choose the NS equations as a foundation for extending standard mechanics to encompass more of biology. One must start *somewhere*! Uffink points out that these equations have been "part and parcel" of conventional physics for more than a century and a half and scoffs at my invoking them now. Yes, they are old, but they are still rich in unexplored possibilities! To suggest that they are now fully illuminated is misleading. Their nonlinear, partial differential character makes them, if not intractable, then at least extremely difficult to solve exactly. I'd like to see Uffink's account of turbulence, if he has one, or of G. I. Taylor vortices, or Bénard cells (see Koschmieder, 1993). In my opinion, the NS equations are the richest equations of motion in all of physics. It is sobering that even with them, in spite of strenuous theoretical work, we fail to come up with a model sufficiently comprehensive to capture all the observed features of fluid behaviors, even in a simple apparatus with only one chemical component!

CONCLUDING THOUGHT

Relying on standard physics (Newtonian mechanics, special or general relativity, quantum theory, quantum field theory or chromodynamics, string, M or loop quantum gravity theories), we are not going to achieve a comprehensive, detailed physical model of the regular trajectory of a human life from conception through development and maturation to senescent decline and death. (The revealed truths of "standard" physics up until 1969 are in Landau and Lifshitz). Nor will we ever be able to derive analytically a phenotype from a genotype.[1] If there is to be a strategic physical biology for complex systems (as opposed to tactical biophysics that does indeed work well), a new extension of standard physics will be required. *Homeodynamics* is offered for consideration here. However, it may be that biology cannot ever be profoundly "physicalized," in

[1] The difficulty can be seen in the new book by Kirschner, M. W., & Gerhart, J. C. (2005). *The plausibility of life. Resolving Darwin's dilemma.* New Haven: Yale University Press.

which case we have two separate universes within the range of our observations. Monism or dualism? Your choice.

REFERENCES

Abraham, R. H. (1983). Dynamical models for physiology. *American Journal of Physiology, 245,* R467-472.

Garfinkel, A. (1983). A mathematics for physiology. *American Journal of Physiology, 245,* R455-R466.

Koschmieder, E. L. (1993). *Bénard cells and Taylor vortices.* Cambridge: Cambridge University Press.

Landau, L., & Lifshitz, E. (1958-1969). *A course in theoretical physics* (9 vols.). Reading, MA: Addison-Wesley.

Monod, J. (1971). *Chance and necessity.* New York: A. A. Knopf.

Monod, J., & Jacob, F. (1961). General conclusions: Teleonomic mechanisms in cellular metabolism, growth, and differentiation. *Cold Spring Harbor Symposium on Quantum Biology, 26,* 389-401.

Pattee, H. H. (1968). The physical basis of coding and reliability in biological evolution. In C. H. Waddington (Ed.), *Towards a theoretical biology* (Vol. 1, pp. 69-93). Edinburgh: Edinburgh University Press.

Pattee, H. H. (1977). Dynamic and linguistic modes of complex systems. *International Journal of General Systems, 3,* 259-266.

Pattee, H. H. (1987). Instabilities and information in biological self-organization. In F. E. Yates (Ed.), *Self-organizing systems: The emergence of order* (pp. 325-338). New York: Plenum.

Pattee, H. H. (2001). The physics of symbols: Bridging the epistemic cut. *BioSystems, 60,* 5-21.

Rosen, R. (1991). *Life itself: A comprehensive inquiry into the nature, origin, and fabrication of life.* New York: Columbia University Press.

Zak, M., Zbilut, J. R., & Meyers, R. E. (1997). *From instability to intelligence. Complexity and predictability in nonlinear dynamics.* New York: Springer.

CHAPTER 10

The Integration Problem: Toward Multilevel Explanations

Henk Visser

> Man does not grow old at the same rate all over. His vital organs, his glands, his bones and muscles, his senses and his psychological abilities age at different rates. (Boring, Langfeld, & Weld, 1948, p. 86).

Gerontology, the scientific study of aging, is a multidisciplinary study which is characterized by all sorts of temporal phenomena, each of which is attendant to any one of the disciplines involved. These phenomena may have different characteristics as well as rates of change, but may also be somehow linked, and this might not be the first concern of scientists working within a certain discipline. Yet it is clear that it would be very desirable from a theoretical as well as metatheoretical point of view if the various results could be brought together and integrated. The practical importance of integration is also obvious: when aging is accompanied by, or even consists of a loss of a variety of possibilities, a one-dimensional fixation is not very helpful. In this chapter, I will discuss this *desideratum* from the point of view of a philosopher of science: dealing with the obstacles for solutions of the "integration problem" and presenting conceptual means that may further multi- and interdisciplinary gerontological research.

OBVIOUS OBSTACLES

Old age doesn't come alone.

As in all proverbs, there is a grain of truth in the saying that old age doesn't come alone. But the distance from scientific truths is evident. Scientifically speaking, it is not enough to say that getting older is accompanied by mental, physical, and emotional changes, for better or for worse; and it is required that the different changes are described as precisely as possible, explained, and linked together. The latter requirement is the most difficult, because it requires so-called multilevel explanations with the help of laws that explain the occurrence of changes on more than one "level"; that is, laws, which traditionally belong to different (sub)disciplines, about successive processes. Perhaps it is helpful to elucidate the subject with a simple illustration. It is borrowed from the philosophy of science in which multilevel explanations are dealt with on a metalevel (cf. Darden & Tabery 2005).

The philosopher Bunge once gave a clear example, starting with the following question: "Why does thirst increase upon drinking sea water?" The obvious answer to this question is "Because by drinking sea water part of it goes into the blood so that the larger concentration of salt produces osmosis whereby the blood becomes more watery and the body's protoplasm dries up. As a result, the hypothalamus is excited and the "psychological partner" of this neural condition is the thirst sensation" (Bunge, 1967, p. 21f).

The different levels are the physical, the biological, and the psychological. Since the different explanations in terms of "thirst," "hypothalamus excitation," "cell hydration," "water diffusion," and "osmotic pressure" are linked by laws, we may call it an *interlevel explanation* (Bunge, 1967, p. 241). The fact that these concepts belong to a certain level of description and can be lawfully or regularly linked to concepts of another level is expressed by calling these concepts "systematically significant." This does not exclude systematically significant concepts being found within the reach of a single discipline. Such is the case for higher order explanations (e.g., the molecular theory of heat).

Unfortunately, the temporal concepts of the multidisciplinary science of gerontology are too often not systematically significant. We can distinguish physical aging, biological aging, physiological aging, psychological aging, and cognitive aging, but precisely how are these processes related?

There are obvious obstacles to the *desideratum* of finding systematically significant temporal concepts that enable us to *integrate* the results of different levels and so partially solve the integration problem. I will mention three of them.

In the first place, there are additional levels involved in the description, explanation, and prediction of phenomena of aging. There are also the sociological and the historical levels, each with its own terminology. This makes the problem of integrating the different results even more difficult. It seems that each level has its own problems, and yet these problems do not stand alone. It is easy to take for granted that foreknowledge of the legal date of your retirement may influence your behavior, which in its turn may alter your physical condition. How does one explicate the causal notions in such cases?

In the second place, the explanations would require so-called process laws or, at least, process models in which reference is made to temporal sequences of states of a system, including past states, which enable us to predict properties of future states, under the assumption that the system is relatively closed. However, the human body consists of various interfering systems and their developments are described with different time intervals, ranging from very small (in physics) to very large (in evolutionary theory). (This may sometimes be overcome by the distinction of *phases*. The overlapping phases of postmenopausal or senescent bone loss in women after menopause shows that it may be difficult to establish correlations between different levels solely on the basis of phases.)

In the third place, there are differences between the disciplines themselves. The concepts of the natural sciences are data oriented, whereas the data have been gathered in controlled observations and well-designed experiments. Against that, many, if not most concepts of the social sciences have their origin in common-sense notions, and it is doubtful whether the former are sufficiently dissociated from the latter in the present state of the art. The fact that gerontology is a relatively young field of research—Stanley Hall's *Senescence* appeared in 1922—is by no means foreign to this situation.

The third obstacle can be serious if it prevents social scientists to come closer to natural scientists. In that case, the difficulty of linking the different levels remains because of intrinsic qualities of one or more of them, notably of a methodological nature. In psychology, the method of operationalization is the dominant approach, whereas the data-oriented method is almost entirely restricted to mathematical psychology. The following example from the psychology of aging may elucidate the difference.

Stanley Hall once said that "there is a certain maturity of judgment about men, things, causes and life generally, that nothing in the world but years can bring, a real wisdom that only age can teach" (Stanley Hall, 1922, p. 366). Some recent studies are indeed concerned with the problem whether wisdom comes with age. How is this problem to be scientifically tackled?

In the operationalization approach, there are two steps to be taken: first, the concept of wisdom is operationalized; and second, tests are designed and carried out. The outcomes of the tests, in this case certain correlations between scores and age periods, should prove the fruitfulness of the approach. However, the first step may lead, and has in practice led, to different and admittedly vague definitions, whereas the question of the validity and reliability of the corresponding tests is still open, notably when these are artificial (cf. Brugman, 2000). Moreover, if the notion of age is conceived as calendar age only, and the investigations remain isolated from other, natural scientific results, then they do not even reach an explanatory level. What do we learn from a conclusion that age is (or is not) a factor of (whatever feature you want)? Can such results be adduced to support Schroots and Yates' claim that "psychological processes of change do not necessarily parallel biological changes along the life span" (Schroots & Yates, 1999, p. 417). Should we not base such a conclusion differently on a comparison of these processes themselves? But this presupposes systematically significant concepts instead of the mere notion of calendar age.

As I remarked before, the operationalization approach is the standard method in psychology for gaining more insight into the phenomena, while the data-oriented approach is closer to the procedures of the natural sciences. Here one does not start from existing common-sense concepts, but proceeds the other way around. Scientific concepts are derived from the outcomes of experiments instead of being borrowed from common-sense notions. Consider again the problem of the alleged wisdom of older people. We don't know how to make this notion precise. We have the impression that older people are better at solving certain complex problems than youngsters. Suppose that in a well-designed experiment persons of different ages are asked to solve some of these problems and that statistically significant differences are found between properties of the solutions given by persons of different age groups. This may give rise to the forming of a *new* and *significant* concept, depending on whether tests result in new data. Dittmann-Kohli's sentence completion method (SELE) presents a promising example of this approach. It enabled her to derive *new* concepts of subjective time, such as "limited continuation" and "preservation" (Dittmann-Kohli, this volume).

Of course this does not mean that *systematically* significant concepts will be found in this way. Again, chronological age does not by itself determine a scientific level (Baars, this volume). Moreover, the approach is not without difficulties. How do we acquire relevant experiments when *artificial* tests such as the notorious IQ tests are to be excluded? The complex problems should be derived from experience. This requires that the scientific researcher has acquired specific professional intuitions about the achievements of persons of different ages.

In this book, the integration problem of finding systematically significant concepts is preeminently about *temporal* concepts that occur at different levels; that is, the concepts that are used by scientists from different scientific gerontological subdisciplines in order to describe and explain the phenomena of aging. This means that we are not concerned with temporal concepts as used by persons of different ages *unless* such data lead to scientific concepts. This is not wholly unrealistic, as van der Meer claims for her notions of "past- and future-oriented." Similarly, Schaie's proposal for "event time analyses" may offer related concepts (Schaie, this volume).

LINKING OF LEVELS

The spiritual eyesight improves as the physical eyesight declines.

Plato's idea that human beings are inclined to think more deeply about things when their visual faculty is declining is perhaps the first attempt to link the physical level with the psychical level. In his time there was hardly anything that merited being called scientific research, let alone concerning physical and psychical "mechanisms." Plato was not troubled by the above-mentioned obstacles, which block bringing together findings from different areas in gerontology. Things are different in (interdisciplinary) scientific research. Is there a way out?

We should restrict the scope of this problem. Yet even if only time-related concepts and conclusions are considered, the approach would still be too broad. It would probably include philosophical notions that ask for further explication, such as certain conceptions of self or person. Admittedly, time is traditionally an ingredient of these ideas. That these notions are ignored is based on the argument that there is no reason to assume that the corresponding conclusions in their present state (without scientific studies) can at all be linked with scientific findings. Of course, outside philosophy, notions such as "ego identity" may be scientifically significant (cf. Erikson, 1959).

Linkage of results at different levels can still be a question of speculation, as we learn from Dittmann-Kohli's overview in her section on time perception as a biological given. There is nothing wrong with this, since speculations may lead to new explorations. Therefore we take suggestions on this point seriously; for example, when Dittmann-Kohli concludes that her results, based on narrative self-reports, "are pointing strongly to the view that there are developmental, ontogenetic changes over the adult life span" (Dittmann-Kohli, this volume). A difficulty is, of course, that we do not know which ontogenetic changes correlate with the found changes in certain attitudes toward past and future, assuming that the latter results are not biased (cf. Schaie, 1988). Fortunately, van der Meer mentions some results that indicate in which directions suitable answers may be sought. She reports several results concerning past-oriented and future-oriented attitudes, although she also notices discrepancies: age groups that are past oriented according to one result may be future oriented according to another (van der Meer, this volume). Apparently the notion of future oriented is too general and must be restricted as to what is or is not expected in the future. For example, econometric findings about the relation between (calendar) age and income satisfaction have shown no statistically significant differences between the patterns of age-related changes in the temporal orientation of working people in different Western European countries. It appears that persons younger that 40 and those older than 60 are more past oriented in a well-defined sense, whereas middle-aged persons are more future oriented (cf. Van Praag & Ferrer-i-Carbonell, 2004). The suggestion of a linkage with regularities on the sociological level is ready at hand.

The scientist may also be urged to distinguish between distant and not-so-distant future (Dittmann-Kohli, this volume). But this makes the challenge of looking for correlations with cognitive aging even bigger. Van der Meer (this volume) may be right when she holds that "there is empirical evidence pertaining to the description of losses, gains, and maintenance in the underlying cognitive abilities with aging," but it seems obvious that restricted concepts referring to "planning abilities" and "prospective memory" are needed. She rightly remarks that Park's four hypotheses about "the basic mechanisms accounting for age-related decline in cognitive function" require further research, optimistically including research that is meant "to link the behavioral constructs to their underlying neural substrates." Park is talking about mechanisms, but he has not outlined the temporal sequences of steps. Compare this with what is known of such phenomena as the type of cell death called apoptosis.

There are more serious difficulties with this program. Future orientedness in a restricted sense, attributed to someone who is anticipating intended activities after retirement—this example is credited to Dittmann-Kohli (this volume)—does not seem to be systematically significant for finding an interesting correlation with the higher order psychological level on which the development of the "contents of the working memory" is described. (It is again easier to point out that there is a relationship with the sociological level.)

Connecting the psychological level with the neurological level seems promising in the case of decrease in short-term memory at a later age. There is a parallel with the "thirst upon drinking sea water" example, because of the established effects of marijuana and nicotine on short-term memory. That short-term memory performance can be measured is beyond doubt, just as activities in different parts of the brain can be diagnosed by Positron Emission Tomography (PET scans) (cf. Reuter-Lorenz, 2000). Moreover, it is claimed that hormone replacement therapy (HRT) has proved to be effective with a group of post menopausal women, aged between 50 and 80, when compared on memory tests with those without HRT (Burkhard et al., 2004). Accordingly, optimists believe that the problem of integrating results at different levels will in the long run be solved. However, the results mentioned do not directly take into account developmental *processes*, and this means that the second of the above obstacles is still present.

AGING PROCESSES

> In old age there is a coming into flower. My body wanes; my mind waxes.

The time that authors distinguished as overall different "life phases," say *pueritia*, *iuventus*, *virilitas*, and *senectus*, lies long behind us. But also classifications of periods of life with respect to one aspect are too rough to bring us further. Therefore, the study of aging *processes* seems more appropriate for partially solving the problem. These processes can be described in several ways, metaphorically, as the quotation from Victor Hugo shows, but the obvious scientific way is the use of explicit temporal notions, although different levels of investigation may employ different temporal concepts. It makes sense to direct the attention to such different concepts. Schroots and Birren's distinction between physical time, biological time, psychological time, social time, and intrinsic time, quoted by Schaie, may serve as a first approximation (Schroots, 1996). It suggests that a scientific discipline may have special temporal concepts for dealing with changes, though it is not excluded that it also uses temporal concepts from another discipline. In fact, physical time and its direction is presupposed by all other disciplines than physics, whereas the direction of time in physics is based on the *entropy principle*, holding that natural changes occur in the direction of increasing total entropy.

The results of physical time measurements are also taken for granted in other disciplines, although certain properties of time intervals such as equality of length may not be relevant for their own purposes. According to Schroots, the fact that there is no physical difference between, say the period of the first 30 years of a human being and the second 30 years, "makes sense only from a purely clock or calendar time perspective" (Schroots, 1996, p. 584). The fact that the second period comes after the first makes sense from a thermodynamical point of view, but the biological processes that occur in the subsequent periods are another matter. Thermodynamics deals with increases of entropy of the *universe*, whereas biology examines the natural processes in which new molecules are formed in the *human body*. There is no conflict: when there is a specific increasing order within living systems, this takes place at the expense of increased disorder in the universe as a whole (Strehler, 1967, p. 661; cf. Sacher, 1967; and also Atkins, 1986).

Moreover, living systems as well have a propensity to increased disorder. However, there is as yet no integral theory of biological aging processes, let alone a unifying theory in which purely physical and biological processes are attuned to each other. Yates' attempt to extend or modify physical theory in order to incorporate biology is audacious, but the proposals remain pure hypotheses as long as the (postulated) process of "self-organization" of "dissipative structures" is a mere heuristic description and remains unexplained (Yates, this volume). In other words, this top-down approach to the problem of integrating physical and biological results is at best still in an initial stage. Even Bunge's paradigmatic example of the multilevel explanation of the empirical generalization that thirst increases upon drinking sea water shows that there is no unified theory that comprises the different levels.

Nevertheless, some of Yates' empirical findings deserve a closer look. He reports that for most organ systems, loss rates for variables are clustered between 0 and 2% per year, and this seems a good starting point for attacking the integration problem (cf. Sehl & Yates, 2001). It resembles the famous Gompertz law, or better, curve, stating that for most human populations, except for advanced ages, the probability of death increases in a logarithmic fashion as age increases linearly (Strehler, 1967, p. 663). However, the various attempts to explain this law already show that there are still separate levels, and the same seems to hold for Yates' "law." But there is still another lesson from the Gompertz case. The exception clearly shows that a notion of oldest-old mortality is significant. Can this be made *systematically* significant as well? (cf. Gavrilov & Gavrilova, 1991). It is clearly not sufficient to define oldest-old in terms of calendar age. What does it mean if one confines it to older than 85, or 90, or any age? Neuropsychological examinations and autopsies of people who live past a 100 reveal that many brains were "basically healthy looking" with "a nice size, normal weight, and little or no evidence of atrophy" (Ferguson, 1998). So it is reasonable to believe in the significance of a notion of biological age in one or another sense. However, there are different measures of the processes that contribute to aging, and none of them can be regarded as *the* determining factor for biological aging. It follows that biological aging is a multidimensional concept based on specific dynamical concepts—concepts referring to processes—such as "cumulative DNA damage," "progressive shortening of telomeres," and "telomeric overhang loss" on the genetic molecular level, and several other concepts on the cellular, the systemic (i.e., tissue and organ levels, the organismal, and even the social level). This does not mean that we should strive at a unifying, let alone a one-level theory, for there is not even such a theory for the "thirst upon drinking seawater" example. Here the laws of one level are linked to the laws on another level in order to get a multilevel and not a reductive explanation (cf. Bunge, 1967, pp. 22, 42).

TOWARD A THEORETICAL FRAMEWORK

Gray, my friend, is every theory, and green alone life 's golden tree.

It is remarkable that Goethe once used age-related notions in order to articulate his skepsis toward theory. In fact, theory formation is reserved for a "mature" phase of scientific research, and a scientific discipline can certainly be regarded as "grown up" when it has a unifying theory at its disposal. The belief in the correctness of such a theory may be strengthened by discoveries that measurements within different disciplines lead to similar calculated values of a theoretical quantity. Avogadro's number is, of course, the most famous historical example. Determination of the number of molecules in one gram molecule with seven different methods resulted in similar values, varying from $5.91*10^{23}$ to $6.22*10^{23}$. As a consequence, scientists were convinced that this close agreement of values from remote fields evidenced the correctness of molecular ideas (Dorn, 1915, p. 248). Can we expect similar successes in the study of biological aging? Putting it in this way is asking for a *theoretical* framework for the ordering and interpretation of the relevant facts of senescence. However, we are dealing with biology and not with physics. Sir John Kendrew (1962 Nobel Prize Winner for Chemistry) once drew attention to a conspicuous difference: "The techniques of physics and chemistry are intended to extricate simple principles from complex phenomena, in biology the complexity is itself an intrinsic condition and characteristic of phenomenon" (Kendrew, 1977, p. 206).

It is not quite clear in how far biological complexity differs from physical complexity, but it is clear that the different "layers" of biological systems—molecular, cellular, systemic, organismal, and social—do not operate independently of one another. If we add the environment, then we understand the difficulty of finding explanations of different aging processes. Hence Yates' call for nonlinear dynamical methods and the like. Yet the existence of different dynamical concepts belonging to different levels shows that the existence of disorders can be demonstrated at particular levels. Moreover, partial developments of biological processes may be significantly described. In fact, this is what one can and should do after the example of physics since, say, Galileo, who substituted piecemeal, detailed, and verifiable results for large untested generalities (cf. Russell, 1914, p. 4). Of course, a higher order theory comprising both physical and biological phenomena would give a solution to many problems, but it should be inferred from lower order theories, as was done by Newton. Do we already have such theories about physical and about biological aging processes?

Besides, the complexity of a biological system is not a constant, it may evolve in time. This would suggest that a promising theoretical framework for the study of biological aging may be sought in the notion "loss of biological complexity" (Lipsitz & Goldberger, 1992, p. 1806f), as if there were no problems with the concept itself. A comparison with the unsatisfactory situation of the different notions of wisdom is forced upon us.

However, if we take a closer look at losses of function in senescing organisms, varying from modifications in the network of cellular defense mechanism to sensory losses, we may infer that their options, that is, *possibilities*, are changing. *Decrease* of biological possibilities, or better, a more neutral, but temporal notion of *change* of biological possibilities over time seems therefore a better candidate, retaining the main ideas of the proponents of complexity. Moreover it can be generalized to other levels. Admittedly we then get umbrella concepts that comprise restricted notions on all different levels. Consider (on the genetic molecular level) those measurable changes in the expression patterns of genes, for example in the liver, that limit the possibilities of the organism for its functioning. Similarly, the shortening of telomeres and the diminution of replication possibilities of chromosomes can be regarded as a reduction of possibilities. On the neurological level, the loss of neurons may further a decline in functional and cognitive possibilities, notwithstanding the fact that the *system* of neural connections does not operate by itself. Neuroscientists distinguish systems and subsystems, even though they exhibit interactions.

How the interaction between subsystems can complicate things is shown by the example of the two neurotransmitter systems: the serotonin system and the dopamine system. Degeneration of the former system seems to *correspond* to the increasing occurrence of depressions, whereas the degeneration of the latter *correlates* with the decrease of memory functions. But the process of degeneration of the serotonin system may be followed by a degeneration of the dopamine system, *after a certain increase in its activity*.

Notice that here different levels are brought together, the psychological and the neurological. But how are the changes in the psychological functions measured? Is the concept of depression itself precise enough for a quantitive approach? Can its dispositional derivative—depressive—be reworded in terms of possibilities? Does the operationalization approach guarantee this? Or should we pin our faith on the data-oriented method? In the latter case, we try to derive systematically significant quantative concepts from data collected in observations of persons during the time intervals that their neurotransmitter systems are degenerating. It appears from all this that the general integration problem is far from being solved; so let us have a look at a particular example in which a temporal concept is involved.

Consider the temporal concept of "speed of information processing," as developed by Salthouse, who contends that practically all intellectual abilities are subjected to an age-related slowing of processing speed (Salthouse, 1996). Longitudinal studies have indeed shown that a decline of processing speed is age-related, at least in such tasks as a Number-Connecting test, a Digit Symbol-Substitution subtest, a Picture-Completion, a Block-Design, and a Spatial-Ability subtest, although these studies also show that speed is just one factor among others (Zimprich & Martin, 2002). Yet it trivially follows that a diminution of someone's processing speed delimits his possibilities to perform certain tasks in a prescribed time interval, just as a diminution of someone's skating velocity in a given time period limits his possibilities to win the 500-meter race at the Olympic games. So there is reason to assume that such possibilities can be graphically modelled and quantified.

So far, so good. But the significance, let alone the systematic significance of this concept is not as great as it looks. I deliberately mentioned the tests that were used, because none of them contains *complex* tasks. Things are different with problem solving in games such as chess (cf. Ericsson & Charness, 1997), where the results of earlier (mental) operations may be forgotten during the search process (cf. van der Meer, this volume); but test subjects still succeed in solving the problems in a short time, because they have retained other possibilities, such as their perceptual skills, and compensate their loss of short-term memory skills with chess expertise based on long-term memory (De Groot & Gobet, 1996, p. 214). Another interesting phenomenon is the familiar fact that certain abilities, such as the correct application of fairly complicated rules, not only of chess and other games, but also of algebra, spelling, and musical performance, may remain intact during one's whole further life, except in case of later dementia. It is also long known that the required "complex psychological functions, such as imagination, reasoning, judgment, and critical powers, [may] remain on the maximum level nearly to the end of the individual's life" (Miles, 1933, quoted by Allport, 1954, p. 396).

Suppose, however, that we are able to establish (1) that human beings with a demonstrable loss of neurons in the cerebral part most strongly activated in the above-mentioned simple test situations have a considerable slower "information-processing velocity" than persons without such losses, and (2) that test subjects of the complex tasks, who do not fall short in this respect, show an increased activity in another part of the brain. (This is not wholly implausible, given similar results with focused attention tasks [cf. Jäncke, Specht, Shah, & Hugdahl,

2003].) In that case, systematic significance is promising, although at least three important difficulties have still to be overcome at the present time.

First of all, the number of test persons that have been subjected to PET scans is as yet very small. Therefore the admissibility of the inductive generalizations requires further investigation. Second, in order to draw conclusions about the increased activity of certain parts of the brain in psychological terms, the problem of finding systematically significant concepts should have, to a certain extent, already been solved. Third, the question of the interdependence of levels, already mentioned in the introduction, deserves closer attention.

Concerning this interdependence, the most interesting fact from several points of view is that human beings are capable of lifelong learning. "You're never too old to learn" is another proverb that is also scientifically meaningful. It is said that the gradual decrease of grey matter in the brain when we grow older and older may be arrested through "exercising our brains" by all sorts of activity (Andreasen, 1993), and also that learning a new skill may strengthen if not form neural dendritic connections (cf. De Haan & Johnson, 2003). This would mean, in our terms, either that still having certain (partial) possibilities and using them are two different things, or even that one's partial possibilities may continue to increase over time. Also it may mean that the biological aging processes can be actively influenced by psychological processes. But how and to what extent this is possible is still an open question.

OVERCOMING THE OBSTACLES

An interdisciplinary study of aging processes requires a framework in which correspondences between regularities that are found in different disciplines are described. A program is suggested in which the findings are reformulated in terms of possibilities. Does this mean that the above-mentioned obstacles can thereby be overcome?

The first obstacle concerns the multitude of levels of description and explanation, each with its own terminology. (Re)formulating results in terms of *possibilities* may at least bring about a conceptual congruence.

The second obstacle concerns the dynamical character of aging processes and the requirement of process laws or regularities. This is accommodated by the concept of *change* of possibilities *over time*. It would be helpful if the choice of time intervals in the process laws themselves could be based on such changes, but the question if this is at all possible can only be answered after the first step of reformulating the results has been taken.

The third obstacle concerns the differences between the disciplines themselves. Admittedly the theoretical framework in terms of *changes of possibilities* corresponds more to a data-oriented approach than to the "operational definition gambit." What the possibilities and impossibilities are cannot be established by common-sense arguments, but must be discovered from well-designed experiments in which the difference between the possibility of performing a performance-based test and its impossibility is precisely defined. Current experiments in which performances are classified as "fully able," "partially able," and "unable" can be used, provided that the diagnosis of partial ability is further specified in abilities and inabilities. And as soon as the latter are ascribed to impossibilities on a different level, we have made a step forward in our program.

The practical significance of this focus on possibilities and impossibilities must not be underestimated. On the one hand, the *acceptance* that some things have become impossible for elders may console them. On the other hand, the *awareness* of their own continuing and even new possibilities may encourage them.

> Most older people don't feel old. Even as bodies and minds become less than reliable, elders see themselves and want to be seen as willing to take on challenges. Helping them explore possibilities and options is life giving and provides the unspoken message that we consider them capable and worthy. Doing so can also be freeing for the caregiver (Anonymous, 2002).

REFERENCES

Allport, G. W. (1954). *Personality. A psychological interpretation.* New York: Henry Holt and Company.

Andreasen, N. (1993). *O brave new world! Exploring the mind and brain in health and disease.* Presidential Lecture, University of Iowa.

Anonymous. (2002). *Elder care solutions newsletter,* March Volume.

Atkins, P. W. (1986). Time and dispersal. The second law. In R. Flood & M. Lockwood (Eds.), *The nature of time* (pp. 80-98). Oxford: Basil Blackwell.

Boring, E. G., Langfeld, H. S., & Weld, H. P. (1948). *Foundations of psychology.* New York: John Wiley and Sons/London: Chapman and Hall.

Bunge, M. (1967). *Scientific research. II. The search for truth.* Berlin: Springer-Verlag.

Brugman, G. (2000). *Wisdom: Source of narrative coherence and eudaimonia.* Delft: Eburon.

Burkhardt, M. S., Foster, J. K., Laws, S. M., Baker, L. D., Craft, S., Gandy, S. E., Stuckey, B. G. A., Clarnette, R., Nolan, D., Hewson-Bower, B., & Martins, R. N. (2004). Oestrogen replacement therapy may improve memory functioning in the absence of APOE e4. *Journal of Alzheimer's Disease, 6,* 209-219.

Darden, L., & Tabery, J. (2005). Molecular biology. In E. N. Zalta (Ed.), *The Stanford encyclopedia of philosophy* (Spring 2005 Edition).

De Groot, A. D., & Gobet, F. (1996). *Perception and memory in chess. Studies in the heuristics of the professional eye.* Assen: Van Gorcum.

De Haan, M., & Johnson, M. H. (2003). Mechanisms and theories of brain development. In M. de Haan & M. H. Johnson (Eds.), *The Cognitive neuroscience of development* (pp. 1-18). London: Psychology Press.

Dorn, E. (1915). Experimentelle Atomistik. In E. Warburg (Ed.), *Physik.* Leipzig und Berlin: B. G. Teubner.

Ericsson, K. A., & Charness, N. (1997). Cognitive and developmental factors in expert performance. In P. J. Feltovich, K. M. Ford, & R. R. Hoffman (Eds.), *Expertise in context: Human and machine* (pp. 3-41). Cambridge, MA: The MIT Press.

Erikson, E. H. (1959). *Identity and the life cycle.* New York: International Universities Press.

Ferguson, C. (1998). Fountain of youth bubbles in brains of the oldest old. *Harvard University Gazette,* March 1998.

Gavrilov L. A., & Gavrilova N. S. (1991). *The biology of life span: A quantitative approach.* New York: Harwood Academic Publisher.

Jäncke, L., Specht, K., Shah, J. N., & Hugdahl, K. (2003). Focused attention in a simple dichotic listening task: An fRMI experiment. *Cognitive Brain Research, 16,* 257-266.

Kendrew, J. (1977). Introduction. In R. Duncan & M. Weston-Smith (Eds.), *The encyclopaedia of ignorance.* Oxford: Pergamon Press.

Lipsitz, L. A., & Goldberger, A. L. (1992). Loss of 'complexity' and aging. Potential applications of fractals and chaos theory to senescence. *The Journal of the American Medical Association, 267,* 1806-1809.

Miles, W. R. (1933). Age and human ability. *Psychological Review, 49,* 99-123.

Reuter-Lorenz, P. A. (2000). Cognitive neuropsychology of the aging brain. In D. C. Park & N. Schwarz (Eds.), *Cognitive aging: A primer* (pp. 93-114). Philadelphia, PA: Psychology Press.

Russell, B. A. W. (1914). *Our knowledge of the external world as a field for scientific method in philosophy.* London: George Allen and Unwin.

Sacher, G. A. (1967). The complementarity of entropy terms for the temperature-dependence of development of aging. In E. M. Weyer (Ed.), Interdisciplinary Perspectives of Time. *Annals of the New York Academy of Sciences, 138,* 680-712.

Salthouse, T. A. (1996). The processing-speed theory of adult age differences in cognition. *Psychological Review, 103,* 403-428.

Schaie, K. W. (1988). Methodological issues in gerontological research. In K. W. Schaie, R. T. Campbell, et al. (Eds.), *Methodological issues in aging research* (pp. 13-42). New York: Springer.

Schroots, J. J. F. (1996). Time: Concepts and perceptions. In *Encyclopedia of gerontology* (Vol. 2, pp. 583-590). New York: Academic Press.

Schroots, J. J. F., & Yates, F. E. (1999). On the dynamics of development and aging. In V. L. Bengtson & K. W. Schaie (Eds.), *Handbook of theories of aging.* New York: Springer-Verlag.

Sehl, M., & Yates, E. (2001). Kinetics of human aging: I. Rates of senescence between ages 30 and 70 years in healthy people. *Journal of Gerontology Series A: Biological Sciences and Medical Sciences, 56,* 198-208.

Stanley Hall, G. (1922). *Senescence: The last half of life.* New York: Appleton.

Van Praag, B. M. S., & Ferrer-i-Carbonell, A. (2004). Oxford, UK: Oxford University Press.

Strehler, B. L. (1967). Cellular aging. In E. M. Weyer (Ed.), Interdisciplinary Perspectives of Time. *Annals of the New York Academy of Sciences, 138,* 661.

Zimprich, D., & Martin, M. (2002). Can longitudinal changes in processing speed explain longitudinal age changes in fluid intelligence? *Psychology and Aging, 17,* 690-695.

Contributors

JAN BAARS, Ph.D., studied sociology and philosophy in Amsterdam and is Professor of Interpretive Gerontology at the University for Humanist Studies in Utrecht and Professor of Philosophy of the Social Sciences and the Humanities at Tilburg University in the Netherlands. He has published and (co-)edited a dozen books and published many articles on philosophical and gerontological subjects in English, German, French, Finnish, and Dutch. His main interests are the theoretical and practical presuppositions in approaches to aging, especially concepts of time and temporality. Dr. Baars has lectured at universities in Europe, the United States, Japan, and South Africa and is co-editor of *Aging, Globalization and Inequality: The New Critical Gerontology* (Baywood, 2005).

FREYA DITTMANN-KOHLI, Ph.D. and habilitation in psychology, is head and professor at the Center for Psychogerontology, University of Nijmegen, since 1992. Courses on psychogerontology and research on human development over the life span with an emphasis on adulthood and aging have been main activities. New methods have been developed to combine qualitative and quantitative study of personal meaning and personality in small and large scale surveys and cross-cultural studies. From 1967-1992, teaching, research, and publications covered fields such as cross-cultural studies, curriculum development and education, vocational development in adolescence, and late life intelligence and wisdom.

ELKE VAN DER MEER is Professor of Cognitive Psychology at Humboldt-University, Berlin, Germany. Her research interests are in human memory and cognition, especially issues related to coding of temporal information in semantic memory, language comprehension, and individual differences in cognition and emotion. She has edited or co-edited nine books and published some eighty research articles and chapters.

K. WARNER SCHAIE is the Evan Pugh Professor of Human Development and Psychology and Affiliate Professor of Psychiatry and Behavioral Sciences at the University of Washington. He received his Ph.D. in psychology from the University of Washington, an honorary Dr. phil. from the Friedrich-Schiller University of Jena, Germany, and an honorary Sc.D. degree from West Virginia University. He received the Gerontological Society of America's Kleemeier Distinguished Research Contributions award, the MENSA lifetime career award, and the American Psychological Association's Distinguished Scientific

Contributions award. His current research interests are the life course of adult intelligence, its antecedents and modifiability, the early detection of risk for dementia, as well as methodological issues in the developmental sciences.

JOS UFFINK was born in Amsterdam in 1956 and trained as a theoretical physicist at the University of Amsterdam. In 1991, he defended a Ph.D. thesis on the quantum mechanical Uncertainty Principle at Utrecht University. Since then, he has published on various topics in the foundations and history of quantum mechanics, statistical physics, and probability theory. He has spent research fellowships at the universities of Cambridge, Oxford, and Pittsburgh, and is currently employed as Senior Lecturer in the foundations and history of science at Utrecht University. Since 2003, he is editor of the journal *Studies in History and Philosophy of Modern Physics.*

F. EUGENE YATES received his medical degree from Stanford University in 1950. After internship he served for two years as a Navy physician during the Korean War. He joined the Physiology Department at Harvard University in 1953, and in 1960 returned to Stanford where he served as Executive of the Physiology Department until 1969. From 1970 to 1980 he was a member of the Bioengineering faculty at the University of Southern California and Director of their Medical Engineering Center, after which he became Crump Professor of Medical Engineering at the University of California, Los Angeles. For seven years he was first Director of their Medical Engineering Institute. His research interests include systems analysis of endocrine feedbacks, thermodynamics of complex systems, design of controlled delivery devices for therapeutic drugs, and mechanisms of aging. He currently is Scientific Advisor for the John Douglas French Alzheimer's Foundation in Los Angeles.

HENK VISSER, Ph.D., became Emeritus Professor at the University Maastricht in 2005. In his professional life he taught mathematics, analytic philosophy, philosophy of the information sciences, and philosophy of science. His systematic research focused on productive problem solving; his historical research concerned the development of scientific philosophy and scientific humanism. One of his more recent works is *Het Forumwaarmerk van Wetenschap* (*The Forum Theory of Scientific Truth*), written with the psychologist A. D. de Groot. Since 1998 Dr. Visser has been president of the Evert Willem Beth Foundation in Amsterdam.

Index